ABBA, FATHER

BONAVENTURE PERQUIN, O.P.

SCEPTER PUBLISHERS

CONTENTS

FOREWORD

God wants to be a Father to all. Yet his Fatherhood needs some explanation, and preferably in a form that is simple and comprehensive. If this is so, it will be adapted to the requirements of anyone who wants to learn more about the heavenly Father and his relationship with his adopted children on earth. A display of learning and scholarship would be incongruous in treating of this subject, with its essential climate of simplicity. That is why the direct approach has been chosen: a selection of conferences, most of which have at some time been spoken, is what this book is meant to be.

The great problem throughout was the use of Sacred Scripture. In the absence of any single satisfactory English translation, it was difficult to find the translation which conveys the meaning of the original text adequately without the obscurity of the translation or the personal idiosyncrasy of style of the translator obtruding itself and acting as a barrier. Consequently different translations have been used. Those quotations which have no letter added to the reference are taken from the Douay translation; those with the letter K are taken from Monsignor Ronald Knox's translation; the letter W indicates the Westminster translation; and C, that of the (American) Confraternity of Christian Doctrine.

Grateful thanks are due to M. M. S. and F. A. M. for their indispensable assistance in preparing these conferences for publication.

BONAVENTURE PERQUIN, O.P.
Blackfriars, Oxford

I

Father and Child

Behold what manner of love the Father hath given us, that
we should be called children of God; and such we are.

I JOHN 3: 1 W

Beloved, now we are children of God.

I JOHN 3: 2 W

In reading the first text, especially in the Greek, one feels
that, after the words "that we should be called children of
God," St. John must have paused while his spirit soared
with breathtaking penetration into the immensity of the
love which the Father has given us in not only calling us
his children but in making us his children in the truest
sense. For this realization made St. John exclaim: "and
such we are." Many years before, he had had a similar
experience, when he saw his Master's heart opened by the
lance, and his Blood pouring out to the very last drop.
That total outpouring of the Precious Blood was for him a
sign of the love that caused it: the immense love of his
Master and of the Father, who was giving his Son for the
redemption of the world. But when St. John was writing
his first epistle, it was not directly the contemplation of
the crucifixion and death of his Master which evoked his
astonishment at the immensity of the Father's love. It was
rather the thought that the Father should have gone so far
as not merely to call us his children, but to make us *be* his
children in the most absolute sense of *being*: that of living
with his life. It is as if St. John was saying, in his amazement: "See, realize, what stupendous love the Father has
given us, that we should be called God's children—and
indeed we are!"

9

St. John, speaking to the people of his own day, urged them to remember their baptism and to try to realize what this baptism had meant to them, what it had brought them, and what it had done in them and for them. He wanted them to acquire a deeper understanding of baptism itself and, even more, to go beyond it and appreciate the immense love of his Master's Father, which it manifests and communicates.

For what had the Father given them in their baptism? In making them *be* his children, he gave them, above all, his love. It was not a symbolic or token gift of love, nor was it a passing gift, but definitive and lasting. As always, the Father took the initiative in giving them his love, for they did not deserve it in any way. Far from it: before he gave it, men were his enemies, unworthy of his immense love. They could not possibly merit it by themselves, for no one can merit anything without having that love for him which is the gift of the Father's love. The Father has to love mankind first, gratuitously, for we are all utterly undeserving: "Herein doth lie the love, not in our having loved God, but in his having loved us" (1 Jn 4: 10 W).

St. John makes it clear to us, as he did to his first readers and listeners, that the initiative in the exchange of all love between the Father and his children must necessarily come from the Father, since "God *is* love" (1 Jn 4: 8). Now, in us there is a distinction between our love and our person: love is part of us, something we do. Only God *is* love. His whole being is love, just as his power, wisdom, faithfulness, all his attributes are one in him: he is his attributes. And because God is love he cannot act out of anything but love. The supreme manifestation of his love is in the Incarnation, the gift of his only-begotten Son for our redemption. "What has revealed the love of God, where we are concerned, is that he has sent his only-begotten Son into the world, so that we might have life through him" (1 Jn 4: 9 K).

When the Father gives his immense love to us in and through baptism, he does not merely promise it; he actually gives it at once in all its fullness: with its divine tenderness, its loving care, its infinite power and wisdom, its unfailing desire to forgive. St. John wanted all his readers and hearers to share the light that had been given him so that we should all see our baptism as the gratuitous gift of the Father's love and that we might always remember that love and its transcendent dimensions, dimensions which we cannot measure but in which we must believe. And so, later in the same epistle, St. John wrote: "we have learned to recognize the love God has in our regard, to recognize it, and to make it our belief" (1 Jn 4: 16 K).

The Father's own life is the gift of his love to us at baptism. Through this gift of life we are truly "born of God," truly his children. For to give life is to be a father, and to receive life is to be a child. Therefore in and through baptism the Father begets all those who receive his life, and we the baptized are in a true sense his children from the very moment of our baptism. It is not something we may become at some future date: we are God's children here and now. "Beloved, now we are children of God" (1 Jn 3: 2 W).

After the supreme gift of his only-begotten Son, that of his own divine life is the Father's greatest gift to those who thus become his children (see Jn 1: 12–13). Nor is the gift of baptism ever isolated from the gift of his Son: these gifts cannot be separated, because it is only those who are baptized in and into Christ who are true children of the Father. In giving his divine life the Father so to speak extends his love for his Son to all those who through faith and baptism are united to his Son: it is their faith in the Son, sent by him, which enables them to share the Father's love for his Son. It also makes them share the Son's love for the Father, and thus they are able to return the love of the Father with and through the Son's love for him. It is through the gift of his divine life that God's Fatherhood and love penetrate into the inmost depth of his children. Each of them carries within him the seed of the Father's life (1 Jn 3: 9) and, with it, possesses the most impressive proof of the Father's love.

The divine life, however, which the Father gives us in and through baptism, is not natural to us; it is not homogeneous with the life which human parents communicate to their children. We are not children of God by nature, and we are not born with the divine life already in our soul. The only-begotten Son of God alone has possessed from all eternity the Father's life in all its infinity. But human beings cannot possibly be children of God in this sense. They cannot by nature belong to the Father's family. They need to be adopted, and the Father adopts them in and through Christian baptism. It is in virtue of this baptism that God is our Father, we his children, and Jesus Christ, the only-begotten Son, our Brother. Yet we do not have to wait till after death for our adoption into the Father's family, for it takes place in this life, with the promise of a more glorious future beyond. "Beloved, we are sons ["children" is St. John's word] of God even now, and what we shall be hereafter, has not been made known as yet. But we know that when he comes we shall be like him" (1 Jn 3: 2 K). Baptism gives us the right and privilege to say to God: "You are my Father," and to each one of his adopted children the Father says: "You are my child. In and through baptism I have begotten you."

Baptism, then, is the act by which the Father adopts us. That this adoption consists of the Father's communication of his divine life to us shows us how different adoption by God is from adoption by human beings. For what takes place in adoption as we know it in human society? Let us imagine that a rich and mighty king is visiting a poverty-stricken and primitive village in his country, and there notices a little child playing in the gutter, poor, starved, and unkempt. The king decides to adopt that child and to take him back to his splendid palace. Not only his own people but the whole world would be agog. Many would admire him, others would criticize him according to their different points of view. A gutter-child to be put on an equal footing with the king's own children, sharing their inheritance, their amenities, their family life! And what an entirely new situation it is for the urchin himself.

But the Father's adoption of us involves infinitely more. He is God of immense majesty—*"immensae majestatis"*. His is not the majesty of an earthly king, only on a vastly grander scale: his is an altogether different kind of majesty, a majesty which cannot belong to any creature even if he were king of the whole world. His is the infinite, transcendent majesty of God. And yet it is he who says to us when he adopts us: "Henceforward you are my child. My Son is now your Brother, and all my other adopted children are your brethren. Be perfectly at home with us. You have now a new life, a new family, new surroundings. You have much to learn. But listen to my Son: he will tell you everything you need to know. Model yourself on him, for the more you become like him the more pleasing you will be to me, the more you will feel at home with us, and the more you will share our intimate life, wisdom, and love."

When we look at ourselves we hardly recognize the children of infinite majesty, nor do we always behave as such. And yet we must believe that it is true, because the Father sent his Son to tell us this: provided we are born again of water and the Holy Spirit, we are children of God. The fulfillment of this condition is essential because there is a still more radical difference between human adoption and God's adoption than that of earthly and divine majesty. We can call the adoption of an urchin by the king in our example a legal fiction, because the boy never becomes the king's own true child. He cannot change within: the change is only external. It is true that the adopted child is given the right to share the royal inheritance, but the king cannot touch his inner life; the child can never be re-born of the king. A human person cannot give to an adopted child what he has given to the children of his own life and blood; that deep sharing of his innermost being is impossible. But this is possible to God. He can infuse his own life into the children he adopts, no matter how numerous they are. He can give them a new life in addition to what they receive from their human parents, and the life he gives is so much the more real and true because it is his own.

It is then a reality: God is our Abba, Father. There is no pretense about it, his Fatherhood is infinitely more real than the fatherhood of a human parent could ever be. Yet the great problem of the adopted children of God is to remember that they are his children. This is difficult because the life he gives them is invisible and the essential effects of the adoption remain invisible. Faith alone enables them to see themselves as children of God and to see him as their Abba, Father. But if they truly live by faith, their whole person, their outlook, thoughts, and desires will all be re-molded and re-fashioned by the fact that he is their Father. Their adoption can make an enormous difference to them if they become more intensely alive to it and carry out all its implications.

Moreover, as each form of natural life has its corresponding pattern of vital activities: animal life its special pattern, or human life its natural one—so the divine life communicated in baptism also has its specific pattern of activity springing from its divine origin. And so as the divine life is allowed to grow and mature in the baptized person, he will behave more and more in a way that befits his dignity as a child of God. His behavior will more and more follow the pattern of the incarnate life of the only-begotten Son, his brother, and a likeness to the Son will gradually develop in him.

At first however, the person adopted by God is like the child adopted into the human king's family: placed in a completely new environment, he has to begin life all over again, acquire new habits of life, conform to a new code of behavior. The urchin has to behave always and everywhere as a member of the royal family, and in view of his past it will involve a complete transformation of his personality and his conduct. The human being adopted by God is in a similar predicament: his past is all against him, and he has tendencies within him that incline him to behave in a way that does not befit a child of God. His life too has to be completely transformed if he is to grow up and mature as a child of his heavenly Father, for whatever he says and does must now be worthy of him. If he responds to his Father's love and does all he can to make the spirit of the family completely his own, if he listens to the Father's only-begotten Son, then his adoption will deepen and mature; so much so that, if we could have a perfect knowledge of Christ and of a fully mature Christian, we should see a striking resemblance between them: a resemblance that is most pleasing to the Father and glorifies him greatly.

Another important feature of the divine life in us, is that of itself it is everlasting. For in that life there is nothing subject to wear and tear or even to death: it is eternal. It does not become everlasting simply when we die but begins at baptism and goes on for ever. "He that believeth in the Son, hath life everlasting" (Jn 3: 36; cf. 5: 24, 6: 40). Nevertheless, the adoption of the children of God while they are on earth can be rejected, although it can never be obliterated. God never repudiates it, but his children can do so: they can refuse to remain his children. They can even turn against the Father and repay his love with indifference or worse: hatred and contempt. In fact, every mortal sin is a repudiation of the adoption, because in committing it the adopted child rejects the Father's gift of life and love, his very Fatherhood. And yet this child can never undo the fact that he has been adopted once: he sins as a child, and not as a stranger; he leaves his home, but it is as one who was a member of the family.

The sinner, then, turns his back upon his Father because he does not want to be a child of his family any more and refuses to live as such. He takes what belongs to him, his sinful nature, and goes his way. Yet God will always be the Father who adopted him in the immensity of his love and will always look upon him as his child. Although he rejects and scorns his adoption and the Father's love, that love will follow the wayward child, unknown to him, wherever he goes; and if he returns, his Father's arms will receive him once again.

To receive his child back is so different from receiving him for the first time in the act of adoption. It is his own child: the Father has never forgotten that, and now he rejoices with unspeakable joy because his child was lost and is found again, was dead and has come back to life. What a profound difference their past relationship makes to the child when he returns in repentance, and to the Father in his forgiveness. The child is penitent, remembering who he once was: "Father, I have sinned against heaven and before thee: I am not worthy to be called thy son" (Lk 15: 21). The Father forgives him as one who was once his child and receives him once more into his family.

Even this cursory glance at the Fatherhood of God and our adoption as his children brings out clearly what a wonderful gift the sacrament of baptism is. It is the gift of life from him who is not only God of infinite majesty but also a Father of infinite love and mercy, wisdom and power. Once baptism has established this Father–child relationship, everything else in life falls into place in the magnificent pattern that could only have been devised by a God who is also an infinitely loving Father.

★ ★ ★

In the Old Testament, God's wondrous deeds and gifts to men, such as the Exodus from Egypt and his constant presence in the midst of his people, never ceased to arouse in the Chosen People their deepest admiration and gratitude. Do not his yet more wondrous deeds and gifts of the New Testament invite the same response from us? If we respond fully we may recapture something of St. John's amazement at the thought that the God of transcendent majesty should love us sinners so much, and should desire our adoption as his children so much, that he sent his only-begotten Son into the world to make it possible through his Passion, death, and resurrection. "What has revealed the love of God, where we are concerned, is that he has sent his only-begotten Son into the world, so that we might have life through him" (1 Jn 4: 9 K).

So vast, however, is the Father's bounty that any consideration of the manifestations of himself. and of the wondrous deeds and gifts he has lavished upon his children, must inevitably be limited. We shall select those which best give an understanding and appreciation of his Fatherhood and our adoption. Therefore we shall treat first briefly of those which he bestowed upon his Chosen People in the Old Testament, and then more fully of those which the new Israel received from him in the New Testament. We shall try to keep in mind the fact of God's Fatherhood and to see all the "*mirabilia Dei*," these wondrous deeds and gifts, as those first and foremost of a Father toward us, his adopted children.

At the same time we shall see that even if we must restrict ourselves to general truths and their general practical applications in our daily lives, every adopted child of God has his own deep personal experience of the wondrous deeds and gifts of God in his own life, his journey toward the promised land. Each of us travels through this world as a child of God, guided and wrapped about by his

Father's loving care, just as was each of the Chosen People of old. And so we can all say with the Psalmist:

> How numerous have you made, O Lord, my
> God, your wondrous deeds!
> And in your plans for us there is none to equal
> you;
> Should I wish to declare or to tell them, they
> would be too many to recount.
>
> —PSALM 39: 6 C

2

God's Fatherhood in the Old Testament

For I am a father to Israel, and Ephraim is my first-born.

JEREMIAH 31: 9

*. . . who are Israelites, to whom belongeth the adoption
as of children.*

ROMANS 9: 4

It is possible to draw such a sharp contrast between the Old and New Testaments that no continuity of any sort seems left. Yet the study of God's Fatherhood as it is revealed in the Old Testament shows how misleading an excessive emphasis on the contrast between the two Testaments is. The New Testament does not belie the concept of God's Fatherhood which we find in the Old. On the contrary, the New Testament perfects it and gives new dimensions to the features already revealed. The only-begotten Son alone could make known these new dimensions, expressing them in his own life, death, and resurrection, but his way had been prepared. Between God's Fatherhood as revealed in the Old Testament on the one hand, and as revealed in the New Testament on the other, there is no conflict, no dichotomy. Instead there is a marvelous continuity which made the immense enrichment achieved by the Son possible and all the more striking and enlightening for us.

All through the history of the Chosen People, God revealed himself constantly as possessing those qualities which are generally associated with fatherhood. He revealed to them his power, his wisdom, his mercy and love, and how they were combined into a wonderful providence, unsurpassed in its faithfulness and tenderness. God

19

showed a loving care for his people which not even the most loving father of a human family could show for his children. This loving care reminded his people of human fatherhood at its best, while at the same time they realized how unlike it was in its unique perfection.

What else had God shown himself to be to the Patriarchs Abraham, Isaac, and Jacob but a most loving Father? He had been their strength, their comfort, their guide: a true Father to them. Not only did he reveal his Fatherhood to them, but he caused it to be reflected in themselves: he made them the fathers of his Chosen People not so much in virtue of their physical fatherhood of innumerable descendants but in a much deeper sense by reason of the promises he made to them, which they were to hand down to their posterity. Their fatherhood was to be seen above all as a spiritual fatherhood: the transmission of a spiritual inheritance. This inheritance would enrich their descendants not only with the promised land of milk and honey but with the promises of the Lord their God: the promises of his loving care, lasting protection, and constant defense. Their fatherhood "according to the flesh" (Rom. 4: 1) was to be the vehicle of their spiritual fatherhood, of a fatherhood which was not to be restricted to their physical descendants but was to be universal, to be shared by all who made God's promises their own regardless of race or time. Nowhere, perhaps, do we find this Fatherhood of God shown to the Patriarchs of his Chosen People described so movingly as in the Book of Deuteronomy 10: 14–15 K:

> This Lord God, that is master of the heavens, and the heaven above the heavens, of earth, too, and of all that they contain, would yet knit thy fathers closely to him in his great love, and make choice of you, their son, above all other nations in the world; the proof of it is before you.

After the deaths of the Patriarchs, God did not cease to lavish his loving care upon his Chosen People. He continued to be their Father because his Fatherhood was not subject to death, as was that of the Patriarchs: his was lasting. "For thou art our father, and Abraham hath not known us, and Israel hath been ignorant of us: thou, O Lord, art our father, our redeemer, from everlasting is thy name" (Is 63: 16). In other words, the fatherhood of the Patriarchs was temporary: they had lived and died, whereas God's Fatherhood was permanent and not bound up with any human person be he patriarch, prophet, or king.

It was especially during the period of the Exodus and afterward that God's Fatherhood was revealed to his people in most striking ways. Again in the Book of Deuteronomy we find the Father's love in all its strength and tenderness best described:

> In the wilderness (as thou hast seen) the Lord thy God hath carried thee, as a man is wont to carry his little son, all the way that you have come, until you came to this place (1: 31).

> He kept him as the apple of his eye. As the eagle enticing her young to fly, and hovering over them, he spread his wings, and hath taken him and carried him on his shoulders (32: 10–11).

Indeed, this nation was his "first-born Son" (Ex 4: 32). Similarly, Isaiah speaks of them as children the Lord has brought up (Is 1: 2ff.).

The Chosen People, then, had to be taught how to conduct themselves as the children of the Lord their God. "Be ye children of the Lord your God," they were told, "a people set apart for the Lord, chosen out of all nations on earth to be his very own" (Deut 14: 1–2 K). Although they often went astray, God never tired of "healing their rebellion," keeping them as his children. Jeremiah gives his message to them: "How shall I put thee among the children, and give thee a lovely land, the goodly inheritance of the armies of the Gentiles? And I said: Thou shalt call me father, and shalt not cease to walk after me" (3: 19). His heart always went out to them.

Nevertheless, God chastised them "as a man chastises his own son." He trained them to keep his commandments, to follow the path he chose, and to live in fear of him. The commandments he gave were exacting, but they were the "leading-strings of love." These were not arbitrary impositions: they were meant to guide their first steps and impart wisdom to them. For these commandments and laws embodied their Father's wisdom. This is why his love for them urged him to give them those laws and insist on their obedience. Their filial obedience was the sure way of imbibing their Father's wisdom and thereby learning to live wisely. So in constantly transgressing those laws they proved themselves not only disobedient, ungrateful, and unloving, but foolish too. This was preferring folly to wisdom, darkness to light, death to life.

Never did their Father accept their disobedience as final. No doubt he punished them for it severely, but, the punishment over, he forgave them. In the Book of Hosea we find: "I carried them in my arms: and they knew not that I healed them" (11: 3). Even before punishing them he would almost plead with his children to repent and make amends, that punishment might not be necessary:

Come back, and make amends for all this guilt of yours, that shall else be your undoing; away with them, your defiant rebellions against me; a new heart, a new spirit! Why must you choose death, men of Israel? Die who will, his death is none of my contriving, says the Lord God; come back to me and live! (Ez 18: 31–32 k).

When they disobeyed, it was as children, not as strangers or slaves. This is why they wounded their Father's love so deeply and provoked his anger so frequently; but even their punishment was that which is meted out to children, and the forgiveness they received was the forgiveness of a Father. For it was life that God as Father of his Chosen People wanted to give them. If he gave them laws and relentlessly insisted on their obedience, punishing them grievously for disobedience, it was not to bring them death. "Death was never of God's fashioning; not for his pleasure does life cease to be" (Wis 1: 13 K). From this we too learn that he wants his children to live, to grow to maturity.

The history of the Chosen People can therefore give us deep insight into God's Fatherhood and into the infinite power, wisdom, love, and providence that went into the wondrous deeds, "*mirabilia Dei*," that accompanied his adopted children throughout the Exodus. Upon them the revelation of his Fatherhood at this time made a deep impression. Then they were fashioned into a nation, for this was when "Juda became his sanctuary, Israel his domain" (Ps 113: 2). This was when they became his Chosen People in the fullest sense, and his adopted children. He, the Lord God, was their God and their Father.

Upon us likewise, meditation on God's Fatherhood can make a deep impression. It will prepare us, as nothing else can, for God's Fatherhood, as revealed to us by his only-begotten Incarnate Son. It will enable us to see more clearly the even more wondrous deeds which unceasingly accompany the new Israel, the Chosen People of the New Testament, on their exodus from exile to their promised land. We shall recognize too the waywardness of the old Israel in the children of the new Israel. But above all we shall recognize the same infinite tenderness in God's loving care for his Chosen People, made so much more tangible through the incarnation, Passion, death, and resurrection of his only-begotten beloved Son, Jesus Christ, our Brother and Savior.

What a mistake it would be, then to neglect the Old Testament in an attempt to enter more deeply into the mystery of the Fatherhood of God. The books of the Old Testament are an indispensable introduction and a necessary preparation of mind and heart. Through them we can become attuned to the Father-child relationship, which was the normal one between God and his Chosen People in virtue of his adoption of them as his children. This adoption, implicit in the relationship described so strikingly and movingly in the Old Testament, becomes explicit in the New Testament. This is why we who possess the fullness of adoption through Christ find our understanding of it enriched by meditating on God's preparation for it in the Old Testament. There we find God as an infinitely powerful, wise, and loving Father to each one of his adopted children.

For not only was the Lord God the Father of his people as a people: he was the Father of every faithful Israelite who saw himself as a child of his God and prayed to him as a child speaks to his father. In Ecclesiasticus, for instance, we find that the prayer of a man in temptation begins: "O Lord, father, and sovereign ruler of my life, leave me not to their counsel: nor suffer me to fall by them" (Ecclus 23: 1).

The Book of Wisdom shows that many a man must have prided himself openly on being a child of the Most High: "He glorieth that he hath God for his father. Let us see then if his words be true and let us prove what shall happen to him, and we shall know what his end shall be. For if he be the true son of God, he will defend him, and will deliver him from the hands of his enemies" (2: 16–18). But God did defend and deliver him in his own way. Those who were his enemies had to acknowledge this: "We fools esteemed their life madness, and their end without honour. Behold how they are numbered among the children of God, and their lot is among the saints" (Wis 5: 4–5).

If this was true of all faithful Israelites, it was especially true of the kings of Israel, who represented God's people and through whom God so often demonstrated his fatherly love and protection: "I will be to him a father, and he shall be to me a son," said God of David to Nathan the prophet in the Second Book of Kings (7: 14). And how could this special Father–son relationship between God and the king of his Chosen People be more concisely expressed than in Ps 2: 7: "The Lord hath said to me: Thou art my son, this day have I begotten thee"? No text could show more clearly than this how the revelation of God's Fatherhood in the Old Testament was meant to prepare Israel for the revelation of Jesus Christ as the only-begotten Son and as the first-born among many brethren. To them he would make known his Father's name, and to them he would send the Spirit of adoption, the Spirit who was to make them cry out: *Abba*—Father.

3

The Father's Power

Then Moses and the Israelites sang praise to the Lord,
and this was their song: A psalm for the Lord, so great he
is and so glorious; horse and rider hurled into the sea!
Who but the Lord is my protector, the pride of my song;
who but the Lord has brought me deliverance? Shall I not
praise him, my own God; shall I not extol him, the God of
my father before me? The Lord, the warrior God; whose
very name tells of omnipotence! That power could hurl
Pharao's chariots, Pharao's army, into the sea; drowned
in the Red Sea, the flower of all his chivalry; the depths
closed over them, and they sank to the bottom like a stone.
How magnificent, Lord is the strength of thy right hand;
that right hand which has shattered the enemy!

EXODUS 15: 1–6 K

As God's adopted children, the new Israel, we need to be
reminded that all our strength lies in the power of our
Father, just as much as did that of his Chosen People in
the Old Testament. Our Father never changes; his ways
are the same throughout the ages, for it is only the human
circumstances that are different.

We read in the account of the Exodus that the Father
determined to show both his Chosen People and the
Egyptians who enslaved them that he alone was God. The
plagues, the hardening of Pharaoh's heart, the final magnificent story of the escape from Egypt, all help to reveal
his power used on their behalf:

> I will lay my hand upon Egypt and will bring forth my
> army and my people the children of Israel out of the

land of Egypt, by very great judgments. And the Egyptians shall know that I am the Lord, who have stretched forth my hand upon Egypt, and have brought forth the children of israel out of the midst of them (Ex 7: 4, 5).

This continued throughout their history: God, having chosen his own people, showed them how he was prepared to use his power to liberate them, to protect them, to fight their wars. He was "the mighty one of Jacob" (Gen 49: 24), the leader of its armies, of its "sabaoth" (Ex 12: 41), "the Lord mighty in battle" (Ps 23: 8). Whenever he fought for his people, they were assured of victory, whether it was under Moses, under Josue, the Judges, or the Kings. At times, however, in order to chastise and punish them, God fought against his people, and then of course their defeat was certain. Victory was theirs when God fought with them, but they must never forget that it is his victory rather than theirs: they were not to become inflated by it and think that though the victory was easier with God's help they would have won it in any case, if at a greater cost. Nothing was further from the truth. By themselves they were powerless against their powerful enemies: only God could enable them to win the victory which they should receive as a favor. It was a gift, and they should be grateful for it, deeply and humbly so:

> Thou hast girded me with strength unto battle; and hast subdued under me them that rose up against me. And thou hast made my enemies turn their back upon me, and hast destroyed them that hated . . . Therefore will I give glory to thee, O Lord, among the nations, and I will sing a psalm to thy name (Ps 17: 40, 41, 50).

The better the Chosen People remembered God's wondrous deeds on their behalf, the more readily would they put their trust in him, ask him for his help, and praise him after receiving it. This is why the wondrous deeds, the *"mirabilia Dei,"* had to be recorded, their stories learned by heart. We find this made clear in Psalm 77:

> Great things have we heard and known, and our fathers have told us. They have not been hidden from their children, in another generation. Declaring the praises of the Lord, and his powers, and his wonders which he hath done. And he set up a testimony in Jacob: and made a law in Israel. How great things he commanded our fathers, that they should make the same known to their children: that another generation might know them . . . That they may put their hope in God and may not forget the works of God (77: 3–6, 7).

Therefore they praised their Father for his deeds in hymns and canticles. Such wonders were recorded not only for their benefit but also for ours, because nothing will help us so much to put our trust in God as the vivid remembrance of his mighty deeds.

This is why the Exodus is so important. The Father wanted to impress the remembrance of his power indelibly upon the minds of his children, so that they and future generations should remember and trust in him. He manifested his power in the deliverance of his "first-born" from Egypt, just as he had manifested it in the lives of the Patriarchs, for to him nothing is impossible. Abraham had understood this so well: "Is there anything hard to God?" (Gen 18: 14). How deep was his insight into God's limitless power! And how well he had understood that God always used his power to bring about whatever he desired for his People. Thus in the Exodus he delivered them with "mighty hand" and "stretched-out arm." In that deliverance he showed himself once and for all as the one who is Almighty in heaven and on earth, as Moses told the Israelites:

He brought thee out of Egypt, going before thee with his great power, to destroy at thy coming very great nations, and stronger than thou art, and to bring thee in, and give thee their land for a possession, as thou seest at this present day. Know therefore this day, and think in thy heart that the Lord he is God in heaven above, and in the earth beneath, and there is no other (Deut 4: 37–39).

God made the Exodus, then, as dramatic, as forceful as possible on purpose, so that they should be impressed. Also he inspired Moses, David, and others to write about it so that the memory of it should never fade. Later, when they were tempted to doubt or complain or forget, they could look back at what he had done and trust him. He wanted all his children to enjoy his power, to know it and love it, to see themselves as sheltered, protected, armed, in the shadow of his wings. And he wanted to move their hearts to praise, to acknowledge that shadow with joy and gratitude, as Moses did.

We have our Exodus too: our life is a journey, and like the Israelites we have hope in proportion to our faith in God's power. Without hope we may approve in theory of holiness, but we shall not seek it, really wanting it. We cannot long for God, for holiness, unless we have some pledge of success. We have to be certain of our Father's love and its efficiency; otherwise the possibility of disappointment would be too much for us. The more certain we are of our destination and of our means of getting there, the more promptly we shall step out on the journey. Like Moses, we need to recognize the harmony that exists between God's merciful love and his power: "Thy mercy had delivered Israel; thy mercy should be their guide; thy strong arms should carry them to the holy place where thou dwellest" (Ex 15: 13 K). The power of God, as we know it, is the exercise of his love in our lives, the power to redeem, the power to sanctify. God can do what he wants, and he wants us to be saints.

For God there is no distinction between what he wants and what he is able to do: "Whatsoever the Lord pleased he hath done" (Ps 134: 6). For us it is different: the deeper our desires, the more we want, the sharper the distinction becomes. By ourselves we cannot realize in the smallest degree any of the hopes which alone make life in this world supportable. By ourselves we are utterly helpless, wholly unable to do any good. Without our Father's help we are unable to turn to him, even to acknowledge our need. We have to learn that all our strength is from him, all our capacity for good, and for this we have to be made little, brought low, to the very ground. It may be by sickness or by failure or any other means, it does not matter how, as long as we learn that our self-reliance is an illusion.

It was God's power alone which freed us at baptism from the power which the devil has over those in original sin. That was an exodus for us, and our adoption by a powerful and loving Father. It needs his infinite power now to keep us from sin, to make us persevere and live as his children. His strength is with us each moment, supporting us. Without him we can do nothing. We may be very conscious of our failings and yet be unable to overcome them. Yet to discover our powerlessness is to discover the depth of our need, and this is a blessing. For we find that our need is God himself. and we are absolutely dependent on him to supply it. How deep is that need if God alone can fill it! It is a great gulf in our being: as unfathomable as the power of God. The Psalms constantly express this sense of need and the confidence of the child in his Father: "I am needy and poor; O God help me. Thou art my helper and my deliverer: O Lord, make no delay" (Ps 69: 6).

For we are not meant to despair, though we could easily be discouraged by our sins, our weakness, our countless failures in generosity, in faithfulness, trust, and love. It is easy to build up a picture of our miseries, especially as we tend to confuse them with our disappointed pride in having failed. Such confusion shows that we suppose ourselves to have a right to some power, some capacity or strength of our own. But we are poor. We have to rely on our Father, who knows what we need before we ask him. As soon as he feels in us the slightest acceptance of our powerlessness, then he gives, for he knows we are willing to receive. It needs faith to accept God's power to supply all our needs: we have to believe that he can, and that he wants to, supply us, because he loves us. Then we shall be enforced in his strength: we shall feed on it, shelter in it, act in it, and rest in it.

Our own strength, then, is an illusion. The minor failures we make are not as big as the fundamental mistake of supposing that we have ever succeeded in anything at all by ourselves, especially our sanctification. So many times we have taken to ourselves the praise, the honor, which was due to God alone. We cling to our desire to be important in any field. But we are not necessary to God. As his children we can please him, but only by becoming like his only-begotten Beloved Son, not by giving him anything. We get so excited about action: we think we are achieving something if we feel overworked, or if we have said much about many things. We are always hurrying to save time; but what are we saving it for—eternity? We are afraid of the apparent uselessness of stillness, afraid of being empty-handed, afraid of having nothing to show. But we are poor, we have only what we have been given. Our Father teaches us this by our failures. As we appear more and more useless, we see that our idea of utility was too narrow. He knows what is best for us. He may simply want us to fail, to make that our success. Or he may want us to suffer, and that can be the most efficient employment of all:

They that sow in tears shall reap in joy. Going they went and wept, casting their seeds. But coming they shall come with joyfulness, carrying their sheaves (Ps 125: 5–7).

We are given light to see these things in order that we may trust in God, hope in him and in him alone. Our sufficiency is from God, our adequacy, our proficiency. The more we recognise our nothingness, our powerlessness for good, the more we look to the Father for strength: "Deep calleth on deep" (Ps 41: 8). St. Paul, who was a son both of the old and of the new Israel, learnt much from his own weakness: "I besought the Lord, that it might depart from me: And he said to me: My grace is sufficient for thee: for power is made perfect in infirmity" (2 Cor 12: 8–9).

He understood that this is why the Father sent us his only-begotten Son: we needed him to redeem us and bring us the fullness of adoption. Our Lord sums up in himself the powerful love of the Father, shown to his children through the ages. And so St. Paul could say joyfully: "Gladly therefore will I glory in my infirmities, that the power of Christ may dwell in me" (2 Cor 12: 9).

The Church prays at the beginning of each hour of the Divine Office: *Deus in adjutorium meum intende: Domine ad adjuvandum me festina*, "Incline unto my aid, O God. O Lord, make haste to help me." The early Fathers knew the deep need we have: we could not even say one Little Hour as we should without God's help. We should constantly call upon him for help, whenever we see our need. If we love the Father and want him to be all-powerful, then we shall be grateful for every occasion which teaches us our weakness, because in this way we have the joy of calling him God Almighty.

The virtue of faith coupled with the knowledge of our helplessness brings us the glorious freedom of the children of God. This liberates us from fear and envelops us with confidence. "When I am weak, then am I powerful" (2 Cor 12: 10). The more helpless we are, the more readily we forget our ideas of importance or ability or strength. If we have hope in nothing created, nothing can disappoint us: we put our hope in God, who will not be moved. Infinite Truth, infinite Power, infinite Love notices our smallness and utilizes what is most little, most weak, to manifest his strength. The less there is of us, the more room for him, and since we are all not merely inadequate but also deficient, we have all great opportunities for holiness, for expressing God. He will be "Raising up the needy from the earth, and lifting up the poor out of the dunghill: that he may place him with princes, with the princes of his people" (Ps 112: 7–8).

He wishes us to find joy in this, as the Israelites did in the Exodus, when they felt how their Father carried them in his "strong arms." We have additional joy in the gift of his Son: infinite Power united with the impotence of creation. And he did not come merely to console us for our weakness, but to give us joy in it. There is no reason at all why we should not become saints: it is what the Father wants; nothing else will satisfy him. But we must put no obstacle in the way, certainly not the least suggestion of self-reliance. We cannot become saints by ourselves; we are nothing. Yet our Father is omnipotent; all things are possible to him. He can make us holy, and we cannot even begin to be holy before we are deeply penetrated with the conviction of his power. His power works in us: this is the grace which is given by his merciful love. We need to remember our Father's mercy at the same time as his power, for in his dealings with his children the two go together.

God's awe-inspiring power is an instrument of his mercy. It was always so: Moses and the Israelites knew this: "Thy mercy had delivered Israel" (Ex 15: 13 K). His power was always used for a loving and merciful purpose, even if at times it seemed more an instrument of anger and punishment. But did not God punish out of mercy? For he loved his people and had to secure not only their military victories but more: their victory over their besetting temptations to infidelity, to idolatry, stiff-neckedness, to allow themselves to be morally overcome by their enemies and won over to hideous sins. His love compelled him to chastise his people. After all, he was their Father and they were his children; he had to do all he could to save them, even from themselves.

Indeed, God's power needed to be commensurate with his mercy: mercy without power is of no avail. Infinite mercy needs infinite power, and power without mercy is inconceivable to God. The Father's infinite power is at the service of his infinite mercy. It was, then, as one of the great manifestations of God's mercy, as well as his power, that the Psalmist saw the Exodus:

> Who smote Egypt with their first-born: for his
> mercy endureth for ever.
> Who brought out Israel from among them: for
> his mercy endureth for ever.
> With a mighty hand and with a stretched-out
> arm: for his mercy endureth for ever.
>
> —PSALM 135: 10–12

4

The Father's Merciful Love

Give glory to the Lord, for he is good: for his mercy endureth
for ever. Let them say so that have been redeemed by the
Lord, whom he hath redeemed from the hand of the enemy
and gathered out of the countries.

PSALM 106: 1–2

Moses, we are told in the Book of Exodus, was much loved by God. The Father even spoke with him "as a man is wont to speak to his friend," and this growing intimacy with the unseen God gave rise to Moses' desire to see his face. Now, man cannot see the face of God and live, and so the Father in his merciful love promised to place Moses in a cleft of the rock: "There I will station thee . . . while my glory passes by, and cover thee with my right hand till I have gone past. So, when I take my hand away, then thou shalt follow me with thy eyes, but my face thou canst not see" (Ex 33: 22–23 κ). The Father thus tempered the unbearable splendor of his glory and power with mercy. It is indeed his mercy which is particularly stressed in this conversation with Moses; for his answer to Moses' demand for the sight of his glory was that all his splendor should pass before him, he would pronounce in his presence his own name, Yahweh, and especially, he said: "I will have mercy on whom I will, and I will be merciful to whom it shall please me" (Ex 33: 19).

The attributes of the Father, seen in his dealings with his Chosen People, were all at the service of his mercy. In the Old Testament we find many examples of his merciful love directing his power, his wisdom, his fidelity, his

35

patience. It is the same in our own lives if only we could see it. "Who is wise, and will keep these things; and will understand the mercies of the Lord?" (Ps 106: 43). Divine wisdom gives us a deeper appreciation of our Father's mercy, and yet it is that merciful love of his which gives us his wisdom. The Father is merciful to us whether we know it or not, but to be able to know it, to recognize it and thank him, is a superabundance of mercy, a gift greater than we can fully understand.

The Psalmist often looks back on the mercies of the Exodus, and exclaims in wonder: "Let the mercies of the Lord give glory to him: and his wonderful works to the children of men" (Ps 106: 8). That is how we should look back on the mercies of our Father to us: all the means which divine wisdom has devised to bring us to him. The sacraments are given us by his merciful love. Who would have dared to think of eating the Body and drinking the Blood of Christ? God's mercy and wisdom thought of it. It is a mercy of God that he lets his justice purify and temper us, that his power should sanctify us. It is a mercy of God that he should exercise his patience and fidelity continually, in spite of our meanness and lack of trust. Just as in the time of the Exodus, he is giving to his children, giving without end.

There is not only the mercy of his forgiveness which overlooks and blots out our unfaithfulness and ingratitude in penance, but also the mercy of his love for our little-ness. There is the mercy of that divine jealousy which demands that we attend to him alone, rivets us to him, and tears us away from all those things from which we long to be free but from which we cannot free ourselves because of our weakness. These are the mercies of the wilderness. His merciful love gives the intimacy of every moment of trial or struggle, of invitation and consent, of reluctance and reconciliation. He wants to be wholly ours, and yet he wants to give himself wholly to each of his children, and he is able to. What human love can be compared with this?

The Father's transcendence is the measure of his mercy. Why should he, who is so utterly unlike us, so far above us, condescend to care about us? But he is Infinite Love, Infinite Mercy. The realization of it would be hard to bear if he did not at the same time give us a way of satisfying our longing to respond to his merciful love by giving, putting ourselves and our whole existence into his strong and gentle hands. He lets us love him. We should treasure the little acts that his wisdom inspires us to do for him, even though they are gifts from him before they are gifts from us. For without him we cannot do the least good thing, not even think a single good thought.

Even in the natural order the Father's merciful love gives us food, shelter, all we need, all day long, all night long. He is acting as he did when he looked after his People in the desert, feeding them himself, sheltering them with his presence. In the supernatural order it is still more wonderful. He stoops down to us so that *audemus dicere: Pater noster*: we dare to say "our Father." He wants to call each of us "my child," and wants us to call him "my Father." For, above all, what merciful love he has shown to us in our baptism: our adoption as children of God.

So, in his merciful love the Father blesses us, as only God can bless. All his gifts to us are blessings, and all his blessings are gifts. They are there in an unending sequence from the beginning of time, an everlasting outpouring: Creation, the Exodus, the establishment of the Kingdom, the coming of Christ, the Church, the blessings in our own lives, light, water, beauty—all are blessings given by our Father.

We do not always see everything as a blessing. Sufferings and frustration are just as much the blessings of his merciful love as are sunshine and music. We need to acquire the sensitivity which will enable us to see God's blessings everywhere: in health or sickness, poetry or pots and pans. Who can give us this sensitivity? The Holy Spirit, no one else. We have to become sensitive to him. He will help us to look for God's blessing in everything, for there is nothing that we cannot learn to regard as such. Suffering is a great blessing, but so often self-love makes us see it all out of proportion, we murmur like the Israelites in the desert. If only we could see it as a blessing, as an opportunity of becoming Christlike, we should see it in the right proportions. God's merciful love, touching us with some blessing whatever it may be, ought to make us react to it: seeing, we can bless him in return, as his creatures and his children. We find people reacting in the right way in the Old Testament: Moses singing his canticle of praise, Tobias when he received his sight, the three young men in the fiery furnace, all of them bless God for his mercy to them. Above all we find it in the Psalms.

On Thursday at Vespers the Church sings Psalm 135, a whole litany of thanksgiving: "Praise the Lord, for he is good: for his mercy endureth for ever." When we are more sensitive to the Holy Spirit, we come to a deeper realization of the Father's mercy to us all through our lives, in the Church, in the world, and we want to sing our thanksgiving, even if it is in silence. Could we not make our own song? We must make it sooner or later because we shall spend all eternity singing it. We can make our own the words of the Church, of Scripture. Over and over again in the Old Testament, the New Testament, and the liturgy, the most spontaneous response of men to their Father's merciful love is *Benedictus Deus*—Blessed be God.

Could not this be our song, too? It can express a compound of different elements, which vary according as the soul is richer or poorer in the appreciation of God's mercy and in its own insight into God himself. Gratitude may be dominant, and how much we need to thank God for his gifts! The world in general is so forgetful, so ignorant of his mercy. We ought to be aware of it in our own lives and those of others, that we may praise and thank him in a way not too disproportionate. Dependence may be dominant: a recognition of the mercy of the Father's will for us. In this world of confusion and darkness, his will is our life, and it includes all his mercies to us, past, present, and future. Adoration may be dominant: simply thanking God for being himself: "We give thee thanks for thy great glory." Made up of so many different elements, our "Blessed be God" can express so many movements of our soul.

What were all those people in the Bible doing if not expressing their gratitude to their loving and merciful Father? So often, for instance, he saved David and gave him victories. His response was always to bless God:

> Blessed be the Lord my God, who teacheth my hands to fight, and my fingers to war. My mercy, and my refuge: my support, and my deliverer . . . Happy is that people whose God is the Lord (Ps 143: 1, 2, 15).

Tobias was a man who recognized God's hidden mercies: "He repined not against God because the evil of blindness had befallen him, but continued immovable in the fear of God, giving thanks to God all the days of his life" (Tobias 2: 13–14). And when rewarded with the gift of his sight, he immediately "glorified God" and said: "I bless thee, O Lord God of Israel, because thou hast chastised me, and thou hast saved me" (11: 17). Again, Tobias and his family recognized the merciful love of God their Father in the sending of Raphael to them. Their immediate reaction was adoration, praise, and the blessing of God.

Blessings are found in the New Testament too. The Incarnation, greatest proof of the Father's merciful love, is surrounded by blessings. Our Lady was called blessed by

Gabriel. Zachary saw his son John and recognized God's mercy: *Benedictus Dominus Deus Israel.* His song is so rich, full of things otherwise inexpressible: adoration, praise, gratitude, and joy. Simeon, holding the Messiah in his arms, blessed God. This tremendous event inspired these just men, who in some way link the Old Testament and the New, to bless God. Adoration, wonder, gratitude, amazement, are expressed in the blessing of each in different proportions. Each used the same word, but it expressed an individual soul, and all that had gone on in that soul in the past. Suddenly they saw the mercy of God, and into their blessings went all the riches of mind and heart.

All these elements, when man blesses God, are woven by love into a garland—because these children of God loved their Father so much they were sensitive to his mercy toward them. So they felt urged to bless him for it as soon as they saw the wonder of it. St. Paul was the same; his cry of wonder seems to pierce heaven: "Blessed be the God and Father of our Lord Jesus Christ, who hath blessed us with spiritual blessings in heavenly places, in Christ" (Eph. 1: 3).

The saints in their severest sufferings said, "Blessed be God." The Holy Spirit put on their lips what he had put on the lips of people in the Old Testament, for they all saw in suffering their Father's merciful love. We too can learn to say it in success or failure, after a rebuke that hurts, in monotonous or uncongenial work, if we see all these things as gifts from our Father's hands. We can thank him for all the circumstances of our lives, for his mercy directs them.

The great act of thanksgiving for the new Israel is the Mass. To be united with the sacrifice of the Son and his dispositions toward the Father, this alone makes endurable the smallness of our gratitude compared with what we receive. It alone makes acceptable to the Father the smallness of our offering. We are not poor in thanks who offer his Son, nor does our Father see it so. *Quid retribuam*

Domino pro omnibus quae retribuit mihi? Calicem salutaris accipiam et nomen Domino invocabo? "What shall I render to the Lord, for all the things that he hath rendered to me? I will take the chalice of salvation; and I will call upon the name of the Lord" (Ps 115: 12, 13). The sacrifices of the old Israel were expressive of gratitude, but this Act alone is proportioned to our debt. It is infinite and inexhaustible. The Divine Office too is a means of thanking God for his mercy. We ought to thank him not only through but for the Mass and the Divine Office because in them he has given us words and acts of thanksgiving which we can make our own.

Do we really feel a spontaneous urge to thank God for his merciful love? If a person becomes sensitive, pure, childlike enough to see blessings in all that God gives, then there is an unceasing desire to say, "Blessed be God." There is something alive and stirring in the soul of that child of God which needs to be expressed. Then many of the words of Scripture, especially the Psalms, correspond to this movement of the soul. As soon as the Holy Spirit finds a truly childlike heart, sensitive to God's blessings, then he in his infinite mercy fills the words with new meaning. They are always loving words, because the Spirit of Love is behind them all. But we must love deeply, for a superficial love of God only makes the words seem to belong to someone else. So often we do not respond to the Holy Spirit because we are failing in sensitivity to his touch. Alertness to him means at the same time purity of heart, faithfulness in little things, generosity, silence, and recollection, day after day, whatever we are doing. In this way we grow sensitive to the Spirit, and to our Father's merciful love. Then we can exclaim with Moses, in the words of his Canticle of praise and thanksgiving:

> Who is like to thee, among the strong, O Lord? Who is
> like to thee glorious in holiness, terrible and praise-

worthy, doing wonders? . . . In thy mercy thou hast been a leader to the people which thou hast redeemed: and in thy strength, thou hast carried them to thy holy habitation (Ex 15: 11, 13).

So too we shall long for heaven in order to thank our Father for his merciful love "face to face" for all eternity, and to wonder for ever at the wisdom of his condescension.

The mercies of the Lord I will sing for ever. I will shew forth thy truth with my mouth to generation and generation. For thou hast said: Mercy shall be built up for ever in the heavens; thy truth shall be prepared in them. Blessed be the Lord for evermore. So be it. So be it (Ps 88: 1, 3, 53).

5

The Father's Wisdom

For my thoughts are not your thoughts: nor your ways my ways, saith the Lord. For as the heavens are exalted above the earth so are my ways exalted above your ways, and my thoughts above your thoughts.

ISAIAH 55: 8, 9

O the depth of the riches of the wisdom and of the knowledge of God! How incomprehensible are his judgements, and how unsearchable his ways.

ROMANS 11: 33

To the Israelites, escaping from Egypt, the way God took them through the desert must have seemed foolish. He did not lead them by a straight and easy route along the Coast but by a roundabout way so that they would not meet the hostility of the Philistines and be tempted to return to Egypt. In his wisdom their Father foresaw all possible difficulties, and he "went before them to shew the way by day in a pillar of cloud, and by night in a pillar of fire: that he might be the guide of their journey at both times" (Ex 13: 21–22). So often God's wisdom seems folly to us as we see it in the circumstances of our lives, and yet looking back afterward we see that he was right: he always knows best. This is what happened when later writers, like the author of the Book of Wisdom, looked back on earlier events. This author, possessing richly the gift of understanding, was able to recognize God's wisdom in creation, in the history of Israel, and in God's care of his children. He recognized that to acknowledge the Father's wisdom is to become wise. It is the fool who abuses his knowledge of the world by recognizing only

43

creatures: "For if they were able to know so much as to make a judgement of the world: how did they not more easily find out the Lord thereof?" (Wis 13: 9). For the wise man the whole of creation reveals its Creator and his beauty, the whole history of Israel its Father and his wisdom.

We need to be deeply purified in our minds to understand God's ways, to appreciate the pattern of his wisdom in the ordering of our lives. Our insight is obscured by original sin, and we have acquired, often painfully, a wisdom of our own. This is the wisdom of fallen nature, an understanding of things, a way of judging, a worldly outlook quite different from divine wisdom. Every one of us to some extent needs a deeply penetrating purification which is exceedingly painful, to force us to give up our own way of thinking for God's way. Somehow our own knowledge and understanding seem to have become almost identified with our minds themselves: that is why it is painful to give it all up. We are full of our own opinions, and often we think we are being asked to give up what is wise. But we have to learn that our human, worldly, often selfish wisdom is not really wisdom at all. The only true wisdom is God's wisdom. "All wisdom is from the Lord God, and hath always been with him, and is before all time" (Ecclus 1: 1).

Once we grasp this, we can begin to strip ourselves of our illusions. We can absorb divine wisdom only to the extent that we give up our own. We have to learn to be detached from all our own preferences, even in spiritual things, so as to be sure that we are open to our Father's wisdom. Few people allow themselves to be completely possessed by divine wisdom because so many are unwilling to be different from the world. They want to think and be as the people around them, and yet they want God's wisdom at the same time. But this is impossible. A thirst for God and a thirst for wisdom cannot be separated, and so we are wise if we abandon our worldly outlook and seek only God, who is Wisdom.

In Scripture the Father speaks to his children in their own language: his wisdom is at the service of his merciful love. We cannot help loving the words of Scripture if we think of them as coming from him: "Eat honey, my son, because it is good, and the honeycomb most sweet to thy throat: so also is the doctrine of wisdom to thy soul" (Prov 24: 13–14). In Scripture, Infinite Wisdom is speaking. Let us always approach him, then, as he speaks to us, with open minds, completely, unconditionally, ready to hear, to understand, and be penetrated by the words of life.

It is above all through the Person of the only-begotten Son of the Father that we must seek his wisdom. He fulfills all the old revelations of divine wisdom. Now that he has come into the world as man, we can read new meanings into old texts, seeing the Father's wisdom be-hind past events. The author of the Book of Wisdom, for instance, looking back on the slaying of the first-born of Egypt just before the Exodus, sees God's wisdom in the sending of his word, the "fierce conqueror" of Israel's enemies:

> For while all things were in quiet silence, and the night was in the midst of her course, thy almighty word leapt down from thy royal throne (Wis 18: 14–15).

The Church, with her wonderful capacity for accommo-dating scriptural texts, now applies this to the Incarna-tion. In mid-silence, suddenly, the Word of God leapt down to earth, sent by the Father in his infinite wisdom, to take up his abode with men. The Word spoken by the Father from all eternity, was spoken in time and entered the world not only as the "fierce conqueror" of sin, but also to show forth his Father's love for men. Thus the Incarnation is the supreme manifestation of the Father's wisdom. The sweet Word, Incarnate Wisdom, came to speak to us about his Father and himself, about our adoption and salvation from sin and death. In the Gospels we find Eternal Wisdom speaking about God in human language. The Word as it were breaks himself up into little words for the children of God. St. John often speaks of the Word speaking words. Our Lord is breaking up wisdom into little pieces to feed us, the hungry children.

The crucifixion sums up all the apparent foolishness and supreme wisdom of the Father's dealings with his adopted children. His plan was made "before the foundation of the world," St. Paul tells us. He chose us to be "holy and unspotted in his sight in charity: who hath predestinated us unto the adoption of children through Jesus Christ unto himself, according to the purpose of his will, unto the praise of the glory of his grace, in which he hath graced us in his beloved Son" (Eph 1: 4–6). The folly of the cross is the wisdom of God.

The Son came for the glory of his Father, for the fulfilling of his will, to make known his name, so that we might glorify him, too. And yet he willed to be despised, to be condemned to death like a slave. This is wisdom in action. When Christ acts and speaks, Wisdom acts and speaks. Moreover, when our Lord makes exacting demands, it is Wisdom that makes exacting demands. "For the word of the cross, to them indeed that perish, is foolishness; but to them that are saved, that is, to us, it is the power of God. For it is written: 'I will destroy the wisdom of the wise, and the prudence of the prudent I will reject' . . . hath not God made foolish the wisdom of this world?" (1 Cor 1: 18–19, 20).

The counselors of our Father's kingdom are the poor of heart and the single-minded, the childlike, those who take up the cross and follow his Son. The vain, the untruthful, and ungenerous are the wise men of this world. The two wisdoms are irreconcilable. Our Lord, Eternal Wisdom, told us to become little children, to learn from him gentleness, patience, humility. His yoke is light, but we must sacrifice all our pride. If we disdain his words, are we not scorning our Father's love, as well as his wisdom? If only we could recognize this to the full and accept all the consequences.

The more contemplative we become, the more the Holy Spirit takes hold of our minds, particularly by the intellectual gifts, and makes the acceptance of divine wisdom easier. In order that he may do this, we need to get rid of our impatience and vanity and learn to be docile. "Whosoever is a little one, let him come to me," says Wisdom in the Book of Proverbs; but also we must "forsake childishness, and live, and walk by the ways of prudence" (Prov 9: 4, 6). Childishness is vanity, childlikeness is wisdom.

The world, however, expects people to be self-opinionated, to have fixed ways of judging, to have a false respect for individual opinions and judgments, as if truth were a flower found in a great many varieties which each man could cultivate to his own taste in his own garden. But the wise children of God find truth only in him: they listen to him with open minds and hearts. The world does not expect us to be childlike. Nevertheless we must be very eager to be little and to be taught the wisdom of God. We need to be very detached from our own way of thinking, humble and pure, very dependent on our Father:

> And who shall know thy thought, except thou give wisdom, and send thy Holy Spirit from above: And so the ways of them that are upon earth may be corrected, and men may learn the things that please thee? (Wis 9: 17–18).

We know that God uses human instruments to help us to him. Human mediation is the simplest way the Father has of explaining himself: that is why he spoke through

Moses, the Kings, the prophets, and sacred writers. Above all he sent us his only-begotten Son, Incarnate Wisdom, to be our Master. The Church continues his work of teaching, guided by his Spirit. Everything and everyone can in some way bring us closer to God, for as we become more childlike we find that all is relevant to our relationship with the Father; everything brings us news of him.

We too in our turn can be messengers for him. But an apostle must be a wise man, for no one can give what he has not got. If he possesses only human wisdom, he will be able to give people only his own human ideas, knowledge imperfectly extracted from limited experience. We must first learn divine wisdom before we can become true instruments of God. This means hard sacrifices and much humility, for the apostle is a servant, kneeling to wash his brothers' feet, as his Master did. For the wisdom of God which we preach is first and foremost the life of his Son, which we live.

The Father's wisdom enters our lives from morning to night through his will. They are the same thing. We are wise only in so far as we do God's will. The children of the Old Testament learned this at the cost of giving up their own ideas and allowing God to lead them. But then they were led into the promised land. Like them we live out his will in our lives; by being obedient to his laws and responsive to his Spirit we become truly wise:

> The mouth of the just shall meditate wisdom: and his tongue shall speak judgement. The law of God is in his heart, and his steps shall not be supplanted . . . Expect the Lord and keep his way: and he will exalt thee to inherit the land (Ps 36: 30, 31, 34).

Perhaps obedience is difficult: it may not seem to make sense. That is probably because we are judging things from a purely human point of view. We must beware of trying to measure the Father's transcendent wisdom by our own knowledge and experience. He is Infinite Wisdom: if we could understand him completely with our puny human minds, he would he something less.

We need to learn from the example of the Israelites wandering in the desert yet another lesson. It must have seemed a purposeless existence to many of them: they seemed to be doing nothing constructive. But God had a plan which included not only their wanderings and their settling in the promised land, but also the Incarnation and Redemption. All his actions, past, present, and future, are part of the working-out of the plan of his glorification. All things are to be restored in Christ, and the glory of the Trinity manifested. The whole world from its first to its last day serves this purpose, and each generation contributes only a fraction. Yet each individual has his part to play, as if each were a little stone in a mosaic.

The purpose of our existence is to make our insignificant but nevertheless indispensable contribution toward the beauty of the whole mosaic, designed by Divine Wisdom to reflect his beauty. As we do not see the whole design, nor even his plan for us as individuals, our part is bound to appear meaningless sometimes, or at least puzzling. At most we see our lives in the context of a small fraction of the whole: a family or community or group of colleagues. So we have to learn to accept the mystery. The wanderings of the Chosen People, meaningless as they seemed, played a very important providential part in the building up of the messianic kingdom in preparation for the Incarnation and ultimately the glorification of God by mankind in his Son.

Let us try to rise above the appearances of things to the Source: our Father in all his wisdom and mercy. Of course we have to recognize the limitations of our life, but we need also to see it as playing an indispensable part in the mosaic of God's plan. If our life does not glorify God, if it does not fulfill the purpose God intended for it, the mosaic will to that extent be marred. Our stone may be a very tiny one, insignificant in itself, yet seen from God's point of view the picture is defective without it. We prevent God to that extent from manifesting his glory perfectly, because we were not there to contribute our little part.

Acceptance of God's wisdom in planning our lives and submission to it in the events which we do not understand bring great peace of soul. To accept a mystery we must submit—*Fiat*—and then ponder in our hearts, as our Lady did. Not ponder first and then submit if we understand. God may give us some understanding later, but even if we are left in darkness our *Fiat* remains, and we are fitting into his wise and beautiful design. No human being can ever deprive us of our share in our Father's glorification; that is a great consolation. We can look forward to the day when we shall see his design fulfilled, including our own little part in the context of the whole.

The danger is that we shall want to know too much now. If we insist on knowing God's reasons for things before submitting, we shall never be given understanding. The only way in which we can learn something of divine wisdom now is by being very docile, anxious to be taught in his way alone. God will enlighten us, by degrees, by his gift of Wisdom, whereby we know more of him because we are becoming more like him. We shall begin to see things more as he does. But we must remember that we are in the presence of God and take off our shoes: detach ourselves from our worldly knowledge and our own preconceived ideas. Then the Holy Spirit is given freedom to work in us.

We say in the Advent liturgy: *O sapientia, suaviter disponensque omnia fortiter et suaviter. . . .* Irresistibly and gently, our Father's wisdom graciously orders everything from one end of the world to the other. In the coming of his Son, we find a wonderful combination of infinite power and gentleness. Only Infinite Power and Love could make itself as helpless as he did in the crib. Only Infinite Wisdom could be so obedient. In making the obedience of the only-begotten Son theirs, the adopted children can begin to learn something of their Father's wisdom.

6

The Father's Providence

The beloved people has a God great as no other; he rides in heaven to deliver thee, the clouds making way for his majestic coming; there, on high, is his dwelling, and yet the eternal arms reach down to uphold thee.

DEUTERONOMY 33: 26–27 K

God has care of us. His transcendent majesty and power must not make us think of him as a distant God; rather we should be very aware of his majesty stooping down to us with the most extraordinary, detailed care. "I am a beggar and poor: the Lord is careful for me" (Ps 39: 18).

Throughout the Bible, parables and images are used to convey to us the reality of the Father's loving care. Moses uses those of the eagle and its young, and a nurse with her little charge. Our Lord says: "Are not two sparrows sold for a farthing? And not one of them shall fall on the ground without your Father. But the very hairs of your head are all numbered. Fear not therefore: better are you than many sparrows" (Mt 10: 29–31). And it is more than anything God's command—"Thou shalt call me father" (Jer 3: 19)—which makes us appreciate the Infinite Love that makes Majesty stoop so low.

The Father carries his children "as a man is wont to carry his little son" (Deut 1: 31), now, just as much as he did the Israelites in the wanderings of the desert. It was in order to show the Chosen People the detail with which he planned their liberation from Egypt that God insisted on the ritual of the Passover being performed so exactly. They were told precisely what they should eat and how, what they should wear, both at the time of the actual Passover and in the ritual which would later commemorate it. Thus they would always remember his detailed care of them and would continue to trust him:

And thou shalt tell thy son in that day, saying: This is what the Lord did to me when I came forth out of Egypt. And it shall be as a sign in thy hand, and as a memorial before thy eyes (Ex 13: 8–9).

We need to be reminded of God's care of us, for in a sense there are none others who have the power to care. If they do care for us, it is because the Father is using them as the instruments of his care. His providence exercises itself through human instruments: he gives them the charity to care for us unselfishly. That is what charity is: God's love and care being given through human instruments to his children. Ultimately there is only God's care, and that never fails. His promises to his Chosen People are put in images of human tenderness, which in some way convey his tenderness: "You shall be carried at the breasts, and upon the knees they shall caress you. As one whom the mother caresseth, so will I comfort you, and you shall be comforted in Jerusalem" (Is 66: 12).

How grateful we should be for the Father's tender care, and how contrite for the many times we have forgotten it. So often we have claimed for ourselves the independence and strength of God, and yet we can never be independent of him in truth. For the providence of the past we can only be grateful and contrite: for the providence of today we must have acceptance and submission. "My son, give me thy heart: and let thy eyes keep my ways" (Prov 23: 26).

We need to see the working of the Father's providence in our daily life, no matter how unsatisfactory it may seem. His care for each of us is personal and individual, though we may not feel anything or seem to experience his loving kindness. What could be more reassuring than his words in the Book of Isaiah: "Can a woman forget her infant, so as not to have pity on the son of her womb? And if she should forget, yet will not I forget thee" (49: 15)? Every moment is precious, a gift direct from his hands. It is very sad if we are occupied only in examining the gift to see if it gives us pleasure or not, turning it upside down with our understanding to see if it has the hallmark of God on it. There is no need of a hallmark when there is only one smith, and he is our Father. No need in fact to examine the gift at all, since no pleasure it gives us can equal the sweetness of receiving it from him.

Our Father's providence is never the same each day. He arranges a marvelous variety in our lives so that they may never settle and become stagnant. He does not want us to forget him by losing ourselves in the enjoyment of his gifts. The prophets saw clearly that whenever the Israelites settled down and became prosperous, they became un-faithful to God. They looked back with longing to the time of the desert wanderings, because they saw that there the relations of the children with their Father were at their best. There was no created support or protection in the desert, and the people were intensely aware of their utter dependence on God: led by Moses they constantly turned to their Father for help. His providence cared for them day after day, month after month, and the people served him in spite of their murmurings. It was when they became prosperous that they forgot him.

As to future providence, we know from past experience all God's loving care of us, and we can be therefore quite assured that the same care will be lavished on us in the future. We can welcome it already with wide-open arms. God will never cease to care: "He will overshadow thee with his shoulders: / and under his wings thou shalt trust" (Ps 90: 4).

If it is true that each of us has a place in his great plan, it is also true that he has a plan for each one's life individually. He supplies us with all we need both materially and spiritually to fulfill his plan for us: that we should glorify him by becoming like his Son. From our point of view, our life is like a book whose pages have not been cut. The most exciting chapter comes at the end, but our Father is wise and merciful and will not let us read it in advance. He cuts the book, page by page, for us; and only he knows how many pages there are to come, or whether the end will come quite suddenly. Of course, as we read only a page at a time, there is much that we do not fully understand, we miss some of the significance, and we shall appreciate the story as a whole only when we have reached the end and are able to look back on it. But we do know that our Father's providence watches over it all. Whenever the end does come, we shall die with the glorious likeness of his Son in our soul if we have been faithful to him all along. Page after page he cuts, saying: "This is my will for you." His will is the instrument of his fatherly love by which we reach the full maturity of children of God. He does not leave us at the mercy of illusions or the play of circumstances—he loves us too much for that. We are not to be in a constant state of perplexity, for the life of his adopted child is of its nature simple. if we trust him and obey his command, he will always let us know what he wants of us.

Our Father's care of us, then, is very different from the care we have for ourselves because he is confident in the infinite means he has to exercise that care. Our caring is born not of the power of Divine Love, but of fear, anxiety, and lack of confidence. But this becomes completely changed when we put our confidence in him: the true child of the Father is like the just man in the Psalm: "His heart is ready to hope in the Lord: his heart is strengthened, he shall not be moved" (111: 7–8).

The certainty of the Father's care develops in us the attitude of abandonment. The abandonment of individuals, of families, or of the whole Church to Divine Providence is an unreserved, peaceful, continuous abandonment to his care. It is important at all times, but most of all as regards the spiritual life. God never leaves us in complete security while we are in this world because, if he did, we would begin to forget our complete dependence on him. We would then substitute our own thoughts and ways for his and become too attached to this life, forgetting that it is only a journey. His merciful providence will not allow that.

This sense of being looked after by our Father in all circumstances is essential. Each moment he comes to us, each moment he gives himself to us. To doubt his care is to cast a reflection upon his goodness. We ought not to live in a state of perpetual worry, we ought to be able to go to bed each night as children without a care in the world, for we really have no cares, no reason for sleepless nights. "The Lord ruleth me: and I shall want nothing . . . For though I should walk in the midst of the shadow of death, I will fear no evils, for thou art with me" (Ps 22: 1, 4).

We should be grateful for that element of insecurity which keeps us always turned toward God. The precariousness of our existence, the inevitability of separations, deprivations, sufferings, interior as well as exterior, all this is good, because it makes us more aware of our dependence on God. In times of danger public or private, in need or distress, nations, families, individuals turn to him and pray for help. They recognize their helplessness then. But after the danger is over they forget him again. His most loving children, however, are truly abandoned to him, with the greatest and most unreserved generosity, and this abandonment is lasting. It is the lesson that God teaches us through St. Thérèse of Lisieux, which shows that he regards it as very important.

In the eyes of the world, abandonment is foolishness, and it is possible for us to develop the instinct of self-preservation to a very high degree. But we must be as children trusting their Father to the utmost: "Although he should kill me, I will trust in him" (Job 13: 15). He will take everything from us, tear it from us if that is necessary, to teach us to rely on him alone. Self-love is a great obstacle. Even when we have stopped admiring ourselves, we still cling to that from which we want to be freed, fearing to make a complete surrender in case it leaves us nothing. But faith can make it, faith in the loving power of our Father, especially as it is incarnate in his Son.

We have not a care in the world. If we have cares, they are of our own making and, so, against God's will. We have to ask him not to soothe our cares, but to teach us to forget them, so that we may lose ourselves in the security of his arms. Moses hesitated for one moment when he beat the rock for water: for this failing in trust, he was denied more than the sight of the promised land. For lack of faith, Zachary was struck dumb. But our Lady, with her perfect faith, her unquestioning *Fiat*, "Let it be," became the Mother of God. The world today is lacking in faith, full of anxiety: there is nothing like enough abandonment to God.

We must abandon to him our whole life, materially and spiritually; our death too, with all its circumstances and the time of its coming. We must abandon to his care all those we love: he loves them, too, for it is proper to the lover to love those whom the Beloved loves. The Father will look after them-their health, their sickness, their prosperity, their sufferings, are all in his hands. We have to live a life-long Passover: "your loins must be girt, your feet ready shod, and every man's staff in his hand" (Ex 12: 11 K). For we are in flight from ourselves, passing over the summits of the land, in the security of faith, to the security of vision; in flight from sin, journeying through the desert of the spiritual life. No danger, material or spiritual, can touch the life of a baptized Christian, for he lives with his Father's life. If we fear for an instant that the waves will engulf us, it is because we are looking at them instead of at the way of faith and trust, which is perfectly dry. We too are in the shadow of our Father's providence, just like the Israelites:

> For a cloud overshadowed their camp, and where water was before, dry land appeared, and in the Red Sea a way without hindrance and out of the great deep a springing field: Through which all the nation passed which was protected with thy hand, seeing thy miracles and wonders (Wis 19: 7–8).

Sometimes we can see nothing else but our trials and temptations: the waters seem to threaten our life, and yet we know that our feet are dry, our Father is with us. We can always say: "I have put my trust in thee, O Lord: I said: Thou art my God. My lots are in thy hands" (Ps 30: 15–16). Spontaneously, then, we call on him as our Father: it seems the only name which fully expresses our love and our trust: "Thou, O Lord, art our father, our redeemer, from everlasting is thy name" (Is 63: 16).

7

The Father Forms His Children

Do not forget the long journeying by which, for forty years,
the Lord thy God led thee through the desert, testing thee by
hard discipline, to know the dispositions of thy heart, whether
thou wouldst keep his commandments or not.

DEUTERONOMY 8: 2 K

The Chosen People, God's adopted children, had much
to learn about their Father and about themselves during
their wanderings in the desert. How often their Father
found them a "stiff-necked people," always trying to go off
on their own, refusing to trust and obey him. In the Book
of Deuteronomy, Moses reminds them of his descent
from Mount Horeb, bearing the tablets of stone with the
commandments written on them, when he found the
people worshiping a molten calf. How quickly they had
forgotten God's words "from the midst of the fire." Only
through his prayer had the Father kept patience with them
and spared them. Moses reminds them of the wonderful
deeds of God on their behalf at the time of the Exodus,
and tells them that they must remain faithful to him if they
are ever to enter the promised land.

All this time of exile was their time of training, of
discipline, of their preparation as the nation from which
one day the Messiah would come. But first they had to
learn some hard lessons: they had to recognize their own
weakness, the futility of their own attempts at independence.
The Father had to bring them low so that they
would recognize their total dependence upon him:

Because they had exasperated the words of God: and
provoked the counsel of the most High: And their heart

was humbled with labours: they were weakened, and there was none to help them. Then they cried to the Lord in their affliction: and he delivered them out of their distresses (Ps 106: 11–13).

In his patience he was willing to teach them slowly, step by step, and he never failed to supply them in their needs, once they turned to him again with repentant and humble hearts. He is just as patient with us. He is willing to spend a whole life-time to train each child of his to behave as a member of his family. In fact his wisdom disposes all the events of our life precisely for this purpose.

For us the great test is life itself. As will be seen, God sometimes sends us specific trials which test particular virtues, but as a rule it is our daily life which is the most searching test. It is so continuous, so inescapable, so deep-going. And yet that is the most natural way of teaching us: it can be a steady growth in childlikeness. Through everyday things we can be shown hidden faults that we never knew, or weaknesses we never suspected. That is why such testing is so valuable. Life-long, varying from time to time in intensity, the trial of life on earth is our Father's patient way of training us to be mature members of his family.

Therefore we should never want to be free from this discipline of his. That would be foolish: to want to be free from trials is to want to be free from the Father's love. His love is a fire, a purifying fire, and that is bound to burn and hurt us; it will be so especially when that fire must consume something that resists it, that will be purified only with difficulty. But we have to trust the Father's wisdom, remembering that he tests only those he loves:

And dost thou doubt that the Lord was chastening thee, as a man chastens his own son, training thee to keep the commandments of the Lord thy God, and follow the path he chooses, and live in fear of him? (Deut 8: 5–6 к).

We do not read that God tested the Hittites or the Egyptians, or that he was patient with them. His justice often scourged them, but he did not discipline them in the sense of training them; that was reserved for his Chosen People, his "first-born." Moses, their leader, had first to be purified and taught God's ways. It is the same for all the adopted children, old or new: we have to be prepared for trials, seeing his love behind them.

The Israelites were in the desert for three days without water. This was a severe trial at the very beginning of their journey. But the Father knew to what limit he could go at that stage and did not press them further: as soon as they complained, he "shewed Moses a tree whose wood turned the waters sweet when it was thrown into them" (Ex 15: 25 к). Sometimes God seems to try us to the very limit of our endurance. We feel that if it lasts a moment longer we shall not be able to bear it. Yet he well knows what we are capable of, and we learn that in a second he can remove all tension by supplying exactly what is needed. The purpose of such trials is to make us trust him, but he can try us only to the extent that we let him love us. That is why the greatest saints had great sufferings: they were the Father's most loving and beloved children.

Trials rightly accepted also have the effect of emptying us of self-love. This is necessary because if we are full of self we can never be filled with God. We should ask him to empty us of self-love so that we may have a greater capacity for his love. Then we shall be free to love him with all our strength. But to be loved by God to our fullest capacity will mean much self-denial, and few people really want this. They want the consolations at least of love, the good things, like wisdom and knowledge, which come from love; they do not want the suffering, they want to choose.

But it is no good selecting what we want: we have to want what love wants. Our Father's love will teach us the necessity for greater purity. The new Israel must outstrip the old by asking to be cleansed, but also for the strength to bear the trials. If the Father is to fill us, he has to deepen our capacity for him: we need great fortitude to bear it. Our mind, our will, our spirit, our faith, hope, and charity, the very deepest parts of our soul: all must be purified. And so there must be willingness on our part, too, there must be no "murmuring" from the new Israel as there was from the old.

We can learn much from the behavior of the Israelites in their trials and the Father's dealings with them. Their great defect was lack of faith. The Church reminds us every day at Matins not to follow their example, in the Invitatory "Today if you shall hear his voice: harden not your hearts: As in the provocation, according to the day of temptation in the wilderness: where your fathers tempted me, they proved me, and saw my works" (Ps 94: 8–9). They were trying to put God to the test. The Hebrew word used is exactly the same for God putting the Israelites to the test as it is for their putting God to the test. But the Father has the right to test his children; the children have no right to test their Father. Their special test was hunger and thirst. They "murmured," complained to Moses and Aaron: "Would to God we had died by the hand of the Lord in the land of Egypt, when we sat over the flesh pots, and ate bread to the full. Why have you brought us into this desert, that you might destroy all the multitude with famine?" (Ex 16: 3).

We too have often murmured, perhaps not so seriously as this, but by asking whether the trials God sends are compatible with his love. Trials may take different forms: sickness, aridity, failure, misunderstanding—it does not matter what—and they may last a long time. Yet we must not doubt the Father's merciful love and power, nor judge him by our human standards. This is what the Israelites were doing, and Moses had to explain that their complaints were against God, not against himself. Likewise their trust had to be not in him but in God. We have to accept the fact that our Father's wisdom surpasses all our understanding. We must not ask from him an account of his doings, for it is foolish to try to penetrate the mystery every time something happens that we do not understand. Not only in order to satisfy us would God be obliged to enlighten us about his plan for our own life, but also about the details of his whole providential design. Instead of causing a disturbance in our own soul by seeking to understand too much, let us peacefully accept the trials his wisdom has devised for us. Our trials are very often the way he chooses to teach us to practice the virtues we have been praying for. The man who prays for patience, for instance, does not wake up in the morning completely changed, made patient overnight. No, it is through the violence of temptation and the efforts taken to overcome it with God's help that we grow in virtue.

The Israelites were tempted to think that the Father no longer cared about what happened to them. They doubted the love of One who could give what seemed essential, but did not do so. But they were to have the promised land in virtue of their faith, not their own strength: he reserved to himself the means of getting them there. The Father knew that their faith was very weak, in spite of all they had seen of his power, and so he taught them the same lesson over and over again; he allowed them to feel the severest need and then supplied them with more than they could wish for. Yet their continued lack of faith displeased him deeply; so much so that he would not let any of that generation enter the promised land except Joshua and Caleb, whose trust had never failed.

There was no justification for their lack of faith, for they had seen so many *mirabilia Dei* to strengthen it, and yet "they forgot his works: and they waited not for his counsel" (Ps 105: 13). We too have seen *mirabilia Dei*, and even greater ones: the Incarnation and the Redemption. From a purely natural point of view the Exodus may have been more striking, but the Incarnation is an infinitely higher manifestation of God's love and power. Consequently, God expects of us at least as much faith as he did of them. We must not harden our hearts; let us remember the *mirabilia Dei* in our own lives: the gift of faith, the sacraments, especially baptism, and all the signs of love that the Father has given us personally. The least lack of faith is a slight to him, a sin which greatly displeases him. We need never engage thoughts of doubt, even if the devil tempts us with them; we only make them worse by dwelling on them. We ought to focus our contrition sometimes on our failures in faith; certainly we should never take it for granted that we never fail thus. Of course, charity is the greatest virtue, but still in this life it rests on faith, and the more steadfast our faith, the more we shall love.

We need never despair: our Father's power is enough to make us saints if only we trust him and want it enough. He will lead us to the promised land. If we were the worst sinners imaginable, with all the sins in the world on our consciences, it would be nothing to him to wipe them all away. It is a small matter to Infinite Power. Our Father wants to make us saints: when he disciplines us we have to believe that, and keep our eyes fixed on him. If we get too absorbed in ourselves we lose sight of God. Then, discouraged by our own failures, we are tempted to say: "What is the use of trying, considering my past record?" No, we must trust in the love and the power of our Father, and in his Son sent to redeem us and strengthen us. His love is always there, patient and faithful, waiting for us to turn to him.

Our Father alone is to guide and teach us, just as he reserved for himself the guidance of his Chosen People.

He showed them each day how far to go; they never knew beforehand, but moved with the Pillar of Cloud and stopped with it, following wherever it led them. The people may have rebelled, but they had no positive way of their own: they did not know where the promised land was or how to get there. They were entirely dependent on God's guidance and had no alternative but to go his way. It is a most important lesson for us: we too must travel in God's way and not choose our own. There is only one way to heaven for the children of the new Israel, and that is to follow the Son of God, who said, "I am the way."

To follow our Lord means following him in suffering. It means utter dependence on God; and like the Israelites, if we try to go off on our own we shall certainly die in the desert. Just as he gave them the food, the strength they needed every single day for forty years, our Father will give us all we need each day of our life. The Luminous Cloud is commonly taken as a symbol of the light of faith, obscure in the daylight, bright at night, yet always guiding us in our exodus from earth to heaven. Our Lord calls himself the Light of the world, and St. Paul sees in the cloud a symbol of the Holy Spirit. All these meanings are true: all show us how the Father is drawing us to himself, to eternal beatitude in the promised land.

So few people recognize that our life here is in a wilderness. No natural food or water can ever satisfy our souls—it is wrong to expect it; and therefore we have to be made to feel our need of God, who alone can satisfy us. We are exiles and strangers here on earth: this is brought home to us when darkness falls upon our souls. We follow the light of Jesus Christ whether we are in darkness or in consolation. All the trials which make up the one great trial of life itself teach us that our only security is our faith in the Father's power and merciful love, his wisdom and providence. He is always faithful, even though he may take away from us all natural security.

Our Father wants us to hunger and thirst for him. He feeds us, and we hunger the more; he quenches our thirst, and yet it becomes more intense. We cannot be satisfied fully until in heaven we possess him and he possesses us. The nearer we come to the end of our journey, the more we shall long for him. But we must always desire God ardently, from the beginning to the end of our journey, even if we are in darkness. The foretaste that we are given while we are in the desert is only enough to sustain us for the present, for there remains a hunger and thirst for God alone, and a cry to the Father from the very core of our being to take us to him. Our time of trial is a blessing: it is the Father's way of training us to depend on him, to seek him alone, so that one day we may come home to him and he will recognize us as his children, because we have in us a likeness to his only-begotten Son.

8

The Father's Faithfulness

*The Lord is faithful in all his words and holy
in all his works.*

PSALM 144: 13 C

For it is a perverse generation and unfaithful children.

DEUTERONOMY 32: 20

The Father is faithful and true: these two aspects of his
goodness cannot be separated. In many versions of the
Psalms the two words are interchangeable, both meaning
the same thing: God is Truth, constant, unchanging, reli-
able. He always lives up to the expectations of his children, for "the Lord is the true God: he is the living God,
and the everlasting king" (Jer 10: 10). His word is true,
and he is always faithful to it: "God is not a man, that
he should lie, nor as the son of man, that he should be
changed. Hath he said then, and will he not do? Hath
he spoken, and will he not fulfil?" (Num 23: 19). When he
passed before Moses, hidden in the cleft of the rock,
Yahweh proclaimed himself "rich in kindness, faithful to
his promises" (Ex 34: 6). He meant at the same time: rich
in goodness and truth, supreme in veracity and constancy.

It is not surprising, then, to find the faithfulness of God
such a favorite theme in the Psalms. The Father's faithfulness is closely linked with his mercy, for they both express
his loving care of his children. "His faithfulness is a buck-
ler and a shield" (Ps 90: 4 C) to them, because it provides
an assured protection. "All the paths of the Lord are
kindness and constancy" (Ps 24: 10 C), that is, all his ways
of dealing with his people are inspired by goodness and
faithfulness to his promises.

67

When the Father began to make known to men something of his providential plan for them, he bound himself by certain promises: he promised Noah that he would never again destroy mankind, and gave the rainbow as a symbol of his "covenant"; Abraham received for himself and his descendants the divine promise of salvation, and circumcision became the symbol. In return Noah, Abraham, and their descendants were bound to God by ties of loyalty and obedience. Now, when the Father had proved his power and love still further by delivering Israel from Egypt, thus making them his particular possession, he made them a nation with himself as their king. The reasons are summed up with perspicuity by Moses in the Book of Deuteronomy, for he had been enlightened by the Father himself:

> Yours is a people set apart for its own God, chosen by its own God, out of all the nations on earth, as his own people. If the Lord has held you closely to him and shewed you special favour, it was not that you overshadowed other peoples in greatness; of all nations you are the smallest. No, it was because the Lord loved you, because he was true to the oath which he had sworn to your fathers (Deut 7: 6–8 K).

Fifty days after the crossing of the Red Sea, on the day which was henceforward called Pentecost, God offered the Israelites a new covenant, an alliance. Israel was to be for him a domain over which he would exercise his royal and fatherly power, and was made up of those who had access to him and served him. It would be a holy nation, consecrated and belonging to him on condition that Israel obeyed him and observed the laws of the covenant. This was sealed by the people's promising obedience to God and being sprinkled with blood by his representative. It was thus both a gratuitous gift and an obligation: the

Father adopted them as his children, but they would have to behave as such, in order that he could carry out his part of the undertaking in its fullness.

The children of Israel expressed their filial love and obedience by fidelity to the precepts of the covenant: it was the proof of their own genuine desire to be God's people. Faithfulness is reciprocal, as Moses explained to them:

> And thou wilt find it ever the same; the Lord thy God is God almighty, is God ever faithful; if men will love him and keep his commandments, he is true to his word, and shews mercy to them while a thousand generations pass; if they make him their enemy, his speedy retribution overwhelms them, without more ado, the reward they have deserved (Deut 7: 9–10 K).

It was a wonderful condescension of God, his alliance made with mere creatures, giving them not only obligations but rights. He promised to be their Father, their Shepherd, to lead and protect them. And yet he knew that only a remnant would remain faithful: the majority were stiffnecked, self-reliant, unfaithful. He reminded them again and again of their obligations by means of their defeats, their trials, or the messages of the prophets, but throughout their history the Father's faithfulness stands out in striking contrast to the fickleness of his children.

We, the children of the new alliance, are descendants of the faithful remnant. Jesus Christ, Son and Word of God, the True and Faithful One, has come to fulfill all the promises of his Father. He communicates to mankind, redeemed by his Blood and thus adopted by his Father, the grace which he possesses in plenitude. The grace of his faithfulness is given to the adopted children who by imitating him in fidelity until death merit the crown of life and the promised land. The Holy Spirit, who is also the

Spirit of Truth, was sent by the Father and the Son on the old feast of Pentecost to ratify the new covenant of charity. Thus the old covenant was fulfilled by the new, and once more the Father's faithfulness was proved more stable, more perpetual than the firmament itself: "Forever, O Lord, thy word standeth firm in heaven. Thy truth unto all generations" (Ps 118: 89–90).

It is not a matter of giving up the good things of the old alliance—all that was good and holy and sweet in the old is found even more fully in the new. We are closer to the Father than ever before. His Chosen People are now all those who are baptized in his Son. The new covenant continues the old: at baptism we promise obedience and receive not only obligations but the Fatherhood of God in a new and perfect way. Every Christian is made holy by baptism. We are, as it were, sprinkled with the Blood of Christ, whose every drop is enough to wash away all the sins of the world. We receive his Blood indeed in Holy Communion in order to intensify our alliance: it gradually transforms our sense of obligation into friendship, deepening into love. Our Lord himself, the Faithful One, comes to live in us that we may live in him. He purifies our love, shows us the love of the Father, unites us to the Father, and himself, and the Holy Spirit.

If the loving faithfulness of the Son dominates us through the Holy Spirit's action, it will not be so difficult to carry out our part of the alliance by living up to our baptismal vows. The Father will give us all we need to grow in holiness and to meet all the demands he makes of us. He gives us the sacraments: deep living waters against temptations and the powers of evil. He gives us a Mother, who intercedes for us all and cares for us all as her children. And in return, we are to do his will. As long as we do not deviate in the slightest, we can be sure that he will become ever more intimately our Father and shower on us the mercies he is always anxious to give us.

The Old Testament thus helps us to understand our new covenant made with the Father. It is an alliance based on reciprocity: he cannot carry out his part unless we do ours. And yet if we fall away, when we return he will receive us back, as the father of the prodigal son did. In fact it is his faithful love which calls us to return: that is its very beginning—and his forgiveness goes beyond our hopes and dreams.

Yet all the tenderness and intimacy of the Father's faithfulness could not be adequately conveyed in terms of the Alliance between him and his Chosen People. In order to bring it home to them more vividly, the Father's faithfulness toward Israel, both old and new, is expressed also in the imagery of the Beloved and his spouse. In some of the prophets, especially Hosea, we are shown God taking Israel out into the wilderness far from temptations to infidelity, to teach her his love. The prosperity of Israel's pagan neighbors and their rich lands was a constant temptation to infidelity, but out in the desert the Chosen People had to rely on God alone. They were even unfaithful there, but it was usually through their lack of trust in his love and wisdom and mercy, and only sometimes through a leaning toward idolatry. Prosperity was dangerous: when they recognized their helplessness, they turned to God, and so he had to teach them through their failures and his faithful answers to their calls for help. There was thus a continual cycle of prosperity, infidelity, punishment, contrition, forgiveness, and prosperity again. Though the lessons of the desert were hard, prophets like Hosea looked back longingly at this time when there were such clear proofs of God's predilection for Israel:

> Behold I will allure her, and will lead her into the wilderness: and I will speak to her heart . . . and she shall sing there according to the days of her youth, and according to the days of her coming up out of the land

of Egypt. And it shall be in that day, saith the Lord, that she shall call me: my husband (Hos 2: 14, 15, 16).

God is the Spouse of his Chosen People of the new covenant even more than of the old. He shows us the same unfailing divine faithfulness, in spite of our infidelity. We may no longer be guilty of sins like idolatry, but we are unfaithful in little things. We are certainly very much lacking in the generosity required of us if we are to respond fully to the initiative of God's love. Each Christian is intended to be a spouse of God, and he gives each of us all the graces we need in order to be faithful, if only we will take them. Fidelity in little things is tremendously important in the spiritual life, where God and the soul are alone together, and this fidelity gathers up into itself all the other virtues, such as fortitude, faith, hope, and love.

The spiritual life is a school of love, just as marriage is in another sphere. But with us only one party has to learn, to be trained in divine love. At the beginning of the spiritual life we concentrate mostly on God's gifts to us, and we try to respond faithfully. Yet we must learn to go beyond this, for perfect love concentrates more on giving, giving as much as it possibly can, with the utmost fidelity, and without looking for anything in return.

In the Canticle of Canticles we have a much fuller picture of God as Spouse of his Chosen People and of the individual soul than anywhere else. It is also a description of love maturing from that which rejoices in receiving to the pure love of giving. At the beginning the spouse sings of the gifts she receives from her Beloved. But the Beloved sees that she is attached to his gifts to her, and withdraws the sensible manifestations of his love. He withdraws himself too, so that his absence may bring her to desire and seek him. He loves her so much that he wants her to become perfect in love. Her love is strong enough to stand the test, and when he returns to her, her love is purer though not yet perfect: she must yet thirst for his love and his presence more.

God acts in this way with the soul. By his apparent absence he empties her heart of all but the truest love for him. He gives no sensible manifestations of his love, though it is this very love which inspires him to "leave" her. It is now that she must be very faithful indeed, continuing to love him though all feeling has disappeared, and trusting in his faithful love for her. She must not allow the temptation to turn to other consolations or to lose herself in activity, to conquer her. This trial comes from her faithful Lover, and she must remain faithful to him; thus it will strengthen her love. Our Lord told his apostles that it was better for them that he should go; otherwise they would not have become strong enough for the labors of spreading the Gospel, for martyrdom—for they would have relied too much on his physical presence.

We read that the spouse in the Canticle becomes capable of greater love through fidelity in her trials. The Beloved has deepened her capacity for love, but if she had been unfaithful, this deepening would have been impossible. Now, however, there can be much greater intimacy between them. To perfect her love finally, the Beloved absents himself again, and again she proves faithful, seeking him everywhere. The intensity of her love grows, and her purity of intention increases; when the Beloved comes back this time, he gives himself to her completely.

God accepts our love, but that does not mean he is immediately satisfied. He loves us so much that he wants to increase it and to intensify our desire for him. When he finds us remaining faithful in love, in little things, he comes back, bringing gifts which we are now able to appreciate but which before we could not have received. He withdraws again in an ever more painful absence, for shorter or longer periods, even for years. Our love is measured by our faithfulness; it is a pale reflection of his faithfulness, which is measured by his love. There is nothing so important as this fidelity in the spiritual life if we are to become perfectly united to God. We have to remain faithful in spite of his apparent indifference and seeming neglect, going on year after year, as long as he wants us to, even if he never manifests himself to us again in this life. This is the attitude he longs to find in us. His absence is necessary to us. If it does not perfect our love, it is because we are not being faithful; we may be growing weary of the exertion it needs to remain faithful. But it is a thing he loves: fidelity to his will, his love, his inspirations, guidance, initiative, to him in all things. When he is most absent from us in this sense he is showing himself most faithful and loving, for he is giving us a greater capacity for love. It hurts, and often we do not appreciate it, but he is showing himself more than ever our Spouse: he wounds us that we may have a great desire.

This figure of the faithful love of God for his people, and of the faithfulness he requires in return—that of the Beloved and the spouse—is the most intense expression of it possible in human language. The imagery does not conflict with that of the faithful love of the Father for his child, because the reality expressed is more vivid than any picture. Hosea himself uses both kinds of imagery to express God's love for his people. Through them both we recognize the infinite love which surpasses all description, and which dominates all the attributes of the Father. His power, mercy, wisdom, providence, patience, and faithfulness are all in the service of his transcendent love.

9

The Father and Our Lady

Magnificat anima mea Dominum.
"My soul magnifies the Lord."
LUKE 1: 46

As the children of God grow in their awareness of the Father's infinite majesty and his loving condescension toward them, they desire more and more to glorify him. The Mother he has given them shows them by her example how a true child of God responds to all the proofs of love that the Father has shown throughout the ages.

Our Lady, greatest and purest of all God's adopted children, had the deepest insight into the abyss of his holiness, and her own lowliness as his creature. She knew that no one ever owed so much to the Father as herself, for to no one else has he been so generous. He made her holy and pure, chose her from among millions of women to be the Mother of his only-begotten Son: she is his masterpiece. After the humanity of Christ she is the greatest manifestation of God's attributes, for she expresses them through the virtues which correspond to them.

Our Lady's humility sprang from her intense appreciation of the Father's transcendence. She knew that he is utterly unlike us, infinite being. She recognized his holiness: her purity expresses and corresponds to it. His merciful love prepared her to be the Mother of his Son by her Immaculate Conception, not merely taking away original sin but preventing her from ever contracting it at all, so that she was utterly spotless, not even possessing sinful inclinations, let alone sin. No creature has ever shared in the holiness of God as our Lady did. In her too we see his power wonderfully manifested: her fortitude at the foot of the cross, sharing in her Son's sacrifice, was a sharing in his omnipotence. There she was faithful, strong, and patient to the end. Her fidelity corresponds to the faithfulness of God toward his children, and his immutability: human beings are faithful to the extent that they do not change except for the better, remaining faithful to their choice of God and never looking back. Our Lady shared also in the Father's wisdom, for she is the Mother of Wisdom itself, the Incarnate Word. How much she had prepared for this by opening her mind and heart to the word of God in her humility and purity we can tell from her *Magnificat*.

Our Lady was steeped in the knowledge of the Scriptures. She saw the unchanging ways of God in them, and when the supreme moment of her life came, when she became aware of her motherhood of the long-expected Messiah, she recognized his work in her, and expressed her joy in the language of Scripture. She knew that God gave us the Scriptures as a revelation of himself, to tell us what he is like, and how he acts. This is very important because our whole approach to him, our life of prayer, is conditioned by our conception of God. For instance, if we think of him as a Judge who seeks only vengeance, our prayer is one of servile fear; but if we think of him as a Father, our prayer is that of a child, spontaneous, sincere, and trusting.

Our Lady's prayer was perfect for a child of God, because her knowledge of him was so deep. She had meditated on the Scriptures with an enlightened mind and heart aflame with love for God. She had pondered and prayed over them, and so they had formed her mind. Moreover, a process of distillation had gone on in her, which resulted in her *Magnificat*, the very quintessence of the Old Testament. The Scriptures are a collection of various books by different human authors, although of course there was only one Divine Author. Yet our Lady has gone to the very heart of them, giving us the essence of what God has said about himself, unconfused by all the incidents, the people, the wars, the details of the texts.

The Father reveals all his perfections in the Old Testament, as we have seen. We can find a basic, constant pattern of his ways, deeds, and actions which reveal his power, mercy, wisdom, faithfulness, and holiness. He has always acted consistently with mankind, and in her *Magnificat* our Lady expresses her joy, wonder, and gratitude at his marvelous ways: she seems to say, "How characteristic of God to act like this." She has formed a string of quotations and references from the Old Testament into a new pattern with the new purpose, inspired by the Holy Spirit, of reflecting his glory.

At the time of our Lady's visitation of Elizabeth, then, we find that she understood how in her own Motherhood, in the Incarnation, God was acting in the same way as he had always acted, from the first page of Genesis. She expresses this in words springing from her knowledge of the canticle of Anna after the birth of Samuel (1 Kings 2: 1–10), the Psalms, and other words of Scripture. God is unchanging: he still exalts the humble and sends the rich away empty handed; he is still faithful to his promises, as he has ever been. In his immutability lies the secret of the marvelous continuity of the Old and New Testaments. Our Lady is the Ark of the Covenant, the bridge between Old and New. She points forward to the different ways in which the same Father reveals the same perfections in the New Testament and in our own day.

In the past the Father's power, for instance, was shown by events like the victory of David over Goliath. The same power now forgives sins and raises the dead to life. God's arm is not shortened: there is a different context, a different effect, but the same power. Likewise, all his attributes are manifested in a new way in our own lives. God acts now in souls as he did with Adam, David, Samuel, the author of the Canticle of Canticles, or the Psalmist. This truth is what our Lady saw so clearly.

The *Magnificat*, therefore, contains all the lessons God wants us to learn from the Old Testament. It is marvelous to see all those books like grapes going into the winepress of our Lady's mind and heart, coming out as purest wine of the knowledge of God. When we say the *Magnificat*, we are in touch with her in her holiness, as she distills God's perfections for us to taste, purified from all emotion, from all that is irrelevant, in order that our own prayer may be nourished upon truth.

Our Lady's miraculous conception reminded her of Anna, the wife of Elcana, who gave birth to Samuel and sang a canticle of praise. Anna too, like all the saints, had a piercing insight into God's ways. Our Lady's was more perfect, however, and she could give Anna's words a deeper meaning.

Magnificat anima mea Dominum, et exsultavit spiritus meus in Deo salutari meo. "My soul magnifies the Lord, and my spirit rejoices in God my Savior." What does it mean, to magnify God? It means that we recognize him in all his majesty and transcendence and cry out in praise: "O Lord our God, how admirable is your name throughout the earth"; "Who is like you, O God?" Or, "You have made all things in your wisdom." We give him glory for all his attributes and adore him in his beauty and holiness. So our Lady sees his greatness and his condescension to her in her motherhood and exclaims, "my soul is thrilled when I rejoice in God my Savior, not by myself, but through his mercy and goodness." Her words are very like those of Anna's canticle: "My heart hath rejoiced in the Lord . . . my mouth is enlarged over my enemies: because I have joyed in thy salvation" (1 Kings 2:1). But what richness of meaning is added.

Quia respexit humilitatem ancillae suae. "Because he has

regarded the lowliness of his handmaid." Anna had asked God to answer her prayer for a son: to look on the lowliness of his handmaid. She had pleaded with God so vehemently that the priest thought she was drunk. But God heard her anguished and humble words and gave her a son. Our Lady knew her lowliness so well that she was amazed that the Father should stoop down to her. "Infinite Holiness and Goodness looks down on me," she says, "my whole being is filled with love and wonder." She is conscious of the choice of Yahweh himself, and that he should make her the most blessed among all women thrills her. All humble people are thrilled with God: our joy in him is measured by our humility. Our Lady's whole soul responded immediately, fully, to the least manifestation of God; and the more we become like her in humility, the more we too shall be thrilled to the depths of our being by his infinite fatherhood, his providence and wisdom. What a revelation of the goodness of God, that he should look upon us: that is the lesson we learn from our Lady.

Ecce enim ex hoc beatam me dicent omnes generationes. "For, behold, henceforth all generations shall call me blessed." This prophecy is not in the Old Testament, although it is reminiscent of Lia's words when her son Aser was born: "This is my happiness: for women will call me blessed" (Gen 30:13). But our Lady's words are answered by the woman in the New Testament who said to our Lord: "Blessed is the womb that bore thee." What made our Lady say this?

Quia fecit mihi magna qui potens est. "Because he who is mighty has done great things for me." It is not what I am, she tells us, but what God has done for me that matters. I am his creature, his choice, in being made Mother of the Messiah. For the Father had performed another, and the greatest, of those wondrous deeds, which the Psalmist praises him for so often. Our Lady recognized that the wonderful things done in her were all utterly gratuitous gifts of God. He had done this for her because he is powerful. Throughout the *Magnificat* she shows that because she was so sensitive to his manifestations, she thought of God in terms of his attributes.

Et sanctum nomen ejus. "And holy is his name." His supreme attribute is his holiness. He is holy. His name stands for himself and what he is: Infinite Holiness. This idea recurs throughout the Scriptures: God, the "other," the transcendent One, utterly unlike us, is holy. Our response is adoration: a deep sense of his majesty combined with a very great love. Our Lady was quick to recognize too that the Father's holiness includes his mercy toward his children:

Et misericordia ejus a progenie in progenies timentibus eum (see also Ps 103:13, 17). "And his mercy is from generation to generation on those who fear him." Over and over again in Scripture, we find that God showed mercy to those who acknowledged him, reverenced, honored, and obeyed him. This does not mean a servile fear, but the attitude that is in conformity with his holiness and our sinfulness. Our Lady saw that whoever the person is does not matter: God shows himself merciful from generation to generation. Her own motherhood is a characteristic manifestation of his dealings with men: he showers his mercies upon the humble of heart.

Fecit potentiam in brachio suo, dispersit superbos mente cordis sui. Deposuit potentes de sede et exaltavit humiles. "He has shown might with his arm, he has scattered the proud in the conceit of their heart. He has put down the mighty from their thrones, and has exalted the lowly." The Father always showed his power by taking down the arrogant, the conceited, those who thought he would be satisfied with half-hearted service. When his Chosen People became proud and self-sufficient, he punished them, using his power even in supporting their enemies against them. Why? Because they were disobedient, self-satisfied, and thought they were prospering without him. So God allowed their enemies to come in and destroy them and take them away in captivity to Babylon. Yet the same power exalted the lowly, those who were astonished that God should notice them and choose them. The Father's ways are not our ways: he took David away from his sheep and made him king, and a child dear to himself. But those whom God overwhelms with spiritual light and favors are not necessarily known. Our Lady remained unnoticed, and likewise people who have been exalted by God have also passed through the world unnoticed. Yet they are great in the sight of God and his angels.

Esurientes implevit bonis, et divites dimisit inanes. "He has filled the hungry with good things, and the rich he has sent away empty." Our Lady knew what it was to thirst for God, and so he gave her insight into his perfection, and intimacy with the Father, Son, and Holy Spirit. Those who thirst for him he has always given to drink, not only in heaven, but even on earth. He feeds those who hunger for him, and for his will, his kingdom, his holiness, just as he once fed his children with manna. If their hearts are empty of self-love, he fills them with his goodness, his gentleness, and sweetness, but the rich he sends empty away. Our Lady teaches us to go to the Father as a beggar, hungry and thirsty in mind and heart; then he will not send us away empty. She learned these things from Anna's canticle, or from the Psalms, and fits them into her own pattern, which expresses her own experience of God's ways. Thus she prepares us for the words of her Son: "Blessed are the poor"—fortunate, because to them God gives himself.

Suscepit Israel puerum suum, recordatus misericordiae suae. "He has given help to Israel, his servant, mindful of his mercy." The Father adopted Israel as his "first-born" and took care of his children. His merciful love is unchanging from age to age, for it is bound up with his faithfulness:

Sicut locutus est ad patres nostros: Abraham et semini ejus in saecula. "Even as he spoke to our fathers—to Abraham and to his posterity forever." Our Lady sees in her motherhood the fulfillment of the promise made by God after the Fall of man, and repeated to Abraham, Isaac, and Jacob, mindful as he was of his mercy and faithfulness. She sees what Abraham saw: when God promises, he does not fail. First came the Chosen People, then the Chosen One, the Savior. The incarnation, death, and resurrection of Christ are the supreme revelation of the Father's faithfulness to his promise.

The *Magnificat*, therefore, is a perfect summing up of the Old Testament. Even though we can find all its elements there, in the First Book of Kings, in Genesis, Isaiah, and the Psalms, yet it is still our Lady's own canticle. Studying it, we can see the pattern of the Father's ways in the world and in individual souls, his will and his actions. We can see also what wonders are accomplished by him in a soul that is pure and loving, that meditates on the Scriptures. A humble, sensitive heart like our Lady's is, as it were, a finely tuned instrument responding to the touch of the Holy Spirit, and giving to the Father the praise of his glory.

God is as wonderful today as he has ever been, but we need to become more sensitive to him in order to appreciate that as our Lady did. She has shown us by her *Magnificat* how to read the Old Testament with more understanding, and assimilate it as food for our prayer. For the *Magnificat* is a human prayer; it expresses our Lady's adoration and wonder and joy. "Again—his mercy, his condescension: How like him, that is what God always does," she seems to say. We can find this harmony between the Old and the New Testaments too, if we look for our Father in Scripture, and do not merely treat it as a field for study of technical details. Finding him there, we shall become absorbed in the contemplation of him, able to join our Lady in giving him glory, because we shall be learning to share her insight into the double mystery of his transcendent majesty and his Fatherhood.

10

Child-Disciple

I will not now call you servants: for the servant knoweth not what his lord doth. But I have called you friends: because all things whatsoever I have heard of my Father, I have made known to you.

JOHN 15: 15

Jesus saith to her: Do not touch me, for I am not yet ascended to my Father and to your Father, to my God and your God.

JOHN 20: 17

Once we have seen the relationship between God and his Chosen People as a Father–child relationship, our Lord's words about the Father become doubly impressive. So often, for instance, we find him speaking of "your Father," "your heavenly Father," "my Father and your Father" (Mt 5: 45, 48; 6: 4, 8); and he made it clear from the beginning that this relationship was to continue. The new alliance would in no way destroy it; instead it would reveal it in all its fullness, giving it a completely new perspective and an immense enrichment through the incarnation of the only-begotten Son and the revelation of the mystery of the Blessed Trinity.

Yet while our Lord often refers to their heavenly Father and therefore definitely saw his followers as children of that Father, he more frequently speaks of them as his "disciples." "If you continue faithful to my word," he tells them, "you are my disciples in earnest" (Jn 8: 31 K). And, "the mark by which all men will know you will be the love you bear one another" (Jn 13: 35 K). In fact, they soon came to be generally known and spoken of as his disciples, as we can see from the account of the passion: "And now the high priest questioned Jesus about his disciples, and about his teaching" (Jn 18:19 K). Even the maidservant who kept the door at the high priest's house said to Peter, "Art thou another of this man's disciples?" (Jn 18:17 K).

So it seems as though "children of the heavenly Father" and "his disciples" mean the same thing, and as used by our Lord are interchangeable expressions. Consequently we can understand whatever he said to his disciples as being said to the adopted children of his Father with the same appropriateness and force: whatever he demands of his disciples must be seen as demanded of the adopted children, and whatever he promises his disciples he promises them. This is why so much can be learned about the adoption from the Gospels. For how enlightening our Lord's words on discipleship can be for the adopted children. The nature of discipleship is shown in such incidents as this: "One of the scribes came to him, and said, Master, I will follow thee wherever thou art going. But Jesus told him, 'Foxes have holes, and the birds of the air their resting-places; the Son of Man has nowhere to lay his head' " (Mt 8:19–20 K); the conditions and the cost of discipleship are revealed in: "He is not worthy of me, that loves father or mother more; he is not worthy of me, that loves son or daughter more; he is not worthy of me, that does not take up his cross and follow me. He who secures his own life will lose it; it is the man who loses his life for my sake that will secure it" (Mt 10: 37–39 K). And how encouraging are our Lord's words for the children when, turning to his own disciples, he said, "Blessed are the eyes that see what you see; I tell you, there have been many prophets and kings who have longed to see what you see, and never saw it, to hear what you hear, and never heard it" (Lk 10: 23–24 K). Such texts as these, and there are many more, illuminate each other when they are compared with the first Epistle of St. John.

Unfortunately, what often happens in our reading of

Scripture is that the expressions "children of the heavenly Father" and "disciples" are not thought of as meaning exactly the same thing, with the result that they almost appear to mean two distinct categories of Christians. We need to understand more clearly that for our Lord his disciples were children of the heavenly Father, and only such children were his disciples. This becomes obvious when we recognize that having been adopted, the children have everything to learn from the Son, and can learn it from him alone. Only the Son knows the Father: "None knows what the Father is except the Son, and those to whom it is the Son's good pleasure to reveal him" (Lk 10: 22 K); and, "No man hath seen God at any time: the only-begotten Son who is in the bosom of the Father, he hath declared him" (Jn 1:18). So the adopted children can begin to know their Father only by being taught by the Son, by "going to school" with him—that is, by becoming his disciples and accepting him as their Master and Teacher. This is why the Father urged them to listen to his Son: "This is my beloved Son, in whom I am well pleased: hear ye him" (Mt 17: 5). For it is now no longer "at sundry times and in divers manners" that the Father has spoken, but "in these days he has spoken to us by his Son" (Heb 1: 1–2).

The more the adopted children recognize the truth of all this, and that one of the reasons why the Son became man was precisely to reveal the Father, the more they will want to listen to their Master to learn more about the Father who adopted them. There is so much to learn about him, and as they begin to know him, they grow in docility and eagerness as his disciples: the intensity of their desire to learn is the measure of their love for the Father. And so they make their own the pleadings found in the Psalms: *doce me*, "teach me" (e.g., Ps 24: 5); *deduc me*, "lead me" (e.g., Ps 118: 25); *dirige me*, "guide me" (e.g., Ps 118: 133).

The very name Father now takes on new meaning for them, and his children will want to hear as much as possible about him: to hear his ways with them explained, to hear of his power, wisdom, mercy, his care and providence, his own eagerness to forgive, and his insistence on mutual forgiveness among themselves, and the tenderness of his love. Some of these things were explained to the children of the Old Testament, but in the New Testament all are transfigured by the light of the only-begotten Son himself, speaking to them in their own language, using the imagery of their own lives, which he shared. The Son of God was also therefore their Teacher.

Thus it was important for the children of the New Testament to see how utterly different their Teacher was from the Pharisees and Scribes, and that he was not haughty and contemptuous of the weak and ignorant. This is why he told them not to be afraid of him and not to hesitate to become his disciples: he would not reject them, and he was always accessible to them. And so all the children of the new alliance can go to him knowing that however weak and ignorant they are, however clumsily their questions may be formulated, or however inarticulate they may be in expressing their need of him, their need of his love and of his healing, they must have no misgivings. They must not be afraid to approach him, for he is meek and humble of heart (Mt 11: 29). He knows well that this knowledge of the Father will be to them what water is to the thirsty desert traveler. But they need not worry—they do not have to buy it at a heavy price; he will give it to them freely, without charge. "Come, you who are thirsty, take, you who will, the water of life; it is my free gift" (Rev 22: 17 K). Was he not sent to be their shepherd, to lead the children of the Father "to the springs whose water is life" (Rev 7: 17 K)? "Yes, this is the will of him who sent me, that all those who believe in the Son when they see him should enjoy eternal life" (Jn

6: 40 K). And not only is he their shepherd, he is their brother; he is not ashamed to own them as his brethren, for whoever obeys the will of the Father is his brother. There is nothing he wants to give them so much as a deep understanding of their heavenly Father: "I have revealed, and will reveal, thy name to them"; this was how, at the end of his life, he summed up all his teaching and preaching (Jn 17: 26 K).

There were moments when St. Peter was given an exceptional insight into the purpose of his Master's teaching. One of these moments occurred at the end of our Lord's discourse on the bread of life, when many of his followers turned away from him and the Master asked the twelve whether they too wanted to leave him. Simon Peter answered for them all: "Lord, to whom shall we go? Thou hast the words of eternal life" (Jn 6: 69). Yet it was only later that he learned that eternal life was precisely this: to know the Father, "the only true God, and Jesus Christ," whom the Father had sent (Jn 17: 3). This means that knowledge of the Father is not just an intellectual accomplishment but the actual possession of that eternal life which the Son was sent to bring into the world, and for which he died on the cross. It is the life which the Father gives to his children and in doing so adopts them as his own. But he gives it to them through his Son: a child of his must of necessity be a disciple of his Son; likewise, all true disciples of his Son will always be children of his. This is what the Son reveals to the "little ones," his true disciples, and this is what was kept hidden from "the wise and the prudent," the Pharisees and Scribes. His Father's preference for the "little ones" was a source of great joy to his Incarnate Son: "Yea, Father, for so hath it seemed good in thy sight" (Mt 11: 26).

The Incarnation of the only-begotten Son brought to the Father–child relationship as it had been lived by the Chosen People under the old alliance an immense enrichment. While preserving its continuity, he gave it an intimacy which he alone, being the Son, could encourage the adopted children of the new alliance to believe in, to accept, and to respond to. Much will be said further on, directly or indirectly, on this subject, but for the moment one significant detail may be mentioned, which helps to throw light on the new degree of intimacy which the Son wanted to establish between the Father and his adopted children. He taught them to use the word "Abba" in addressing their heavenly Father: the same word which he himself always used when speaking to his Father, as we see for instance in his prayer in the garden: "Abba, Father, all things are possible to thee: remove this chalice from me; but not what I will, but what thou wilt" (Mk 14: 36). Now this word, *abba*, was used only in addressing one's own father; and in speaking in a more distant sense, or of anyone else's father, it was the rule to use suffixes. For example, one would say *abini*, "our father." Reverence made the Jews feel that it would be unfitting to speak to God in the same way in which one spoke to one's own father within the family circle, and so they used the word with a suffix, such as *abi*, "my father," instead of the simple *abba*. After the Incarnation, however, all this was changed. Our Lord taught his disciples to address their heavenly Father as they would their own father in their own family: *Abba*. This shows how insistent our Lord was that his disciples should see in their heavenly Father a true Father with whom they could feel completely at home, and with whom they could live on terms of deep intimacy. It explains too why the Spirit of the Son who brings his teaching to life through the ages never ceases to inspire the adopted children to say "Abba, Father": "And because you are sons, God has sent the Spirit of his Son into your hearts, crying: 'Abba, Father' " (Gal 4: 6).

As we have seen earlier, the Father has to adopt each one of us individually, because no one is born a child of

God. Before they can become the Israel of the new alliance, the children of darkness, of anger, of the devil, enemies of God, have to be redeemed as the Israelites of old were redeemed from Egypt. They must first be reconciled to God before they are entitled to call him their Abba. Only his Son can bring about their redemption and reconciliation; he alone can introduce them into the Father's family. Once he has done this, they are exiles no longer, but "belong to God's household" (Eph 2: 19 κ). Then together with numberless other children they constitute an immense family with the Son as "eldest-born" and with his Father as their Father.

That the Son should become a man and act as Revealer and Teacher would not constitute a redemption, and would not be sufficient to make the adoption of mankind possible: he also had to be their Savior. It was at the highest price possible, that of his Precious Blood, that he obtained for them the power to become children of his Father. If the adoption had been merely a question of a legal undertaking, as it is in human society, such a price would not have been required. But since it involves a real transformation, a genuine regeneration, a begetting into a new life, a re-birth, a re-creation, an infinitely greater price had to be paid. The revelation of the Father was not sufficient, nor was the teaching on how a child of God should conduct himself. For one has to be a child of God before one can truly address him as Abba and can live as a child of his. And so his Son, their Savior, shed his Blood to secure for them this unique privilege. That showed them, as nothing else could, not only his own immense love for them, but also the incredible depths of the Father's love, in not hesitating to give his Son so that in him and through his Blood they might enjoy redemption, the forgiveness of their sins, marking them out beforehand to be his adopted children through Jesus Christ.

But here, as if God meant to prove how well he loves us, it was while we were still sinners that Christ, in his own appointed time died for us. All the more surely, then, now that we have found justification through his blood, shall we be saved, through him, from God's displeasure. Enemies of God, we were reconciled to him through his Son's death: reconciled to him, we are surer than ever of finding salvation in his Son's life (Rom 5: 8–10 κ).

A deep realization of their Father's love, so overwhelmingly demonstrated in the incarnation, death, and resurrection of his Son and constantly kept alive by the Spirit of adoption, urges the children of the new Israel to respond to his love by allowing themselves to be molded into the image of his Son by his Spirit. For they understand that this is the only true response to his love, and that in this way they attain the holiness which will glorify their heavenly Father on earth and for all eternity in heaven. For this they have the assurance of the Son: "In this is my Father glorified, that you bring forth very much fruit, and become my disciples" (Jn 15: 8). And whenever they compare their adoption with that of the children of the old Israel, they will be filled with grateful wonder at the transformation brought about in the adoption by the revelation of the mystery of the Blessed Trinity, by the incarnation of the Father's beloved Son, who revealed to them the Father and reconciled them to him in his Blood, and by the gift of the Spirit of adoption, who makes them cry out, "Abba, Father."

II

"The Word Was Made Flesh"

*God so loved the world, that he gave up his only-begotten
Son, so that those who believe in him may not perish,
but have eternal life.*

JOHN 3: 16 K

And Christ's mind is ours.

I CORINTHIANS 2: 16 K

Jesus Christ, eternal Word of God, became man to save us:
the Father in his infinite love and mercy has given us his
only-begotten Son. Let us take the word "given" quite
literally: our Lord is the gift of God the Father to us; he is
ours. The Father has said to us: I give my Son to you as a
gift; henceforward he is yours. And so we can say: The Son
of God is mine: my Father's gift to me. This is of course
especially true in the Eucharist, when the Father gives him
to us to be our light and strength, our food and drink. But
it is true all the time, after we are baptized, our Father
gives us his Son, and the Son gives himself to us out of
love and obedience to his Father. Indeed we can say to
him: I claim you as mine.

We must see our Lord at all times, in the manger, on
the cross, in the Eucharist, primarily as the Son of the
Father, and as the Father's supreme gift to his adopted
children. If we do not, we misunderstand both Father and
Son. Our Lord came to reveal to us the mystery of the
relationship between the Father and himself, the mystery
of the Blessed Trinity, and how we can share in their life
through the Holy Spirit.

This revelation is at the core of St. John's Gospel, for
there we find our Lord continually going back to his

relationship with the Father, and we learn to see him and his whole life in terms of this. "The world must be convinced that I love the Father, and act only as the Father has commanded me to act" (Jn 14: 31 K). But we need to understand the difference between this relationship and that of a human father and son. The fatherhood of a human being does not involve his whole being, for it is only one aspect of it. The man is a father, but he is also many other things: a husband, a member of a profession, and so on. The same applies to a human son. But God the Father *is* Father and nothing else. His Fatherhood constitutes his whole personality. And it is the same with the Son: his Person *is* Sonship. The Father is utterly and exclusively Father, and the Son is utterly and exclusively Son. Nothing other than this relationship can distinguish between their two Persons, because anything else can apply to both: in God there is only one omnipotence, one beauty, one wisdom, and so on, common to all three Persons of the Trinity. "All that belongs to the Father belongs to me" (Jn 16: 15 K).

The Persons of the Father and Son are directed toward one another: this relationship is necessary to the personality of each, and nothing escapes it because all else is one. The whole Person of each is oriented toward the other. Now, this truth underlies the whole of Christ's teaching: "My Father and I are one" (Jn 10: 30 K). The whole Person of each goes out to the other in infinite knowledge and love, and the Fruit of their mutual, uncreated, infinite love is the Holy Spirit.

At the Incarnation, the human nature of Christ was caught up and drawn into this relationship. The Son, Word of God, became flesh: a man. Therefore a human nature with its human mind and will was assumed by the eternal Word, who himself did not change. The change was all in the human nature assumed by the Word in our Lady's womb, for he took possession of that human mind and filled it with the plenitude of wisdom and knowledge which he is. Therefore we can say that although the knowledge of Christ's human mind was not infinite, it possessed the plenitude. Moreover, his human mind was completely sanctified by contact with the Word of God, his human soul filled with the plenitude of grace.

Since the Incarnation, then, Christ is not only Son as God, but also as man, with all that divine Sonship involves. Through the Incarnation, his whole human nature is drawn into the Son's complete and utter orientation to the Father. This has tremendous repercussions for the adopted children of the Father, who thus become his brethren. This too gives the gospel its true perspective: Christ saved mankind ultimately for the glory of the Father; the saving of creatures could never be the final end, because he was wholly dedicated to the Father. However, as human nature was taken up into his relationship with his Father, and it was by his supreme act of love for the Father that we were redeemed, we too are drawn into that relationship. This is the Father's gift to us. And so the purpose of our adoption is that we should truly share Christ's attitude to the Father: to become like the only-begotten Son in this, and to have his Spirit.

Christ as the Father's greatest gift to us shows forth his infinitely merciful love. We measure the love of a person by what he does. If God gives us his only Son, to bring us to him, what does it prove? What does all Christ's life, and especially his death, prove? That the Father loves us so much, that knowing his Son would be crucified, he gave him whom he loved from all eternity. "How rich God is in mercy, with what an excess of love he loved us!" (Eph 2: 4 K).

How close this brings us to the Father. He seems to be saying to us: "Here is my Son. I give him up to die for you, such is my love for you. Here is proof." Could he give anything greater? The apostles John and Paul suddenly saw it, and their whole being blazed with the thought: "God loves me!" They remembered the crib and the cross, they knew their Master's teaching, and they began to see the immensity of the Father's love. It is not a vague love of mankind in general, but personal, for me. In giving his Son to me, the Father gives everything, all else is insignificant beside such a Gift. And yet I know that I have only to show him my needs and he will supply them too; he loves me.

This is the Gift of inexhaustible riches. This is the Blessing of all blessings from the Father: a Living Blessing. St. Paul sums it up when he says joyfully: "Blessed be that God, that Father of our Lord Jesus Christ, who has blessed us in Christ, with every spiritual blessing, higher than heaven itself" (Eph 1: 3 K).

Now, when a blessing is a Person, all others are blessed to the extent that they receive him. This is why we call our Lady blessed: she received, and brought forth, the Living Blessing. It is hidden, later, beneath the outward appearance of a crucified slave, yet we must recognize there the One who was called by St. Catherine of Siena "the sweet Word of God."

Our reception of him is decisive: generosity, faith, and love are essential. Without him we shall die, for in him is the Father's gift of life and knowledge. Why do we call him the Word at all? It is not merely because at the time when St. John's Gospel was written this was a current expression in philosophy, but more. The Word is the spoken knowledge which God has of himself, in one eternal act. It has infinite life, for the Word of God is dynamic; it is nothing like the word of man, which when spoken is finished and gone. We have seen earlier that the Incarnate Word is the Wisdom of the Father, that everything he did and suffered, and especially his crucifixion, is a profound revelation of that Divine Wisdom, in a form which we human beings can assimilate and make our own. The

Father wants his Son's teaching to penetrate us, making our minds Christlike and holy. Let us now go more deeply into the way he has given us to fulfill this desire.

What is the virtue that enables us to listen to the Word of God? Docility. We must be eager to hear him, to open our minds for him to give them his principles. When he has molded our ways of thinking, we shall reject all the other ways, the worldly ways, that are not compatible with his. We want only those of the Word of God, as we find them in the Gospels, and learn from our increasing intimacy with him. We saw earlier that our minds have to be sanctified before the Father's Wisdom can penetrate them, and that it is through his Word that this is done. When we come face to face with our Lord in contemplative prayer, we see the difference between his wisdom and the wisdom of the world. If his mind is to become ours, we must learn to have the mind of a child and be open to him, ready to let him purify us in his own way. In fact, we can say, with the necessary reservations, that the Word of God has to do to the mind of an adopted child what he did to his own human mind at the Incarnation, communicating to it some of his riches of wisdom and knowledge. But again we must make ourselves ready to receive him; our minds are more shaped by self-love than we recognize, and he has to help us to empty ourselves of it all. It is a pity that sanctification of the mind is often not regarded as absolutely essential. It is only common sense: our hearts and wills cannot be Christlike unless our minds are Christlike.

A simple example of the different points of view of our Lord and the world is the story of the widow and her two mites (Mk 12: 41–44 K). When everyone else displays apparent generosity, the widow seems shy of putting in so little, and everyone else thinks: "poor woman, how small is her offering." But our Lord, incarnate Wisdom, sees the rich throwing their money into the temple treasury and the widow putting in her mites, and thinks something quite different. In his divine mercy he tells us what goes on in his mind:

> He called his disciples to him, and said to them, Believe me, this poor widow has put in more than all those others who have put offerings into the treasury. The others all gave out of what they had to spare; she, with so little to give, put in all that she had, her whole livelihood (Mk 12: 43–44 K).

The poor widow is precious in God's sight because she has given all. Divine Wisdom, seeing, judging, and speaking in simple language, teaches us what is most pleasing to the Father. That is what the Incarnation does for us: it shows us his way of judging actions, gives us his outlook. It is easy for us to be impressed by a display of wealth or culture or charm, and to think that people without them are insignificant, worth nothing to God. But the poor widow is preferable to all the rest, and we learn that the values of the Son of God are not the same as the values of the world. He encourages us to give all, and not to say to God, "You can have this; I can do without it." God is God, and therefore has a claim on all we have.

Now, this can be applied to all aspects of our lives. Whatever we do, whoever we are, we are called to be the Father's adopted children, sharing the attitude of his Son. Our lives must be spent in his service. We are called to communicate to others not the world's judgments of wisdom, but those of the Incarnate Son. That is our vocation, whatever our state of life may be, and we all have some influence on other people somehow. The Word of God wants our lips to continue preaching his wisdom and his knowledge. Unless we are doing that, we are failures; we are not called upon to give people the worldly wisdom and un-Christlike attitudes they already possess. We are to keep alive in the world the teaching of the Word Incarnate and his revelation of the Father's love. To do that truly, we have to be contemplatives, for only in contemplation can the divine wisdom be communicated to our minds. This means gradually learning our Lord's way of thinking, seeing his point of view, making it perfectly our own. Then it becomes second nature to us, and we are able to express it quite naturally. It is ours: somehow in our own speech and behavior, something of the divine wisdom and knowledge is communicated to those with whom we come in contact.

We do not necessarily have to teach or preach in order to do this. It can be done just as effectively by example. Even the example of doing the same dull work day after day can remind the world that the only thing that matters is to do God's will. Perhaps at the Last Judgment many who now appear great will appear insignificant beside the mothers of families or the nuns who dusted and swept and cooked in the same house for sixty years. Few notice their work; it is all taken for granted and seems unimportant, but the Word of God stands by and treasures their toil. Likewise, if we have been given many talents, all must be made vehicles of divine wisdom and knowledge. The gift of all we have, this is what he looks for, in return for the gift of all he is.

We bring the Word of God into the world once more by doing the Father's infinitely wise will. A deep appreciation of this means sincerity and simplicity in our lives, poverty of spirit, faithfulness in little things, kindness and sympathy, all virtues valued by our Lord. In doing our dull work, in using our talents, in nursing or teaching or being ill, we are bringing into the world the Word made flesh. Blessed be God for such an opportunity! If we are perfect echoes of our Master's voice, we communicate his teaching, but we can do this only to the extent that we let his Spirit, who is the Spirit of adoption, form his likeness in us.

Our Lord sends us the Holy Spirit to produce in us his own attitude of Sonship. This is our "family likeness" to him. Our life, our work, our prayer mean nothing if we have not this attitude to God, we too must be oriented toward the Father as our Lord was. Under the influence of the Holy Spirit, therefore, we shall feel the urge, the longing, to turn to the Father at all times, but especially in the Mass. At the Canon it is, after all, chiefly the Father whom we are addressing—*Clementissime Pater,* "most merciful Father"—in uniting ourselves to the sacrifice of his Son. It is by the indwelling of his Son's Spirit that we are able to see God as our Father, and call him Abba. "God has sent out the Spirit of his Son into your hearts, crying out in us, Abba, Father" (Gal 4: 6 K). It is he who will make us share that hunger and thirst for the Father and his glory, which is so striking in his Incarnate Son, because he is the very Spirit of the Son. And the Father is glorified by our growing likeness to his only-begotten Son: "He whose power is at work in us is powerful enough, and more than powerful enough, to carry out his purpose beyond all our hopes and dreams" (Eph 3: 20 K).

12

Child of God

The disciples came to Jesus at this time and said, Tell us, who is greatest in the kingdom of heaven? Whereupon Jesus called to his side a little child, to whom he gave a place in the midst of them, and said, Believe me, unless you become like little children again, you shall not enter the kingdom of heaven. He is greatest in the kingdom of heaven who will abase himself like this little child. He who gives welcome to such a child as this in my name, gives welcome to me.

MATTHEW 18: 1–5 K

When we were adopted as children of God in and through baptism, a tremendous amount remained to be done. The Holy Spirit began then a process of transformation in us, which, if we allow him to continue it, will be perfect by the time we die. It is a process of adaptation to the family life which we now live, and it prepares us for heaven, our true home. The Holy Spirit is at work in us, to reproduce in us the features of the only-begotten Son, whose Spirit he is. Since we share that Spirit, we have the beginning of a "family likeness," but it must be increased until we are completely transformed and our adoption has reached its fullness.

The chief agent of this necessary spiritual transformation is therefore the Holy Spirit. The process of the transformation has two aspects: negative and positive. The negative aspect is that we cease to think and behave as we did before. We cannot cling to the past; we must be detached, renounce many things, if we are not to be hindered in our growth as true adopted children. The positive aspect is that we must assimilate the Holy Spirit, who is given by the Father, just as the Son is, precisely to bring about this transformation.

What is required on our part? First of all, a great willingness to be a child of God, docile, pure in mind, heart, and body, humble and single-minded. The fact is proved over and over again by the apostles and saints, that, according as the Holy Spirit transforms them, they see themselves with increasing clarity as children of God. The spirit of childlikeness is not just an arbitrary devotion; the attitude is essential to adoption. Although all saints may not have it explicitly, the attitude is there, because the Spirit of adoption always produces it in them. He inspires us with the desire to be childlike. This is not childishness, which is exactly the opposite. Childishness is immaturity of mind, heart, emotions, and goes hand in hand with lack of self-discipline. It can go on till old age, death; we can always be childish without becoming childlike. According as a soul matures through the influence of the Holy Spirit, it becomes more childlike, because more Christlike. This means a deep maturity of mind, because it is shaped by the gifts of the Holy Spirit. The childlike person is supernaturally most mature, yet profoundly simple. The childish person is complicated, with all the fluctuations of immaturity in desires, ideas, emotions, one minute on the crest of the wave, the next quite the opposite, and is preoccupied chiefly with self. The childlike person is totally preoccupied with the glory of the Father, just as his Master was on earth: the true child lives and speaks with his *Abba*, Father.

It is very important to understand what our Lord means by being a child, and to take his words seriously. In the incident in St. Matthew's Gospel which illustrates it (18: 1–4), we can see that the disciples were ambitious and that our Lord wanted to teach them to take a different attitude. "Tell us," they say, "who is greatest in the kingdom of heaven?" They often discussed this, and the deep latent ambition in their souls is by no means exceptional. We meet it today: the desire to be great, to be important, to be looked up to by others, to feel that they are dependent on us: we can find these desires in ourselves. Let us not be deceived: we have all felt at some time or another a desire to be accomplished or outstanding, and this is in the world in an excessive degree. Pride represents the kingdom of darkness, and these desires spring from it. It is an effect of original sin. We have enough common sense, probably, to see that we shall never be among the greatest, but we still would like to be important in some way.

"Jesus called to his side a little child, to whom he gave a place in the midst of them." We must remember when we read the Gospel that we are listening to the sweet Word Incarnate, Infinite Wisdom; that is what our memory is for. Everything our Lord does—putting the child there, everything he says—is infinitely wise. He takes a child, and the Greek emphasizes that it is a little child, because he wants to bring out the sharp contrast between his idea of greatness and the disciples'. Now, when we hear our Master say "believe me" (*amen*), we know that he is making a solemn pronouncement, and here he tells us, "unless you become like little children again, you shall not enter the kingdom of heaven."

A change is therefore involved. We are made children of God by baptism, and we know there is a change then, but we have to learn to grow up into the ways of his family. We have to become little children in our Lord's sense: "He is greatest in the kingdom of heaven who will abase himself like this little child." This is the answer to the disciples' question. If you want to know the greatest, it is the person who changes, who "makes himself little, as this child is little," as the Greek puts it. So there is work for us to do within ourselves; recognizing the contrast between the Divine Word's idea of greatness and that of the world, we have to abase ourselves.

We have to take the initiative and set to work. This is where the snag comes in: we cannot hope for the best, that sooner or later it will happen; we must start now. What is smallest in the sight of the world is greatest in the sight of God. What is greatest in the sight of the world is of no importance to God. But because our outlook is so influenced by the world, we still have a kind of ambition for this greatness which has no value in the sight of God. Even the expression "little child" is distasteful to many people: they do not want to be considered little children. It makes them feel rebellious, because they want to be great in the way that the world considers important. This can be half-unconscious, but they pursue it somehow. And yet this is the way of darkness.

There must be an act of self-humiliation: to be a little child in the sight of God, in our own eyes and in those of the world too if necessary. How deep pride goes, that we should resent this. This is because we are not making our own God's way of measuring importance. We have to learn to appreciate what it means to be God's child, and genuinely desire to become little. Our Lord emphasizes this: how far his disciples have to come down if they are to enter the kingdom of heaven. We can each test our own attitude by asking ourselves: how does this strike me? If there is the slightest feeling of rebellion, then our thoughts are not perfectly in tune with God; we still have a certain ambition which pursues that greatness which is without value before God. It is so difficult to keep our minds pure, to see things as our Lord sees them. We drift into the world's way of thinking and have to be pulled back to God's way.

What we have to do, then, is to bring ourselves to the point of saying: our Lord says greatness consists in being a little child, therefore I must make up my mind to be a little child no matter what it costs. The greater I am in heaven, the greater the glory I shall give to the Trinity. The measure of that glory is in my littleness. Our Lady is a splendid example of this: she was so little, so lowly in her own eyes, yet she gives more glory to the Trinity than any angel or saint.

Let us rectify our idea of greatness, therefore, through our Master's teaching. He does not want us to go on thinking as the world does, for that is living in darkness. We must repudiate the darkness of folly and walk in the light of his wisdom, make that our sphere of living. What is greater than to be great in the sight of the Father, great in his sight as our Lady was, if only we abase ourselves?

"He who gives welcome to such a child as this in my name, gives welcome to me." Our Lord goes out of his way to identify himself with the little ones, humiliating himself. He does so again in his Passion and death, being hanged as a slave. The smaller we become in our own eyes, the more we become like our Lord himself. We cannot have the ambitions of the world and be like our Master. Let us take ourselves in hand, then, embrace lowliness, the fact of being a little child, no matter what others may say, or what it may cost. If we desire it, and are determined about it, we gain in stature in our Father's sight: in this way we become mature. When we truly become little children, the Father will reveal himself to us more intimately than ever before, and we shall indeed be at home with him.

Let us now consider more closely what it means to grow as little children of our heavenly Father. This is the growth which depends partly on the Holy Spirit, beginning at baptism, and partly on our own efforts. Our Lord illuminates it for us when he tells Nicodemus: "Unless a man be born again of water and the Holy Ghost, he cannot enter into the kingdom of God" (Jn 3: 5). The baptized person has two lives: natural, according to the flesh, with all its natural resources of mind and body, and spiritual, which is infused by the Holy Spirit and brings about his adoption into God's household. Both these lives are capable of growth to maturity. This presents a grave problem, for it is courting disaster to confuse the two. We are faced by two kinds of growth: that of the human personality with its distinctive body, mind, and talents, and that of the spirit, which can grow and reach maturity just as the other can. But there are differences: one is infinitely superior, and it is possible for one to grow while the other does not. Their growth is not parallel.

Only the supernatural life counts with God. For example: a baptized baby dies almost immediately; it seems hardly human, but because it is baptized it enters heaven. Although lacking the normal human maturity, it has sufficient spiritual maturity to enter heaven and see God. On the other hand, a person who has lived for many years, being naturally very accomplished, yet having no spiritual life and living in sin, from God's point of view is so immature that he cannot enter heaven. He is lacking in the only life that is acceptable to God. He may have brought his human personality as such to perfection, but not in the sight of God; there, he is not even alive, and heaven is closed to the spiritually dead.

The maturity of the human personality and the maturity of the spiritual life cannot be identified. By making a mistake here we can pursue a false ideal of perfection, wasting our time disastrously on the wrong sort of maturation. The problem is how to grow up both spiritually and humanly. The temptation is to sacrifice spiritual growth to the human, because the human is tangible: it is admired, marked by success and fame, and gives a humanistic satisfaction. It has its own nobility, but this must not be at the price of the spiritual life. If possible the two ought to grow side by side.

Spiritual growth is intangible because the Holy Spirit brings it about. It cannot be achieved by ourselves. It needs the infinite power of God, the flame of the Holy

Spirit. Unless we give him an absolutely free hand, surrender ourselves utterly, we may be certain that when we die we shall not be transformed; the image of the Son in us will still be marred, distorted, not true. The slightest impediments hinder him, for he has to go so deep, to the very roots of our being. Then the Christlikeness has to be infused, so that while remaining completely ourselves we become perfect images of the same Jesus Christ. That is one of the magnificent things about the saints: they are all such distinct personalities, and yet utterly Christlike. This is maturity in the spiritual life. The Father's joy is to see his adopted children becoming more and more like his own Son. If we are selfish, mediocre, conceited, and childish, that is, grown up in the worldly sense, we deprive the Father of that joy. And so we can see why maturity in the natural sphere must remain subordinate, for it is not undesirable or evil but secondary. Our maturity in the sight of God is what counts in deciding whether we are to enter the kingdom of heaven or remain outside, for the image of Christ must be so impressed upon our souls that the Father sees in us the likeness of his Son, and our adoption has reached its fullness.

We can then be dead in the sight of God all our lives, yet very accomplished and mature in the eyes of the world. We can be alive in the sight of God and very unaccomplished in the sight of the world. Once again we recognize a difference between God's point of view and that of the world. The world, for instance, will never say, "Blessed are the poor," but our Lord does. How few are the people in the world who pursue poverty and detachment; most often, people pursue money, only to spend more money. It is difficult for children of God to keep their sense of proportion. For this we need a deep, living faith, enlightened by the gifts of wisdom and understanding that come from the Holy Spirit. We must keep before our minds God's standards. When we die, our Father will not ask us whether we have been rich, or whether we have been marvelous painters or violinists, but he will ask: "what likeness to my Son is there in you?" For there can be no aliens in heaven.

Our entry into heaven, then, depends on whether we are little children of God. In that lies our resemblance to the only-begotten Son; his virtues, his humility, self-effacement, suffering, submissiveness, are found only in little children. If a human person stops growing when he is ten years old, by the time he is fifty he is abnormal. We do not say he is "only a child," for he has not developed properly. The same can happen in the spiritual life: we stop growing if we refuse to make the necessary sacrifices. We remain spiritual adolescents with an ambition to be grown up and to make an impact on the imagination of the world.

The true, little, child of God is given something of the divine wisdom, understanding, and knowledge, for he opens himself to the Holy Spirit, who transforms and sanctifies him. But he is not doing God a favor in this: he must thank his Father for giving him the grace to see that he needs to become a little child, to desire it and see what it means. It is a seeming paradox, then, but a vital one: we cannot become spiritually mature, Christlike, holy, unless we become little children. The Holy Spirit will teach us to know Christ himself far more intimately—for example, in the marvelous combination of joy and suffering that no human agent can produce. This is our Lord's own joy because of suffering: we know him in it because the Holy Spirit is beginning to produce in us the same experience. It is not an emotion but something supernatural. A true child of God cannot suffer without joy. Thus we begin to understand our Lord's teaching, death and victory, and also his inexpressible relationship with the Father and the Holy Spirit, because we can in our own way take part in it through the Spirit of adoption. As an artist is free to shape his clay, the Holy Spirit is free to shape us into the image of Christ. The closer we come to this, the more we shall share our Master's outlook, his will, lovingly submissive to the Father's will. We shall have the same willingness to sacrifice self for the glory of the Father, and suffering will become a blessing, from him to us, and from us to him.

It is a question of putting first things first: the sacrifice of everything, but especially all worldly ambition, to the attainment of spiritual maturity. What the world needs first and foremost is saints, not scientists, poets, and musicians, but true children of God. Human maturity is not to be despised, of course, but if it stands between us and our becoming little children, it has to be sacrificed. It is possible that we may be nobodies in the sight of the world, but we can accept this easily once we have learned to see the foolishness of many of the things it esteems. Once we have understood our Lord's words we see that the important thing is to put all our might and generosity into attaining the one maturity that is acceptable to God, to focus all our desires and endeavors on becoming little children. Then we shall see something of the dignity that the Father sees in his little ones. What is greater than this: to enter the kingdom of heaven and share the life of the Trinity? Let us increase our longing to live and die as true children of God, so that when we die we shall go to him and feel at home with him, sharing the utter joy and peace of the Trinity, the life of the Father, the wisdom of the Son, the Holy Spirit's flame of love.

13

"Come, Holy Spirit"

*Who else can know a man's thoughts, except the man's own
spirit that is within him? So no one else can know God's
thoughts, but the Spirit of God. And what we have received is
no spirit of worldly wisdom; it is the Spirit that comes from
God, to make us understand God's gifts to us.*

I CORINTHIANS 2: II–I3 K

The more childlike we want to be, according to the teaching of our Master, Jesus Christ, the more we shall urge the
Holy Spirit to achieve our transformation. He seems to
work too slowly for our liking, so we plead with him to
come, to complete his work before we die. For when we
understand what adoption means, the Father being our
Father, we see to what likeness to the Son it must lead.
And so we shall have a growing devotion to the Holy
Spirit, feeling our need of him, for he alone can make us
childlike. *Veni, Sancte Spiritus!* The Son's coming to us
without his Spirit would be of no avail. The Spirit fertilizes
and fructifies the coming of our Lord and Master.

Therefore our prayer becomes a deep longing of the
soul, a begging for help in our poverty. Now, there is a
tendency for people to look down on the prayer of petition, as if to be really advanced, really "mystical," we must
put it behind us and simply gaze on God alone all the
time. But this is not the teaching of the Church, nor is it
laid down in the writings of the saints. Let us have no
spiritual snobbery, which looks down on vocal prayer and
the prayer of petition as being necessarily inferior. Both
can be extremely deep, coming wholly from the Holy
Spirit. Sometimes one word can be repeated over and over

again without weariness, or the soul may plead for one thing for a long time; these are necessary outlets for longings inspired by the Holy Spirit.

Prayer follows an awareness of dependence: a little child relies on his parents for everything, and a child of God feels like this about his heavenly Father. So his prayer is a need, a life, a way in which the spirit expresses its sense of poverty and trust. The way to learn to be a contemplative is to learn how to ask. Through such an expression of dependence we come to recognize God's mercy, his goodness, his beauty, whatever attribute we are most drawn to, for he fulfills all our longings. Then petition is transcended, for God himself will open our eyes.

Those who are spiritually poor have immense confidence in their Father. They are certain that he will give what they need; it is given, though perhaps not when, or how, it is expected, for his children have to be at his disposal. Seeing ourselves as poor as we are, we long for his Spirit to come and sanctify us. And because we are human, this longing is often expressed in words, sometimes spoken, sometimes imagined. Or else the longing can simply come to the surface of our consciousness without words, for it may be too deep for them. This is genuine prayer of petition: asking for something we long for, personally and intensely.

Such expressions of longing cover all the "stages" of the spiritual life. If the Holy Spirit is doing anything at all in our souls, he inspires longings which we did not have before, of ourselves. They become gradually stronger and more articulate, a form of concentrated spiritual energy planted in the soul by the Holy Spirit, which must somehow be expressed. So St. Paul tells us that the Holy Spirit

comes to the aid of our weakness; when we do not know what prayer to offer, to pray as we ought, the Spirit himself intercedes for us, with groans beyond all utterance: and God, who can read our hearts, knows well what the Spirit's intent is; for indeed it is according to the mind of God that he makes intercession for the saints (Rom 8: 26–27 к).

A genuine inspiration from the Holy Spirit must be in conformity with God's plan for our sanctification. He never inspires a prayer unless he means to satisfy it, provided we respond faithfully to his demands. Often, however, he cannot answer our prayer because we are not ready to make the sacrifices which condition its fulfillment. If this is so, the longing weakens and will probably eventually disappear. We must understand that, for God to answer our prayer, we must be prepared to be generous with him.

Let us look at a specific example of a prayer and the sacrifices which are demanded in order that it may be answered. Someone asks for the gift of knowledge, seeing that it is of great importance in the spiritual life. The Holy Spirit inspires and fosters this desire. But because the purpose of the gift of knowledge is to enable us to see God in created things and thus Beauty himself in created beauty, it first requires detachment from created things in themselves. The person we are speaking of is perhaps particularly attached to the beauty of music. This can remind him of God. Yet if he is not prepared to give up his deep personal attachment to the beauty of music for its own sake, he cannot respond to the gift of knowledge. The paradox is that in order to find uncreated Beauty in music, he must no longer cling to his love for the music in itself. This kind of sacrifice may be lasting—we have to risk that; but often the Holy Spirit leads us back to the thing we had renounced in order to show us Beauty there anew.

This question of detachment is very important if we really want our life of prayer to lead us to intimacy with the Blessed Trinity. We cannot give ourselves wholly to

God if we are still clinging to other things: that would make him just one more of the many things we are attached to. Perfect detachment is necessary if the Holy Spirit is to come to us, fill us, and draw us into union with God. No one must be allowed to deceive us on this: we must be detached from everything created, and always ready instantly to give it up if God were to demand it. Detachment does not mean doing without persons or things, but it does mean that we must not cling to them. Perfect detachment means that we must be instantly prepared to surrender, to give up, anything God demands. This may be very painful and cause us much suffering: our Father knows this, and he accepts it as a gift of love for him. It includes everything, this readiness to give: even life, not to cling to it but be always ready to die whenever God wills it, not a second earlier or later; even health, to be prepared to be ill, perhaps permanently; even friendships, people we love, material things, or our own personal opinions, mannerisms, ways of doing things. We must be ready when called upon by those who make known God's will to us, or by circumstances which are permitted by him, to give up absolutely everything and everybody for love of him. The strange thing is that the more detached we are, the freer we are to love and to be loved, because we need not be detached from God's own love for himself and for his children. This is what we mean by purity of soul.

Without moving toward this perfect response, without this readiness for sacrifice, we remain static. It is as if we wanted to play the piano well but refused to do the finger exercises, and even with the best teacher you cannot make progress without practice. If we do respond, however, the Holy Spirit leads us on, inspiring new petitions, which usually become concentrated eventually into one great longing for the Trinity, or for one Person of the Trinity in particular. Now our prayer will express the maximum of longing in the minimum of words. It is still the prayer of petition, but of what a kind! Inspired by the Holy Spirit, it therefore goes back to God from the soul accompanied by the wisdom and love of the Spirit.

The important thing to remember is this: you can test the sincerity of prayer by a person's willingness to make sacrifices. The greater the longings, the greater are the sacrifices required. For instance, intimacy with the Trinity requires the greatest poverty of spirit, purity, and child-likeness. It demands a searching purification, for only a very little child can become intimate with the Trinity. Only when he is purified of all illusions about his own resources can he go straight to God. To be a contemplative, in this, its true, sense of intimacy with the Trinity, one has also to be very humble and recollected, absolutely sincere in one's desire. We must not underestimate the sacrifices involved in holiness. This is why we talk about the heroic virtue of the saints. The work of the Holy Spirit goes to a far deeper level than we are conscious of, and it is very searching, indeed. But the truly spiritual person is moved, enlightened, and enkindled by him, for he takes possession of that person as Master, Lover, and Beloved.

Now we know that the Holy Spirit takes possession of our soul at baptism. Why, then, do we pray, "Come, Holy Spirit" and long for greater intimacy with him? It is because we are beginning to understand that a deeper relationship with him is possible, and a new aspect of the alliance made between God and his adopted children at baptism is made clear to us.

We have seen that in order to describe the intimacy and intensity of his love for mankind, God called his Chosen People in the Old Testament his spouse. Likewise, under the new alliance, every Christian becomes the spouse of the Holy Spirit, who dwells within him. However, it takes us some time and training before we are able to make a wholehearted identification of ourselves with the new alliance, and a Christian who is not fully aware of the implications of his baptism will never achieve it. But it can and should be a matter of growing understanding. At the beginning of our spiritual life, our relationship with the Holy Spirit was mostly unconscious on our part: he was probably not much more to us than a Person in whom we had to believe.

As our prayer intensifies, we become more aware of him and of who he is: the uncreated Fruit of the mutual Love of the Father and the Son within the Blessed Trinity, a Person. Growing love makes us long for him. We try to surrender ourselves to him as completely as possible, and we soon learn that this surrender is never a completed act. It continues, deepens, becomes more exacting and at the same time more rewarding. For there are different levels of surrender: every time we think we have reached the utmost depth, there is always one deeper yet. There are things, unsuspected before, which we are asked to give. He leads us on, step by step, but progress depends on our fidelity. As soon as we refuse, we stay on one level and can go no further. Therefore we can say that in order to become a true spouse of the Holy Spirit, the first thing to do is to surrender utterly to the Spirit, who is the Love of God, without clinging to our own will any longer. This should be the easiest thing in the world: to surrender to One who is Infinite Love, Wisdom, Beauty, and Power, but it is in fact most difficult. It is part of the mystery of original sin and infinite love. This surrender to Love, day by day, minute by minute, is the most difficult thing a human being is asked to do, and yet: "No eye has seen, no ear has heard, no human heart conceived, the welcome God has prepared for those who love him" (1 Cor 2: 9 K). But what Love demands and what Love gives are a constant source of wonder.

It follows from this that a spouse must be faithful to the utmost degree. The Chosen People in the Old Testament were constantly unfaithful, and so are we, especially in little things. We, who have been given so much more than they had, in many ways are often more unfaithful than we recognize. We acknowledge our obligations, perhaps, but how ungenerous we are in our response. Real fidelity, moment by moment, to the least inspiration of the Holy Spirit, to the opportunities that life offers for showing our love, is exacting. Often we let them slip by because we are preoccupied with self, but if we really wanted to hear him, we should be more aware of his touch.

The true spouse longs for the Holy Spirit. From what we have said earlier we can see that this is so both in the beginning and the end of the relationship with him while we are on earth. He first produces this longing because he wants to give himself to us more deeply. It empties us of desires for other, lower, created things. At first the longing is intermittent, but if we respond it grows stronger and draws us into union with the Holy Spirit. For when we identify ourselves completely with our longing, he gives himself to us more deeply, and then our longing is increased again, for in this life it can never be entirely fulfilled. All other desires fall away: we do not miss the things to which we were once attached. And so when all the longings of the soul are unified, both supernatural and natural ones, they become very deep, indeed. They are often concentrated upon, or are bound up with, one Person but lead on to all three Persons of the Trinity. The soul directs brief, intense appeals, "darts" of her own love, toward the Holy Spirit, who is at the same time producing them in her.

So we plead with him to come, *Veni!*—just as the Chosen People pleaded for a savior. He deepens our insight into God with his gifts to us. The more understanding we are given, the more we long for him and for his gifts. We are given new insight into the mysteries of faith: the mystery of the Trinity, the Incarnation, the relationship between our Lord and our Lady, and more, for there is no end to the insight which the Spirit can give. Yet we must remember that the amount depends on our surrender. This is the measure of his gifts to us. He cannot give insight to a mind that is not childlike, docile, pure, detached from worldly things. We have to *care*, to be ready for any sacrifice, to respond with instant loving submission to him, above all to long for him. If there are two people, one of whom says, "Come," to the Holy Spirit with only a vague appreciation of need, the other saying it with the deepest longing of his heart, with his whole personality entering into the plea, the Holy Spirit will come to both, but what a difference there will be in the fullness of his coming and of his gifts! Only to the extent that he is Master of the soul can he embrace it. He dwells there, and there is the focal point of all our prayer. He will mold and shape, enlighten and enkindle us, teach us the deep things of God, bring us to intimacy with the Blessed Trinity.

14

The Indwelling Trinity

If a man has any love for me, he will be true to my word;
and then he will win my Father's love, and we will both come
to him, and make our continual abode with him.

JOHN 14: 23 K

As a result of the redemption, we are baptized into Christ
and are adopted by his Father. At the moment of our
baptism the Blessed Trinity, Father, Son, and Holy Spirit,
take possession of our soul, and we become consecrated
to them as their temple. As long as we remain in a state of
grace, they continue to dwell within us, for now we belong
to them. This is a mystery whose reality is comparable to
that of our Lord's presence in the Blessed Sacrament. We
are very conscious of that, and we ought to be just as
conscious of the Trinity dwelling within us. For we have
learned to trust our Master's words, and we believe him
when he says, for instance: "The man who has faith in me
enjoys eternal life," or, "If anyone eats of this bread, he
shall live for ever" (Jn 6: 47, 52 K). When he tells us also
that the Father and he will come and dwell within us, we
must take him at his word. We know too, from the theology of the Trinity, that when the Father and Son act
outside the life of the Trinity in itself, the Holy Spirit is
always with them. As we have noted previously, the work
of the Holy Spirit himself in our soul is directed toward
deepening our intimacy with the Blessed Trinity, and we
shall see now that it brings us above all to make their
presence within us the pivot of our spiritual life, and of
our whole existence.

How can we be sure that our soul is in a state of grace,

if this is to be the test of the presence of the Holy Trinity there? We cannot be infallibly certain, only God is, but we can be morally sure. That is, we can know as far as our own conscience goes that we have not committed a mortal sin or let it go unrepented. Thus I can presume I am in a state of grace: the Trinity is in possession of my soul because I am "in Christ," truly their child.

Now in spite of this clear and explicit revelation, in the words of our Lord himself, it is possible for a person to be baptized and to live a Christian life for many years without thinking about the indwelling of the Trinity in his soul, and therefore without even doing anything to make it the focal point of his life, which it is meant to be. It might be illuminating for us to ask ourselves how many times we have been told about this mystery. Perhaps often, perhaps not so many times, but most of us have reason to be sorry for our carelessness in not trying harder to recognize all it means, and for not trying to remember who are the Three who dwell within us.

After all, the reason why our Father gave us a memory was to remember him, his wondrous deeds, his teaching, his commandments, and above all to remember him as the God who loves us and has adopted us as his children. To be given a memory for this purpose and then to re- member everybody and everything except God is obvi- ously a shocking abuse of one of our Father's great gifts. Yet the fact is that for many people nothing is so difficult as to remember God and nothing so easy as to forget him. Love, of course, has a lot to do with it, for it is always so much easier to remember people and things we love: love seems to make our memory alert and responsive, whereas indifference makes it go dead. Therefore people who re- ally and truly love God do not find it so difficult to remember him, while those who are indifferent perhaps only occasionally remember him and then with little real interest.

The difficulty, even for those who love God as his children, is that there is no outward sign to remind us of the indwelling of the Trinity, as there is of the presence of our Lord in the Blessed Sacrament, for instance. And few are those who are reminded of their indwelling by the three divine Persons themselves. Not that the divine indwelling is something that depends on our thinking about it: it is there, provided we live as children of God should, whether we think about it or not. It is not just something imagined by our own mind but a concrete reality, existing in ourselves since our baptism.

Nevertheless, though this mystery does not depend on our thinking about it, obviously it is important that we should. Such a tremendous grace as the continual indwelling of the Father, Son, and Holy Spirit is not to be received lightly. It is given for a purpose, too: that of establishing between the divine Persons and ourselves a genuine intimacy to be sustained and deepened by a constant exchange of loving remembrance, and to be finally consummated for all eternity in heaven: God with us and we with God, both on earth and in heaven. So what we need to do now is to teach ourselves how to remember the indwelling Trinity.

The Church knows that we need to be reminded often of all the great mysteries of our Faith, and this is one of the main functions of the liturgy: to keep our minds focused on them, which enables our memory to awaken and stimulate our faith, hope, and love. Thus the sacrifice of the Mass is a reminder: "Do this in commemoration of me"; so are the sacraments, so are all liturgical gestures, such as genuflections—to remind us of the infinite majesty of God; so are the Church's images, such as the crucifix— to remind us of our Redemption; the church's lights, such as the sanctuary lamp—to remind us of our Lord's presence in our midst. Symbols too are frequently used in liturgical art for the same purpose. Here again we meet a difficulty with regard to the great mystery of the Trinity itself, and also of the divine indwelling: the other mysteries of the Faith are more easily represented imaginatively and so are more likely to make an impact on our daily Christian life.

The answer to the problem lies in learning to use our memory for the very purpose for which our loving Father gave it to us. Once we start training it, he will reward us by the experience of what it really means to live in company with the three divine Persons. A really determined effort to try to be more conscious of the presence of the Trinity in us can make a great difference in our spiritual life. An instance of this is the Carmelite of Dijon, Sr. Elizabeth of the Trinity. She became intensely aware of the indwelling of the Blessed Trinity, centered her whole life upon it, and became very holy in a short time. God seems to have chosen her to help to make this mystery better known, for both during her brief lifetime and since her death in 1906, many have been drawn toward it by her example. If we make up our minds to try, we shall be helped by the Holy Spirit, we can use the reminders that we are already given, or make up our own, for we have all sorts of opportunities. Let us take the sign of the cross as an illustration of this.

We make the sign of the cross so often that it tends to become a routine gesture which is for all practical purposes meaningless and not sanctifying, at least not as much as it should be. We should make it with great reverence, not making an outward display of it, but making it with our minds on the words, accompanying this with our hands. The sign of the cross is meant to express our faith in the mysteries of the Blessed Trinity, Father, Son, and Holy Spirit, and of the crucifixion of the sweet Word Incarnate: it is the briefest act of adoration and faith in these two great mysteries and also in that of the indwelling Trinity. It reminds us of the connection between these mysteries, and that the crucified Word Incarnate is the Way to the Blessed Trinity. We can become intimate with the divine Persons as one and as three only through him, and his cross, and so it is important that we should be reminded of this fundamental truth by the sign of the cross. It is the sign of our adoption, our life, as St. Paul says:

> Through the law, my old self has become dead to the law, so that I may live to God; with Christ I hung upon the cross, and yet I am alive; or rather, not I; it is Christ that lives in me. True, I am living, here and now, this mortal life; but my real life is the faith I have in the Son of God, who loved me, and gave himself for me (Gal 2: 19–21 K).

Let us, then, always make the sign of the cross well. If we "glory in it" as St. Paul did, we shall never make it thoughtlessly, as a routine movement, nor lightheartedly, but really as a sign of our devotion to the crucified Word Incarnate, and to the Trinity dwelling within us in virtue of our redemption.

The more we remember the indwelling of the Blessed Trinity, the more we shall learn to see all the truths and all the gifts of our faith in relation to it. There are so many things that can gradually become associated with it, and serve as reminders. Those of us who say the Divine Office say *Gloria Patri et Filio et Spiritui Sancto*, "Glory be to the Father, and to the Son, and to the Holy Spirit," many times a day: we can say it to the Trinity dwelling within us. Above all, the Mass: we can offer the Mass in honor of the Trinity, the Three Persons who are in possession of us, so that a correspondence of thought is set up. Whenever we are at Mass we shall think of the indwelling Trinity, and whenever we think of them, we shall link it with the Mass, the sacrifice of our redemption and adoption.

The Blessed Sacrament is therefore included. Where is the link there? Our Lord remains with us as *Emmanuel*, "God with us." He instituted the Blessed Sacrament as a continuation of the Incarnation, and he is there for the same reasons as when he was on earth: not only to be with us himself but to deepen and foster our union with the Blessed Trinity in our souls. This is why he feeds us with himself, just as it is the reason why he taught and suffered and died. By shedding his Precious Blood, he established the indwelling of the Trinity in our souls, both on earth and in heaven, for heaven is a continuation of the life we have lived on earth since baptism.

We must understand that heaven is not, primarily, a state in which we gaze upon God forever as if we were in some kind of marvelous cinema. When we talk about "seeing God," it is only a figure of speech, for something that we cannot picture in our imagination. We shall, it is true, see with our own eyes our Lord in his glorious humanity, we shall see our Lady and the saints, but we shall not see the Trinity. We shall not see the Father. Instead we shall *know* the Trinity within our souls, something more intimate, more intense, than any sight, for they will possess us and we shall possess them. We shall be "immersed" in the Trinity. But this is precisely what we are beginning now: we possess the reality, although we are as yet only dimly aware of it; then all will be known and felt intensely, with our whole glorified being.

Our Lord therefore comes to us in Holy Communion in order to deepen our relationship with the Trinity now, as a preparation for what it will be for all eternity. In making us Christlike in soul, mind, and heart, he gives us more power to respond, with greater love and faith. This power of responding to the Blessed Trinity ought to increase with each Communion, from day to day, so that we become more and more completely possessed by each. For Christ comes to give us the Father, himself, and the Holy Spirit:

all Three. We are meant to recognize that we can begin our heaven here and now, while at the same time we work to increase our capacity for the Three to fill.

This is how the Son glorifies the Father and the Father his Son, in the souls of the children of God. Within our soul, the Father and Son are glorifying each other, and this is brought about by the Holy Spirit. The more we allow the Holy Spirit to master us, the more our life will center on this fact: that the Three Persons of the Holy Trinity are glorifying each other within us, thus allowing us to share in the glorification of themselves.

So again we can see, in the context of our own lives, how necessary is fidelity to the influence of the Holy Spirit. If we want this foretaste of heaven, we have to be ready to give ourselves wholeheartedly to the Trinity dwelling within us. We can discover so many opportunities for looking within, adoring and thanking and loving them. Manual work is a privilege for this reason, so is repetitive or monotonous work, and the times when we have to wait for things. Instead of wasting our thoughts on useless things, we can turn them toward the Beloved Three within us. We can think of them at any time, simply by directing our love to them, whilst we are cooking, typing, studying, teaching, whatever it is. If we really want to become intimate with the Blessed Trinity, we shall show our desire for it by disciplining ourselves, by keeping silence when we can, so that we can respond to them with our whole being. This kind of recollection is difficult in the press of everyday life and can mean considerable self-sacrifice, but it is not impossible. Without it, without detachment and the control of our memory, imagination, and senses, we cannot hope to achieve our desire.

When we show our desire by a wholehearted, generous response, the Blessed Trinity will meet us more than half way. It would be a mistake, and a discouraging one, to think that everything depends on our own efforts. Of course, they are important, and yet we know that we are only little children; we have to surrender ourselves into the arms of our Father and allow him to carry us. The little child is possessed completely by the Holy Trinity, and he alone can experience what the Incarnation has brought to us, in intimacy with the three divine Persons. Such a little child begins his heaven on earth, for already he shares the life and love of the Father, Son, and Holy Spirit: he is theirs, and they are his. The little child understands now the words of his Master:

> Father, who art Lord of heaven and earth, I give thee praise that thou hast hidden all this from the wise and the prudent, and revealed it to little children. Be it so, Father, since this finds favour in thy sight. My Father has entrusted everything into my hands; none knows the Son truly except the Father, and none knows the Father truly except the Son, and those to whom it is the Son's good pleasure to reveal him (Mt 11: 25–27 K).

15

The Father's Will

Father, the time has come; give glory now to thy Son, that
thy Son may give the glory to thee. Thou hast put him in
authority over all mankind, to bring eternal life to all those
thou hast entrusted to him. Eternal life is knowing thee, who
art the only true God, and Jesus Christ, whom thou hast
sent. I have exalted thy glory on earth, by achieving the task
which thou gavest me to do.

JOHN 17: 1–5 K

The relationship of the Father and the Son in the depths
of the Trinity is beyond our unaided understanding. This
is why the mystery of the Blessed Trinity was not revealed
until the Incarnation of the Word, the only-begotten Son.
In him we are able to see the relationship between the
Father and the Son in human terms; and because we can
see the constant turning of the Son's human mind and will
toward the Father, we are able to learn from it what true
sonship, true childlikeness, is.

Above all, the mystery of this relationship is revealed in
the Son's accepting and completing the task which his
Father gave him to do on earth. For by accomplishing it,
especially in his Passion and death, he shows what it
means to be Son of God. At the same time, the Father
reveals himself in the kind of task he imposed, with all its
implications and consequences. If now we go back to the
Gospels, and especially St. John's, we can see from the
beginning that every detail of our Lord's life was part of
his task, and its completion was the most perfect glorification of the Father. That task took thirty years to be brought
to its fulfillment, and all this time it was the nourishment

of our Lord's soul: "My meat is to do the will of him who sent me, and to accomplish the task he gave me," he tells his disciples (Jn 4: 34 K).

We can never plumb the utmost depths of our Master's desire to glorify his Father by doing his will, for we know it is the very expression of his infinite Sonship. Christ himself is the Glory of God, that is, the revelation of what God *is*, for the benefit of his adopted children. His very being glorifies the Father, for he is the Son, "who is the radiance of his Father's splendor, and the full expression of his being" (Heb 1: 3 K). All Christ is, as God and man, and everything in his life, teaches us something more about God, and thus radiates and manifests the glory of the Trinity. But the supreme moment of Christ's glorification of the Father, in his utter loving submission as Son, was when he bowed his head and gave up his soul from the cross, saying: "It is consummated" (Jn 19: 30).

Now, in this loving and faithful obedience to the Father, our Lord and Master teaches us the most fundamental lesson we have to learn as children of God. He has demonstrated for us what the filial turning toward the Father means in terms of human life: this is the example we have to follow. There is no reluctance to do the Father's will: instead his child lives on it, and desires that others should know, love, and obey the Father too. He gives each of his adopted children a task to do and complete in the circumstances of his own life; there is a particular one for each, just as our Master had his. We must have therefore something of his desire to glorify the Father, to spend our lives in doing this, in union with his Son.

It does not matter what kind of task we have, or whether it seems important or not. Our Lord could have brought more tangible results out of his work at once, and made a stir in the world as a whole, but this was not his task. He did only what the Father wanted. Some people have more spectacular tasks than others, but we must not assess the value of our lives in the sight of God by the world's values. We may not even be meant to use all our talents in this life, for some may be meant to lie fallow, so let us not fret if our lives do not seem to provide us with much opportunity to display them. We only have to do what we are asked, just as our Lord did: he lived in a corner of Palestine, putting up with the Scribes and Pharisees. He saw infinite possibilities in his work, but some were left undone during his lifetime because he concentrated everything on doing precisely what the Father wanted.

The only way to glorify God is our Lord's way. That is, we the adopted children have to become as much like the only begotten Son as possible, and so in our own little way reflect the loving relationship of the Son and his Father. We can only do this if we grow in sensitivity to our Father's will. His will must become our food, as it was for our Lord: it must sustain and nourish us, give us life, knowledge, and love. But it cannot become our real nourishment until and unless we make frequent acts of union with our Father's will. Thus our wills, through these acts, will become more and more united to his will and endowed with all the perfections of his. Our will too will become wise, faithful, strong, beautiful, just, and, above all, loving, a flame of love.

It is not easy to make deep acts of union with God's will, though it is easy enough to make them on a superficial level, or to say with our lips only: "Thy will be done." Such acts will never lead to intimacy with God, that is, to union of wills with him. His will is unchangeable, for immutability is one of his perfections. It is our will that has to be changed, purified, bent, so as to be capable of union, after the elimination of whatever it is in our will that produces disunion or half-hearted union. We have to train our wills by embracing our Father's will; then his Spirit can purify and sanctify ours.

Now it is a fact that we are much more aware of the

existence and of the "otherness" of our Father's will when
he wants us to do things that go against our own will. We
are then conscious that there are two wills: God's and our
own, and that there is a certain conflict between them or a
reluctance on our part to submit and make his will our
own. We may not intend this to be so, but reluctance arises
within us because we are being asked to go against our
own inclinations.

The occasions when we feel like this can be great blessings: they enable us to see the Father's will for what it is,
holy and most unlike ours, and we can accept it generously and bravely, cost what it may, knowing that this
acceptance will make something more of the wisdom and
beauty of his will overflow into ours and therefore into our
own person. Our will especially will be more loving, more
unselfish and pure, more holy. This is the great, though
often invisible, blessing of accepting God's will, and without this wholehearted acceptance, however much it may
cost us, there can be no Christlikeness, no real holiness,
no genuine contemplation. And so the more opportunities
the Father gives us of seeing his will clearly and of seeing
our will not quite perfectly united to it, the more blessed
we are, provided we make full use of those opportunities
and embrace his will lovingly and generously. That for the
really generous friends of God the acceptance of his will
leads to some kind of Passion and crucifixion is inevitable,
since they are following the Master whose submission to
his Father's will led him to Calvary and death.

In commanding us to hear and to follow his Son, our
Father is gradually forming us into his likeness. All the
words of Christ are thus words of eternal life, as St. Peter
said, and contain the germ of our growth as children into
"other-Christs." That is why our Lord's standards are so
high: they must be, because he is Eternal Wisdom. He
demands much, and it is all for our good, just as in the
classroom the best teachers demand a certain standard of

behavior for the good of the children. Our Master insists on our constant loving submission to the Father's will, because otherwise we should have no capacity to receive his gifts. When we comply with his wishes, he loads us with his gifts and graces. But he knows that the Father is not prepared to accept anything from us: halfhearted service will not do for him, for he is perfect Love. God's exactingness therefore springs from love, for he wants to give himself to us as One and as Three, in the depths of our soul.

In order to be true children of our heavenly Father, true disciples of his Son our Master, we must give them the preferential love of our heart—there is no other way; and this means union of will. No one can be preferred to God, simply because he is God: he is supreme and cannot allow anyone else to supplant his love. When our Lord was preaching and teaching and working miracles, a great crowd followed him, but they were not necessarily his disciples. This is shown by the fact that many turned away when his demands became too exacting. They were not ready to give him the preferential love that would make them his disciples. In the Hebrew idiom, preferential love is expressed by way of extremes: if you love Peter more than Paul, you say you love Peter and hate Paul. Our Lord speaks in this way:

> If any man come to me, and hate not his father, and mother, and wife, and children, and brethren, and sisters, yea and his own life also, he cannot be my disciple (Lk 14: 26).

The depth of sacrifice demanded by our Lord is revealed in the words which follow immediately afterward:

> And whosoever doth not carry his cross and come after me, cannot be my disciple (Lk 14: 27).

We must listen to him and take his words as they stand, seeing that we cannot become saints without mortification. The "little way" is not the easy way, and, just as our Lord did, we must go to heaven by way of Calvary. St. Matthew's account of this incident emphasizes the "taking up" of our cross: this means the will is in it. We must bend down and take it up, as our Lord did, not just accept it passively. And it has to be our own cross too, not someone else's: carrying our own cross is how we work out the task planned for us by the Father.

So our cross is given us, and we must take it as we find it, not pick and choose the one we want, an oak one or a teak one. Other people's crosses often look more attractive, but the one the Father gives us is our very own. Our Lord in the Gospels is always talking about his "hour," his crucifixion; he cannot be separated from it, for his Father wills it. We are disciples of a crucified Master, and so we have to be crucified with him. Our cross is usually given to us in installments, weighing differently at different times: it is made up of small cells, little fatigues and worries and things that go wrong. We have to try to put them together so that one day they will add up to a glorious cross, shaped like Christ's. We cannot see the proper shape yet, partly because we are too close; in our self-pity we see each little bit magnified and distorted, and anyhow our loving Father will not let us see it as a whole yet, we should think it too big and heavy, and so lose courage. But we can carry our little crosses, little parts of the cross, and trust that in doing so we are growing like our Master, that one day we shall resemble him: glorified as he is in heaven, with his cross and his wounds glorified too. "And come after me," our Lord says, because he never asks us to suffer what he has not suffered; he always goes before, we have only to follow him.

The cross has always been the symbol of God's will, because it is the symbol of the most perfect obedience that ever existed. And so it is also the symbol of the most perfect glorification of the Father, although outwardly it seemed such a failure. The cross is a mystery, and yet it is a still deeper mystery that it can be so intensely longed and prayed for by children of God, and so light to those who take it up. Yet our fallen nature is cowardly, easily afraid of suffering, and often tries to escape the cross. Now, of course, strictly speaking, we cannot escape it: God can always place it on our shoulders in the form of illness, failures, and so on. But he much prefers us to accept it willingly and even to desire it because it is the only means that makes us like Christ crucified and therefore, in time, like Christ glorified. And if we are brave in taking it up, it becomes a burden of love.

For many people, their cross is the fear of the Cross: a fear that is easily aroused and intensified by an undisciplined imagination. They think that as soon as they surrender themselves to God, he will immediately strike them down with some terrible disease or suffering. How little do they know their Father! But all of us have to beware of our imagination. It is so sensitive to self-love, and besides, being an organic power, is subject to all sorts of physical fluctuations and influences. Thus it can be most misleading. An undisciplined imagination is also the source of endless distractions, instability of character, and unfaithfulness to promises. No power needs more control, and our progress in the spiritual life depends on this. We need to discipline our imagination and learn to live each day as it comes, remembering that God's will is infinitely wise, merciful, and tender, and that he unfailingly gives us the grace we need to accept his will, but only at the exact moment we need it. Then we really live by faith, trust, and love.

In his tender mercy the Father trains us to carry the cross. He begins with light crosses, and if the soul responds and is generous, he gives heavier crosses, each one bringing so much more light, love, trust, and holiness. He acts in this way because, if he were to impose a heavy cross without preparing us first, we should be crushed by it. Therefore we must appreciate our little crosses as signs of his will so that he can train us for the heavier, more sanctifying ones. People who are unceasingly faithful in little things are always found ready when God tries them severely so as to sanctify them more deeply. This allowing ourselves to be formed and trained is a life-long necessity because throughout our whole life we have to be sanctified, made Christlike.

These basic truths help us to accept our Father's will at all times and in all circumstances, just as our Master teaches us by his word and example. They have life-long applications and are capable of ever deepening acceptance. Often we may think that we have really embraced God's will, and we have, so far as we knew it, but then we find that his will makes even heavier demands and that a new act of acceptance and union is required to meet them. Those ever-increasing demands, made so insistently and yet so tenderly, have but one purpose, a loving purpose: to empty our will of self and make it much more capable of divine love, both in receiving and giving it, for we know that we can give it only in the measure that we have received it.

If we live a truly childlike life, we shall glorify the Father as his Son did; by doing his will in every detail, with the utmost love and fidelity, until the end. At the moment of death, we too should be able to say with our Lord, *Consummatum est*—I have done what you wanted. Let us be ready for that moment; for it should be the crown, the consummation of our whole life, but it can only be such if our whole life beforehand has been a glorification of the Father in union with his incarnate Son.

Even during our lifetime, then, we can become mirrors of the Father's glory, its living image, as his Son was on earth. Then the single preoccupation of our life and love will be to embrace the mystery of the divine will, to recognize that for which we have been chosen before the creation of the world: to serve the praise of his glory. We insert ourselves in this way into the mystery of creation. Our spiritual life is no longer a purely personal problem, limited to our personal relationship with God: it has its place in the immense scintillation of glory, sown by God throughout space and time. For ultimately everything must glorify God, and glorify him not only by words, but by being there, merely existing, by the exercise of its activity. To glorify God, to refer back to God the glory which his love dispenses and sows with profusion, is not that the role and *raison d'être* of every creature, and most of all of mankind, his children? Nothing matters, provided that God be glorified in us. Following the only-begotten Son, we present ourselves before the Father as living praises of his glory. We cannot enrich him in himself, because the plenitude of his riches is perfect. But we can make his glory and his perfection shine before the eyes of others. It is impossible to love God more perfectly than by manifesting his glory by diffusing it, multiplying it, sanctifying ourselves through his will, so that he may be recognized and glorified in us.

16

Christ Our Master

*This, Father, is my desire, that all those thou hast entrusted to
me may be with me where I am, so as to see my glory, thy
gift made to me, in that love which thou didst bestow upon
me before the foundation of the world.*

JOHN 17: 24 K

What kind of Person is Christ our Master? Many scenes in
the Gospel of St. John help to answer this question, because St. John's sensitivity of mind and heart gave him so
much insight into both the divinity and the humanity of
his beloved Master. It was, for instance, St. John's love
which made him recognize Jesus when he appeared to his
disciples after the resurrection, on the shore of the sea of
Tiberias (Jn 21: 1–8). They had gone out fishing, and all
night they had caught nothing.

> But when morning came, there was Jesus standing on
> the shore; only the disciples did not know that it was
> Jesus.

Then, at his command, they cast their net again and made
a great catch:

> Whereupon the disciple whom Jesus loved said to Pe-
> ter, it is the Lord. And Simon Peter, hearing him say it
> was the Lord, girded up the fisherman's coat, which
> was all he wore, and sprang into the sea.

How vivid the scene is. John remains in the boat peacefully, but Peter jumps excitedly into the lake. Our Lord,
though he has taught them so much, has yet preserved

their individual characters. They are a better John and Peter, wiser and more lovable, but the differences in personality have not been abolished. As children of the Father and disciples of his Son, they have become more Christlike, but they still express their love quite differently.

John recognizes our Lord first because he loves him so much, is so alert, ready for the merest glimpse of him, because he is so intimate with him, just as in the garden Mary Magdalen knew our Lord by the way he spoke her name. We need to learn this sensitivity to our Lord's presence in our lives too, especially in our trials and sorrows. Other people may see things from a purely natural point of view, perhaps as chance or coincidence, but we know that nothing happens by chance. Our Master cares for every detail of our lives: "Have you caught anything, friends, Jesus asked them, to season your bread with? And when they answered No, he said to them, Cast to the right of the boat, and you will have a catch" (Jn 21: 5 K).

Then we find our Lord cooking breakfast for them. There is nothing frivolous about this. Our Master is not concerned merely with candles and incense, but with the human needs of his brethren, also. It is a beautiful scene: "So Jesus came up and took bread which he gave to them, and fish as well." They were hungry, and he did not tell them to say long prayers before breakfast! This tenderness of his is a consequence of the Incarnation: as man he is utterly perfect, for his divinity has perfected his humanity. And he understands human nature in all its aspects perfectly. It is a peaceful scene, too: there is no rush, no agitation; even with Peter leaping into the water like that, our Lord is very calm. We might remember this when we are tempted to think that the best way to save souls is to overwork ourselves. It is not always so, and if we are peaceful in ourselves, we are much easier to live with than if we are in a constant whirl of activity.

Our Master loves us, and he is solicitous for our whole

being. How well St. John's Gospel reveals this. Our Master loves everything about us: body, soul, imagination, our whole personality. He arranges life for our sanctification; illness and sorrow, for instance, are allowed not for their own sakes but for the highest reason: our future glory, to be shared by soul and body. Our Lord's perfect humanity is concerned in his attitude toward us now: he has not changed since he protected and cared for his apostles. How they missed this at first when he had gone! He loves us, insignificant as we are. Indeed, the smaller and more insignificant we feel, the more he loves us. He loves each one, adapting himself, so to speak, to each personality. In heaven John is John and Peter is Peter, sanctified, Christ-like, and yet still each himself. Our Master wants us there with all that is good in us, all that makes us truly ourselves, unchanged; only the sinfulness, what is unchildlike, is to fall away.

Our Master wants us to be with him for all eternity. It is again St. John who gives us a glimpse into the desires of Christ's heart, and into the intimacy of the Blessed Trinity. For as we read his account of our Lord's priestly prayer before his Passion, we hear the human words of the only-begotten Son to his heavenly Father: "This, Father, is my desire, that all those whom thou hast entrusted to me may be with me where I am" (Jn 17: 24 K). The Greek expression has the force of "I will that. . . ." It expresses the immense strength of our Lord's desire, in a way hitherto unseen in the Gospel accounts of his words to his Father. It is his deepest, most intense desire, for it is again bound up with his Father's glory. Bossuet says it is positive, lovable, and sweet for us to hear. Why is that? Because we are the Father's gift to his Son. He is gathering us in, he wants us, and he allows us to listen to his prayer to the Father about it.

Now, for us, this is much more satisfying, more explicit, than to be told vaguely that we shall go to heaven, as if it were just a place. For being with our Lord means being united to the Trinity, and at the same time being with him in his glorious humanity. His desire for us to be with him is shown now, tangibly, in the Blessed Sacrament. It is a confirmation of the purpose of the Incarnation: a new way for him to be with his brethren day and night, until the end of time. He is still among us, the same Person, mind, heart, divinity, humanity, and love. When we receive Holy Communion, we receive a Person: exactly the same one who was born at Bethlehem and gave himself on the cross, with the same attitude to the Father and to us. He comes to us every day to prepare us for our life with him for ever. It seems almost unbelievable, when we think of all that he is, that he should want us at all. But that he should want us for all eternity proves his infinite mercy and love, and no one else desires our company as keenly as he does.

He wants us to be there with him in heaven to contemplate his glory. Seeing his glory means sharing it, because no one who does not share his glory can see it. This is what we mean by "the light of glory." In this life we believe in it all, but we do not see it. Our Master wants us to experience it, share his experience, so that it enters the inmost heart of our being. We do not know what it is like; St. John expresses it in tones of wonder, in his first Epistle:

> Beloved, we are sons of God even now, and what we shall be hereafter, has not been made known as yet. But we know that when he comes we shall be like him; we shall see him then as he is (1 Jn 3: 2 K).

We can glimpse this glory in Moses, face to face with God. It left its mark on him; people could not look at him, and he had to cover his face because of the blinding glory. This gives us a remote idea of what the apostles must have seen in Christ's glory at the Transfiguration. But in heaven we shall see our Lord in his full splendor, without being dazzled or overawed by it, because we shall to a certain degree share it, be clothed in it, and know it. We shall see our Master face to face, as he is.

When our Lord speaks of the glory which was the Father's gift to him, he is not referring to the glory belonging to his Divine Person. This would imply a generation of the Son after the existence of the Father, whereas the truth is that he is Son from all eternity. This glory is that which the Father had destined from all eternity for his human nature when he became incarnate, concealed during his life on earth except at the Transfiguration, but now shining forth in heaven. This is what he wants the adopted children, his disciples and brethren, to see and to share.

What have we done to make us so lovable? Nothing of ourselves. He makes us lovable, in his own inexplicable love for us, because it can come only from the good which he puts in us. And so he wants us. This is one of the greatest of all mysteries, and only God's infinite mercy and tenderness can explain it. In heaven we shall understand the mystery of God's love for us a little better, but we can never do anything to deserve it. We have even offended him by sin, by mediocrity and half-heartedness, and yet he still goes on loving us. That is the kind of Master we have.

While he was on earth he was always a loving Master, though, as we have seen, he could also be stern and exacting. We see him in the Gospels not only teaching but inspiring his disciples to accept his teaching. The great secret of his technique is to awaken permanent ideals, high ideals which influence human nature. He himself was dedicated to an ideal, his Father's glory, and he awakens this in others. We have seen how he formed Peter and John to give themselves to the same ideal, in the way which suited the personality of each. His teaching was never purely negative, for there is no inspiration in mere prohibition. He gives his disciples things to do: seek first the kingdom of God, take up your cross, be generous.

Our Master knows the human mind, for he made it. We can see it in this incident:

> Peter came to him and asked, Lord, how often must I see my brother do me wrong, and still forgive him; as much as seven times? Jesus said to him, I tell thee to forgive, not seven wrongs, but seventy times seven (Mt 18: 21–22 K).

Then he tells them the parable of the servant whose own enormous debt was forgiven, but who was punished for not doing likewise to his creditors. Our Lord shows them the reasonableness of forgiveness on our part, since so much has been forgiven us, appealing to their intelligence. For it was not always easy to put the Master's teaching into practice at first sight; it was hard for Peter, whose reason had to be shown the point of it all. Our Lord appeals also to his disciples' experience: when sending them out to preach, he made them leave all but the barest necessities behind them, and then, when they came back, asked if they had suffered need. They had not. But later he showed them the same lesson on a deeper level: the disciple is not above his Master; they would be treated just as he was. This is an invitation to generosity: if we follow a crucified Master, we must suffer; if we live up to his teaching, we shall not find it easy, but we shall always find in it the source of happiness and truth.

Above all, our Master insists on our recognition and acceptance of all that he is: the only-begotten Son of God. This is the real meaning of faith in the gospel-sense: to see him as God and to accept him as the Revealer of the Father. It is fundamental. As an example we could take the Passion: Christ crucified was God as well as man; that is why his sufferings and death are redemptive, and that is why he rose from the dead in glory. To see only his physical sufferings is to miss the point: it is a Divine Person who freely surrenders himself to these sufferings. His infinite love for the Father and for us urged him on to suffering and death. So the crucifixion is the most wonderful revelation of the love of the Father and the Son for each other, as well as of their love for us. It is there that we find all that our Master has clearly revealed.

And that is why we long for him to come to us: we love him, and we have experienced his love for us. In Advent the Church puts on our lips many expressions of longing which come from the Old Testament. Then they expressed the longing of the children of God for the Messiah; they felt their need and pleaded with him to come. But now the meaning is different; the words do not express the same longing any more, because the Incarnation has taken place. What we ought to be longing for now, especially in Advent, but at all times too, is our longing for our Lord's coming in triumph at the end of the world, as Savior in all his glory. This is the meaning we should put into the words of the Old Testament when we use them in prayer. We ought to desire the second coming of our Master just as much as the people of the old Israel desired his first coming. But many people never think about his second coming at all, except perhaps to dread the Judgment. That is surely rather strange: as if it were possible to love our Lord and not long for his coming. The apostles begged him to come again; they were always waiting for it. St. John says at the end of the Book of Revelation: "He who gives this warning says, indeed I am coming soon. Be it so, then; come, Lord Jesus" (Rev 22: 20 K).

It is not surprising, then, to find the Epistle and Gospel of the First Sunday of Advent referring not to Christmas but to the second coming of Christ. Our Master tells us it is imminent, and this is not a question of chronology, for it will take place in God's time, not ours. For him it is certain, for us it is sudden, unexpected, like a thief in the night. Of course, the longing for the glorious second coming was implicit in the longing for the first that we find in the Old Testament. The first coming was for the sake of the second. In fact, all that God has done in the Old Testament and the New, the creation and the redemption, is subordinate to, leads up to, that supreme moment. It is the reason for that marvelous continuity that we have noticed between the Old and the New Testaments. The Incarnation is for the sake of the second coming; this gives it perspective and meaning: the Son of God comes into the world to prepare for his coming at the end of the world, the supreme revelation of the glory of God.

Yet an understanding of this is not enough. When we ask our Master to come to us, to teach us and take possession of us, we mean here and now. We love him and we long for him now, and our longing is measured by our love. The lover wants to possess the Beloved. This is linked with his second coming, because his coming now is to prepare us for that: what we shall be like then, and whether we shall be with him then, is decided now. Our joy in his triumph then depends on our love for him now. Our relationship with him will remain fundamentally the same. If we die in sin, we shall certainly not look forward to his second coming, because for us it will be an everlasting disaster. That is why his present coming is vitally important: we must prepare ourselves so that he will find us with hearts on fire with joy. This will be the time of his undisputed kingship: the full glory of the Son of God will be seen, no longer by faith, believing that he has conquered, but really with our own eyes, seeing the final triumph of our beloved Master.

In a few years time we shall die and meet our Lord with the love we have at the moment of death, no more and no less. After death there is no means of increasing our love, for purgatory is punishment, purification, not a place for learning to love God. The time for growing in love will then be finished: the time that counts is now. This is a very important truth. How precious our life on earth is: each moment has a consequence of everlasting importance. If we fail now, through halfheartedness and mediocrity in our spiritual life, we shall die with little charity and have little for all eternity. Our Master alone can increase our love, and that is why we need him now, to teach us, and sanctify us in mind, will, imagination, body. That is why we long to be united to him now. Each moment of each day is given us by our Master to grow in our love for him, to show love, and so to receive more. But he is with us: his incarnation is continued in the Eucharist, which prepares us for the second coming: "Blessed is he who comes in the name of the Lord."

Our Master comes to us, especially in Holy Communion, to sanctify us here and now. Holiness is to be like him. We can become like Christ only if he gives us what he is and what he has, for it is not to be a superficial likeness, but one reaching to the depths of our personality. To be molded into the image of the Word Incarnate is to be given his features, and these establish in the sight of the Father a genuine resemblance between his Son and ourselves. Now, these features are what we call the infused virtues: our sharing in the infinite, divine perfections of the Word, which he infused into his human nature when he assumed it in the Incarnation. Of course, human nature can only share, and there are some differences: our virtues of faith and hope are drawn from his beatific vision and possession of God; Christ had no need for faith and hope as we have. But other than these two, we receive all our infused virtues from his plenitude, and the image of the Word Incarnate is in us to the extent that we possess the same virtues that he possessed in plenitude. Obviously mortification is necessary if we are truly to share in our Master's charity, meekness, humility, zeal, and so on, and thereby glorify his Father, himself, and his Spirit. We glorify them more in a sense by what we are than by what we do at a particular moment, although of course the virtues have to be exercised.

Virtues are tendencies that incline us to act in certain ways, the ways which correspond to them: a meek man will tend to act meekly, he will be inclined that way, though occasionally he may fail to act thus. These tendencies can be acquired by the repetition of acts, just as we practice when learning to play the piano, because these acts will gradually impress on our powers a certain inclination to act in a particular way and to respond at once to what prompts them to act in that way. This is easiest to see in the acquired virtues, which are more the results of our own efforts and practice, but it is equally true of the infused virtues, which also are habits and tendencies. For instance, the infused virtue of meekness, which we draw from our Master, who is meek and humble of heart, gives us the inclination to act meekly, and the deeper the hold which the virtue has on our will the more instantaneous our reaction will be toward acts of meekness.

Now, we know that our soul is a battlefield: on the one hand we have the tendencies of the acquired and infused virtues, and on the other hand, the sinful tendencies belonging to our fallen nature, inclinations that urge us to act against the virtues. In following our Master, we mortify these sinful tendencies so that their opposition gradually disappears under the influence of the virtues. "If any man has a mind to come my way, let him renounce self, and take up his cross, and follow me" (Mt 16: 24 K).

True mortification aims chiefly at the practice of the virtues, because the only positive and lasting way of overcoming our sinful tendencies is to practice the virtues opposed to them, so that they become strongest and deepest. The only lasting way of overcoming and eliminating pride, for example, is to seize every opportunity of practicing humility, and not to concentrate our efforts on eliminating pride, which is a negative struggle and therefore uninspiring and unstable. The only way of overcoming self-love is to concentrate everything on loving God. This opens up a really intelligent and effective path of mortification for each one to follow, the aim of it all being to increase our likeness to our Master by practicing his virtues. This is truly following in his footsteps.

It is clear then, that in the degree in which we are like him we shall be united to him: like seeks like. And the more we shall know by experience what he is like. For a person in whom infused meekness, for instance, is very strong will not only be like Christ in his meekness, but will also know by experiencing in himself the same inclinations, what the meek Christ was like.

So at his second coming we shall see what it is to be like our Master. We cannot see it in people now; some may have a striking resemblance to him, but it is still hidden. Then we shall see it. And we shall welcome our Lord to the extent that we too are like him. To be loving, to open oneself, to be prepared to leave self and all attachments, is to begin now to be like him. The intensity of our glory, and joy in his, will depend on our love for him now, and for his Father and Holy Spirit. Every moment counts; it is dangerous to put things off, for we shall never be able to change suddenly, simply by making up our minds. Holiness is a matter of growth, of using all our opportunities as they come along. Let us not give in to ourselves. Our Lord must be Master of our whole person; we must give way to him. Every time we mortify ourselves we grow, and every act of charity increases our love for God. Let us increase our longing for our Master now, for his coming in Holy Communion, in the circumstances of our lives, and ultimately for his second coming in glory. How can we love him without saying with the beloved disciple: "Come, Lord Jesus?" And the answer is: "Behold, I come quickly."

17

Children of Light

I have made thy name known to the men whom thou hast entrusted to me, chosen out of the world. They belonged to thee, and have become mine through thy gift, and they have kept true to thy word . . . in them my glory is achieved.

JOHN 17: 6, 10 K

If we allowed another person to listen to our prayers, it would be a sign of very unusual intimacy. But that is what our Lord allows us to do when we read his priestly prayer recorded in St. John's Gospel. It is a sign of his great love for us, this revelation of the close relationship between himself and his Father and of the deepest desires of his heart. So we see the Son in his human nature, lifting up his eyes to heaven, and praying to his Father.

How was it possible for the Incarnate Son of God to pray at all? It is because he had two wills: divine and human. He had human emotions too, and sometimes his prayer was merely an expression of them, not of his will. He enables us to recognize his sufferings, for instance, when, in the Garden of Gethsemane, he allows us to hear him say: "Abba, Father, . . . all things are possible to thee; take away this chalice from before me; only as thy will is, not as mine is" (Mk 14: 36 K). In his priestly prayer, on the other hand, we have what is more important, a strong expression of his human will, always perfectly conformed to the divine will, and therefore infallibly heard. Our Lord need not have put his desires into words like this, but he did so again for our sakes, that we might know him better through them. He begins, as we have seen earlier, with his greatest desire, with which all the others are connected:

145

"Father, the time has come; give glory now to thy Son, that thy Son may give the glory to thee" (Jn 17: 1ff. K).

Let us now turn our attention to that part of his prayer which expresses our Master's desires for his apostles, because it includes all future adopted children who would learn of him through them. Our Lord says: "It is not only for them that I pray: I pray for all those who are to find faith in me through their word." In the background is the fall of Adam. The Father foresaw it from all eternity and had his plan for the redemption which would reveal the immensity of his love for his children. He made his plan known gradually, revealing it through the history of his Chosen People. It was a continuous preparation for the fullness of time when he gave his only-begotten Son for the carrying out and completion of this great mystery. Then supremely, on the cross, the love of the Father for his children shone out. The Father, in order that his redemptive plan should continue to be worked out until the end of time, chose the apostles and drew them to his Son. He gave them to Christ, to be formed by him for the continuation of his own work by preaching, giving the sacraments, and shepherding his flock.

The apostles were therefore a unique body of men, chosen out to be children of the Light who came into the world to dispel all the darkness of sin. They were a starting point in humanity, the core of the Church, and so they lived with our Lord, shared everything with him, so as to imbibe his spirit. They saw all his work, endured the enmity of the Scribes and Pharisees with him, until the end, and then witnessed his resurrection and ascension, and received his Holy Spirit. They were to continue to give his light to the world. So they were precious to our Lord and to his Father. There is a note of fellowship, a mutual "owning" of them, in our Lord's words: "They belong to thee, as all I have is thine, and all thou hast is mine; and in them my glory is achieved." That is why the apostles are greater than, and different from, all other saints.

"In them I have been glorified": their dignity and greatness lie in this. Our Lord knew that they would be weak for a moment and run away, but he also knew that they would be faithful until the day when they would lay down their lives for him. He saw them whole and had a specially intimate love for these faithful friends, his brethren. Our Lord knew what his personal presence meant to them, what a source of strength it was. Now he was leaving them, and they would be outlawed for his sake, because the children of darkness would hate them, just as they had hated him.

And so, in his tender solicitude for them, he prays that the Father may keep them, watch over them as his children: "I am remaining in the world no longer, but they remain in the world, while I am on my way to thee. Holy Father, keep them true to thy name, thy gift to me, that they may be one, as we are one." Our Lord's chief concern for them, his chief desire for them and for us too, is holiness. He is praying that they should be sanctified, united in faith, hope, and charity, all sharing the life of the Father, Son, and Holy Spirit. That is why he begins his petition—and it is the only time he does—with the words: "Holy Father." For the whole theme of his prayer is holiness for the apostles and all those who believe through them. He laid down his life to make this holiness possible, and for this he feeds us.

All the holiness of the Church, of the apostles, of our Lord himself, comes from the Father, source of all holiness, the supremely Holy One. The Greek word for holy is *hagios*: "consecrated," "set aside." And for this reason the Jews of old regarded God in his holiness as separate, set apart from mankind by his transcendent majesty. His holiness seems to express all the transcendence of God himself, the fact that all his attributes are perfect, beyond all measure—indeed, that he is All. The three Persons of the Trinity are each infinitely holy, and the holiness in plenitude in the soul of Christ flows from the hypostatic union of his human nature with the Word. His holiness is then communicated to us inasmuch as we are united to him: we reflect the holiness of God.

Holiness and unity go together. Our Lord asks his Father to unite us all in holiness, and for this we must be protected from evil, kept true to his name. Sometimes we try to keep ourselves, but we are only children; we need to be kept by the Fatherhood of God. Thus we are one family: children of the same Father, kept safe through temptations and persecutions, children of light, learning to suffer in peace and joy in company with his only-begotten Son. All our unity, then, depends on the Father's love and care for us, having its source in his holiness.

Our Lord says: "that they may be one, as we are one." What does he mean by this? The two onenesses are obviously not identical: that is, the oneness of Father and Son within the Trinity, and the oneness of the Son and his disciples together in the Mystical Body. But these onenesses are like each other. The unity of the Father and Son is unique: they are one in substance, one God. The unity of the Son and his disciples, the adopted children of God, lies in their sharing the same divine life, but not the same substance. However, all other comparisons are too inferior to mean anything: the only unity which really helps to describe the deep unity of our Lord and ourselves is that of himself with his Father. That is why our Lord compares the two kinds of oneness, but there is a deeper reason too: we share his life, his love, his holiness, which he has in plenitude. So we share, too, in our own human way, in his oneness with the Father. All unity is true to the extent that it approaches this oneness. There is only a single Church, one Body of Christ, in which the true life circulates. Baptism ensures that this life flows into our souls, and our

Lord nourishes it, and therefore our unity too, with himself. Therefore, the stronger his life is within us, the stronger is our sense of union with our brethren.

Now, in this same prayer our Master says that he has kept all his apostles true to the Father's name except "the son of perdition." This is Judas, the child of darkness. St. John looks back on Judas as a thief, but still as one who belonged to the Twelve. Our Lord knew Judas would betray him, yet he chose him as one of the Twelve, and none of the apostles seems to have suspected him at all. So our Lord knew everything, but he never showed any resentment, nor did he treat him differently from the others. We have no hint of any reproach, except at the very end, with the kiss of betrayal, and yet we are told of his special love for the beloved disciple. We do not hear that he kept anything from Judas which he gave to the others, his teaching or the power of miracles, and he even washed his feet on that last evening. But we notice that before our Lord opened his heart to the apostles in the last discourse, Judas had gone out into the night; he could not have shared this revelation of the Master's love.

How did Judas come to this point? He had allowed the darkness to creep into his soul: the devil took possession of him, but it must have been at his own invitation, because no one is predestined to damnation. We are predestined to heaven, but reprobated to hell on our own condemnation. To enter either heaven or purgatory we must have supernatural life in us, but mortal sin means death. And every priest who hears confessions knows that many people do commit sins, willingly, defiantly, knowing what they are doing. These are the dispositions of darkness, which means that if those possessing them die, they damn themselves.

Judas had lived with Christ and shared everything, just like the others, yet he did not become holy. He was the opposite to all that the others became. His fall was prepared for by little sins, apparently quite unconnected with the final one of betrayal: little thefts. At first he was a child of light, probably just as enthusiastic as the others, but the darkness crept inside him, and no one noticed except our Lord. There must have been little acts of disloyalty, infidelity, resistance to grace, and so he fell when the big temptation came. This holds a very important lesson for all of us: Judas is not the only one who has betrayed our Lord. We need to retain our humility, realizing that we shall fall unless the Father keeps us, unless we struggle constantly to be faithful to the end.

The world of darkness is fundamentally opposed to the light. From the very beginning of St. John's Gospel we are aware of this antithesis: "And the light shines in darkness, a darkness which was not able to master it" (Jn 1: 5 K). And so our Lord underlines the fact that his apostles do not belong to the world, for they are children of light. In the Gospel, the word "world" is used in two senses, first, to mean mankind in general, as in "God so loved the world," and second, more specifically, those who live in the darkness because they prefer it, those who reject God. In this prayer our Lord is using the latter sense, and he foresees the pressure of the world of darkness upon his followers, not only in the form of persecution, but also as an insidious encroachment upon them, an undermining of their faith and hope and love. So he prays to his Father to keep them free from evil, but not to take them out of this world, though it would hate them because it hated him.

For the followers of Christ are to be in the world as leaven, as light-bearers. They will not be treated softly, because, however dangerous and hateful it is, they must stay in the world as followers of Christ crucified. There is for them the same conflict, the same death. The chief danger is to the spirit. Evil is an infectious atmosphere, and it is easy to be contaminated without knowing it. The teaching of the world takes different forms: materialism, search for pleasure, eagerness to compromise, and so on, but it is basically always the same, a rejection of the light. This worldliness is the real danger, much more than active persecution, which is a sign that the Church is making an impact on the world. So the children of light have to keep clear of all that the world stands for and hold out against it. There is always a danger of being converted by what one is trying to convert, and our Lord knew this: to be immune from the poison, his apostles would have to be saints. True children of light are utterly dedicated, in soul, in mind, in body; that is why he asks his Father to sanctify them.

Only a person in whom the Holy Spirit, the Flame of light and love, is Master can resist the world or even see it as it is. We become acclimatized so easily and do not see all that is hidden in the darkness. "Deliver us from evil": we have no idea how much we have to be protected from the world, especially when it appears in its less obvious aspects, often seeming attractive, cultured, and happy. Only the Holy Spirit can give us the light to see the compromises hidden away. The flood of evil in the world means that even grievous sins are not being denounced, yet the love of God is the hatred of sin; and while we love the sinner, we must never be afraid to denounce his sin— this is not to be lacking in charity.

All these words of our Lord to or about his apostles apply to us. "The world will hate you," he tells them; it will think we are odd, displaced persons, not at home anywhere. But we are heirs to the kingdom of heaven, and we have to let the light shine through us, unhindered, unshadowed by any compromise with darkness. The world has never acknowledged our King, but we have acknowledged him, we belong to him. This separates us from the darkness: how black and white it seems, this judgment of our Father on who belongs to him and who does not.

There was a time when the justice of God was preached a great deal; now, perhaps, it is not emphasized enough. It is thought, wrongly, to be incompatible with his infinite mercy. But our Lord, in his prayer for his apostles, clearly finds joy in the contemplation of his Father's justice: "Just Father, the world hath not known thee; but I have known thee: and these have known that thou hast sent me" (Jn 17: 25). It is foolish to see a conflict between God's justice and his mercy: ultimately they must be one, for he is his attributes. Let us try to share his Son's adoration of the Father, who is Infinite Justice, as we should.

We must think of it as being consoling: human beings are so often unjust, for they judge only by outward appearances. The Father, however, will take everything into account, seen or unseen. All will be brought into the light of his wisdom, all the circumstances of our lives, all pressure laid upon us, all our various tendencies which have affected our actions. He knows all his children perfectly and is incapable of a superficial judgment; even the children of darkness will see and admit his justice.

The Father will know his own, and they will know him. The children of light will share something of the knowledge which the Son has of his Father. The Son, in fact, is the infinite knowledge which the Father has of himself and of everything, because the Son is the Word of God: with him it is a case of being, not really of having knowledge. Now the perfect love existing between the Father and the Son, mutually, is the Holy Spirit, and we can enter into their relationship if we are possessed by him. He enables us to recognize the Son as sent by the Father: the distinguishing mark of the children of light. If we believe that the Father sent him, we accept his revelation in every detail, we give ourselves up to him completely: this is to be a Christian.

Where does the Father's justice come into this? It is in this difference between the world of darkness and the apostles who know that our Lord is sent. What shows that the Father is just? That very contrast. If we have the mind of Christ, we shall see the eternal consequence of this rejection and this acceptance. It is difficult for us to acquire such an all-embracing vision, but our Lord, being God, sees things so clearly, with all their fruits and consequences. The rejection of himself by the world he sees in terms of everlasting darkness and death, the acceptance of him by the apostles in terms of everlasting light and life and joy. We have to learn to build up this vision of things, step by step, to the conclusion in God's all-embracing justice. Then the total vision will fill us with peace, as it did our Lord. The Father's justice is lovable. It is not an attribute to be feared or glossed over. We should face it as we face his mercy and enter into it with a desire to learn and adore. Enlightened by our Lord who is the Light of the world, we shall see that the Father's justice is one with his mercy; and if we are truly childlike we shall love to call him "Just Father."

Both light and darkness, then, reveal the Father's justice. The choice between them is everlasting. If people repudiate the light, they show that they want darkness, and this does happen. The presence of evil in the world proves it; darkness makes it easy for people to go their own way, as Judas did. Those who choose God's light and follow it will live in light. They open their minds and hearts to it, and it floods their souls, dispelling all traces of darkness. In proportion as we open to the light, it takes possession of us. When our soul is fully open, fully illumined, it is ready for heaven; and in the wonderful justice of our Father, we are given the light of life for ever.

18

The Spirit of Adoption and His Gifts

But the Advocate, the Holy Spirit, whom the Father will send in my name, he will teach you all things, and bring to your mind whatever I have said to you.
JOHN 14: 26 C

As a child of light living in a world of darkness, every Christian is faced with the formidable task of living and acting as such. It is true that as an adopted child of God he has received the gift of faith and is enabled to see everything in the perspective of everlasting life and the truths revealed by God, but he needs more. To help his children to act on this, the Father has given those good habits that are called infused virtues, and which urge them to behave as his children should in all circumstances. Still more important, the Spirit of adoption is given to them, dwelling within them always to help them with his promptings and warnings. He is the Spirit of the Son, and so he knows how an adopted child of the Father should think and act, and of course he also knows the Father's will.

We have seen that the most constant, and yet often the least obvious, problem of the child of God is to recognize fully all the implications of his adoption by the Father in and through baptism. He needs the light and the promptings of the Spirit of adoption. Yet even the presence of the Holy Spirit is not enough: the child of God has to be given a special sensitivity to his inspirations, and special dispositions to make him capable of receiving them and acting upon them. These promptings of the Spirit are not limited to exceptional circumstances or emergencies; they are gifts that are part and parcel of the spiritual enrichment that comes to every child at baptism. They are gifts intended to enable him to think and act as a child of God in all circumstances, those that are easy to understand and meet, as well as those that are exceptional and perplexing.

Not for nothing, then, is the Spirit of adoption given to us to remain with us and dwell with us always. He reminds us constantly that we are children of God, and the more intensely we are aware of this basic fact, the easier does our practice of the virtues become. For, in the last resort, the Holy Spirit gives us light and insight not merely to impress upon us God's wondrous deeds but, more important, that we may live and act in accordance with that light and thus become more perfect children of our heavenly Father.

Now, to make us capable of receiving the light and promptings of the Spirit, the Father has given us an additional habitual disposition which makes us especially sensitive to the inspirations immediately connected with our adoption. This is the gift of piety, and it is of special importance to the child who appreciates his adoption and wants to make it much more of a living reality and experience. We must not confuse the gift of piety with the inspirations of the Holy Spirit. It enables us to receive his inspirations. Moreover there is a great variety of sensitivity in this gift, depending especially on the measure of our charity, humility, and purity. That is why some people are much more sensitive than others, being thus alive to their adoption and its decisive importance in every aspect of their lives. This is what the Father desires.

The gift of piety is therefore essential to the true child of God. Through it the Holy Spirit will help him to appreciate his adoption as a living reality, not only as something known by faith; more and more will the child see God as his Father and go out to him with ever deepening movements of filial love. These movements can at times be of a very great intensity, making him cry out with his whole being: "Abba, Father." This is not the result merely of charity guided and stimulated by faith: it is the Spirit of adoption himself who produces these movements of the deepest filial love. He produces, too, accompanying movements of gratitude, of astonishment at the Father's condescension, at his love in giving us his Son to make our adoption possible, movements of complete abandonment, and those movements of deepest intimacy and mutual love between the heavenly Father and his adopted child that cannot be described in words.

But above all the Spirit of adoption awakens in the children a desire to know their heavenly Father better. He makes them see that there is much more to be known and understood about their Father than faith can show, and that for this deeper, more personal knowledge they need him who is the Spirit of the Father. *Per te sciamus da Patrem*: Give us a deeper knowledge of the Father. As this desire grows in each child, his pleading for the coming of the Holy Spirit will also grow in intensity and insistence. There is no limit to the desire, for with each fresh insight it is strengthened, and the child's capacity is deepened. At last a moment comes when with an almost violent impact the realization comes to the child that only the beatific vision can possibly satisfy his longing to know the Father. It is then that the desire to know him is transformed into the desire for heaven. He sees heaven as being the vision of his Father dwelling within himself and loved with a consuming filial love.

Although this knowledge and love of the Father is of its nature personal, it must never be thought of as excluding the knowledge and love of other persons, be they angels or men. For the adopted child knows and loves his Father not only as his own, but also as the Father of countless other children. The Spirit of adoption never allows us to forget the immensity of the all-embracing Fatherhood of God; he will not countenance anything like possessiveness. The Father's love is such that its immensity is perfectly compatible with its intimacy, for though he loves so many, he loves each one for himself as if he were the only child. In this the Incarnate Son is a perfect mirror of his Father, as in all else, because he loved all his disciples and yet his love was perfectly adapted to the needs and aspirations of each one individually. Thus the inspirations that come to us from the Holy Spirit through the gift of piety give us a true conception of God's Fatherhood, and in this way he gradually widens our vision and our heart until they embrace the vast family of all the Father's adopted children. And in this family we can include our Lady, while at the same time we love and honor her as Queen and Mother.

All these children who share the adoption are therefore brethren. What an inspiration, then, toward fraternal charity is the prompting of the gift of piety meant to be. How difficult it is to practice this vital commandment unless we really see our fellowmen as children of the same Father and have grasped something of the intensity of the Father's love not only for ourselves but also for them. Then we see clearly beyond any doubt how impossible it is to love that Father and at the same time to be indifferent toward or to hate any of his children. The commandment of charity is the inevitable outcome of the common adoption of countless children by one and the same Father.

> And everyone who loves him who begot, loves also the one begotten of him. In this we know that we love the children of God, when we love God and do his commandments (1 Jn 5: 1, 2 c).

Now, the more he understands his Father and what his adoption means, the more anxious the child will be to avoid anything that might come between the Father and himself, either to weaken their mutual intimacy or, worse, to cause a breach between them. The child will always have that fear of offending his Father, of hurting him, of being separated from him, of betraying him or being ungrateful to him, which springs from love. Filial love breeds filial fear. It is not the fear of punishment—the child simply does not want to offend, because he loves his Father. The gift of adoption must therefore necessarily bring with it the gift of fear of the Lord: the fear of displeasing the Father, who has adopted us, of behaving in an unchildlike manner.

This is why the Spirit of adoption often uses his gift of fear to help the child to avoid sin, to resist the temptations of the flesh and of the world, because to succumb to them would offend the Father. Once again it is clear how much the frequency and force of the inspirations of the Spirit depend on the intensity of the child's love for his Father. If he loves little, his fear to offend will be weak and perhaps unequal to the attractions of sinful pleasures; whereas if he loves deeply, he will find it so much easier to resist and to conquer them, for the thought of offending his Father fills him with a horror that far outweighs the attractions of sin.

In the matter of temperance, self-discipline, and moderation, the promptings of the Spirit of adoption are important. The virtue of temperance is given a wholly childlike character by the gift of fear, because it permeates the virtue with filial love and filial fear. This is how the child of God can reconcile the most radical detachment from worldly pleasures with the most delicate respect for human values. Nothing is more alien to the gift of fear than Puritanism or Jansenism. If the child of God detaches himself from created things, it is not because he despises them and sees sin lurking everywhere, but because he loves his Father and wants to avoid everything that might come between the Father and himself in the slightest degree. At the same time the Spirit of adoption will help him to guard against despising the gifts which the Father has given to enable him to live a life worthy of him. This means not only supernatural but also natural gifts, gifts of incomparable beauty and delight which the child now receives as coming from the hands of a most loving Father, who cares for him with a solicitude that includes both gifts of grace and gifts of nature.

We have seen how many difficulties have to be overcome, how many hardships have to be suffered by the children of God, if they are to remain faithful to their adoption. And the fear of offending their Father will not by itself lead them to a fully integrated and mature Christian life; it will never bring their baptism to full fruition. They must live, act, and become holy in spite of all difficulties, temptations, sufferings, misunderstandings, reluctance, so that their approach to life must be positive, constructive, and redemptive. Holiness means practicing virtue rather than merely avoiding sin. This demands endurance, perseverance, and courage. It is impossible to grow up as a child of God without fortitude, for each one has to be brave, strong, patient, generous, even heroic perhaps, otherwise he will faint by the way; without fortitude he will never be able to climb his Calvary, where alone his adoption can reach its perfection.

No child of God will underestimate these difficulties and hardships. If he is really doing his best to live as he should, he will know them by experience; and if he has been faithful over a long period, they will be as familiar to him as constant companions: he will have learned how much he needs the inspirations of the Spirit of adoption to overcome them. And it is as a child of his Father in heaven that he has to endure them, not in a spirit of stoic endurance, of complacency or of self-reliance. He needs fortitude constantly, and at times he may need exceptional fortitude. This is why the Father has given him a special gift of fortitude through which the Holy Spirit with his inspirations will actuate and reinforce the infused virtue of fortitude which has already been given to the adopted child. Now he is enabled to meet all possible demands made on his fortitude, however severe and persistent these may be, comforted and strengthened by his Father's Spirit.

It is only natural that a child of God should sometimes be at a loss as to how he should act in conformity with his adoption. There will be moments of uncertainty, hesitation, and doubt, when he needs the aid of the Spirit through the gift of counsel. It is through his inspirations that he makes up for the uncertainties and timidity of human prudence, even that resulting from the infused virtue of prudence. The Spirit enables the child to judge what he should or should not do in particular circumstances. With the gift of counsel, the counsels of God come to him in secret inspirations that far surpass the considerations of human prudence without excluding it altogether. The child of God therefore should act under the influence of these inspirations as far as he is able to recognize them. The lives of the saints often illustrate this in practice, with their firmness and perseverance in the decisions that have been taken, though sometimes they are of an unusual kind. Thus under the direction of the gift of counsel the child of God treads a sure path amidst earthly obscurities and perplexities. How necessary this is, since so much can depend on a single decision! On its prudence or imprudence may well depend the success or failure of the rest of one's life, and the lives of others may also be affected by it. No holiness has ever been attained without prudence, or without far-reaching decisions; and many frustrated lives can trace their failure back to an imprudent, unenlightened decision. A child of God will never cease to plead with the Spirit of adoption to guide him in all his decisions, so that he may avoid any mistakes that will jeopardize his adoption or stunt its growth: *Ductore sic te praevio vitemus omne noxium.*

The child of God needs many other aids in addition to the gifts of piety, fortitude, fear, and counsel. His mind especially stands in great need of enlightenment. But the Father knows this: he always sees his children in the context of their daily life on earth, never in the abstract. He knows that they must learn to judge the things of this world at their true value; otherwise they may be too easily influenced by them, too much impressed by them, and by seeing them independently of their Creator become too much attached to them for their own sakes. The things of this world can be so beautiful, so deeply satisfying, so alluring. For this reason it can be that they conceal their Creator, making us forgetful of our Father, because they capture our hearts and bind them to themselves. The Father must therefore open our eyes to their transitoriness, to their "vanity," to their inability to give lasting satisfaction to the aspirations of the human heart and mind. This is a hard lesson to learn; and to bring it home to his children, the Father sends his Spirit, who through the gift of knowledge enlightens them. He makes them acutely aware of the inherent limitations of all creatures however beautiful or noble; many have recorded the result of this enlightenment, as St. Peter, for instance, says: "Yes, all mortal things are like grass, and all their glory like the bloom of grass; the grass withers, and its bloom falls" (1 Peter 1: 24 K; see also Is 40: 6–8).

Thus this gift shows us the limitations of earthly things, so that it becomes easier to recognize how foolish it would be to allow them to stand between us and the Father, or to blind us to his wonderful power and wisdom. Through the gift of knowledge the Holy Spirit makes us experience the truth of our Master's words: "How is man the better for gaining the whole world, if he loses himself, if he pays the forfeit of himself?" (Lk 9: 25 K).

Yet the gift of knowledge has a more important part to play in our enlightenment by showing us the positive qualities of the things of this world. We are meant to see their goodness and beauty, to be sensitive to them, so that our minds and hearts may be raised to the Father who made them. We must see in them reflections of our Father's power, goodness, wisdom, and beauty. It is as if they bear the print of their Creator's hands, reminding us of him. He made them for this: to lead our thoughts to him, to teach us to respond to his beauty in physical things, and even more in spiritual things. He means us to love him more than the mountains and flowers and water, for, although they reflect his beauty a little, they make us long for the perfect beauty that he is himself.

The Spirit of adoption therefore will give us the light to see creation as it truly is: a revelation of the Father, who has thus surrounded his children with reminders of himself, to help them to remember him, keeping their minds and hearts ever turned toward him. However beautiful the Father's creatures may be, his children must always remember: "How much the Lord of them is more beautiful than they; for the first author of beauty made all those things" (Wis 13: 3).

Of course, the children will plead with the Holy Spirit to give them a deeper insight into the heavenly Father, who is so lovable. We saw that, through the gift of piety, they long to know him better, and this leads them to the sources of revelation. For in many ways the Father has made himself known to his children by speaking of himself, and most explicitly and fully at last through his Son: "God, who at sundry times and in divers manners spoke in times past to the fathers by the prophets, last of all in these days has spoken to us by his Son" (Heb 1: 1, 2 c). Once more the Spirit comes to the aid of the children with his gift of understanding, through which he enables them to penetrate further into the revealed mysteries than would be possible by their own unaided efforts. Beneath the letter he makes them see the spirit; behind the symbol he discloses the divine reality concealed there; and through the wondrous deeds and the facts recorded in revelation, he will show them the Father's glory, his power, mercy, and love. The understanding that the Spirit gives is supernatural: it is entirely independent of study and scholarship and has nothing to do with mere human cleverness. The Spirit does not give the same knowledge and insight to some which others acquire by study. The conditions for this gift of understanding are only the loving desire to understand, humble pleading with the Father to send his Spirit of understanding and openness of mind.

The knowledge given by the Spirit is his own. It can never be separated from love: it is given because of love, it nourishes love, it stimulates love and makes it break forth into more intense acts of love. One can study without love, and without more love as a result of it. But this is not possible with the knowledge and insight that are given by the Spirit of adoption to those who are truly children of the Father: love is its seed as well as its fruit, not the love of knowledge for itself, but love of the child for his Father. This is why one has to ask for it as a child, receive it as a child, and respond to it as a child, with simplicity and docility as well as appreciation and gratitude. The Father gives this knowledge only to the little ones in his sight.

After so many marvelous gifts, what more can the heavenly Father give his adopted children? There is one more gift still, the crowning gift, most sublime of all, and so the most difficult to describe. It is the gift of that wisdom of God, "mysterious, hidden, which God foreordained before the world unto our glory" (1 Cor 2: 8 c), and which is communicated by his Spirit. He instructs them in "the deep things of God," in the things no one knows but the Spirit of God.

The distinctive feature of this wisdom is that it is an

insight and understanding which can be given only to those adopted children who live in deep union with the Father. Union and intimacy between Father and child are its only source, since it is the understanding of and insight into a Person which can be given only to those living in such a relationship. Without this intimacy it would be impossible to understand and to be in perfect unison with the inmost thoughts and desires of the other; it would be impossible to recognize him in his least actions and movements, to know his reactions perfectly and instantaneously. Yet when this relationship exists, one can understand so much, one can enter deeply into the loved one's way of thinking, judging, and acting, although what is deepest and most significant is inexpressible. In this intimacy one's thoughts and desires are identified with those of the loved one; everything is shared. According as the intimacy deepens, so that it includes one's whole personality, one can see everything through the eyes of the loved one, react in the same way, have the same criteria, the same way of thinking, all because the loved one's outlook and way of thinking have become completely one's own.

Now, it is the Father's deepest desire that there should be this relationship of union and intimacy, with all its fruits of wisdom and knowledge, between himself and each of his adopted children. It is the very purpose of the Incarnation and redemption, of the sacraments, to make this intimacy possible, not only in heaven but even on earth, within the context of our own lives and in a measure that surpasses all that we could possibly have dared to hope:"Eye has not seen, nor ear heard, nor has it entered into the heart of man, what things God has prepared for those who love him" (1 Cor 2: 9 c; see also Is 64: 3).

19

"Our Father"

*And it came to pass, that as he was in a certain place
praying, when he ceased, one of his disciples said to him:
Lord, teach us to pray, as John also taught his disciples. And
he said to them: When you pray, say: Father...*

LUKE II: I—2

From love spring desires concerning the person loved.
Thus it is clear that according as a child of God loves the
Father, the Spirit of Love will awaken in him certain
desires. And it is not at all surprising that the child should
experience desires that only his heavenly Father can fulfill,
since he is now mastered by the Spirit of adoption. For
even if our Lord had not given us the "Our Father," the
children of God would have been given those desires,
although they would not have known how to express them
so perfectly and so simply. Therefore the only-begotten
Son in his mercy has formulated for us the desires inspired by the Spirit of adoption in the prayer he has taught
us to say. So at the same time we can be sure that this
expression of our desires is most acceptable to the Father,
guaranteed as it is by the Son of God himself.

"Our Father, who art in heaven, hallowed be thy name."
The more a child loves his heavenly Father, the more
concerned he is with the honor of his Father. His chief
preoccupation now is that the Father should be known,
honored, and loved. He wants his Father's name to be
blessed. In becoming more and more possessed by this
desire, he comes steadily closer to the fulfillment of his
destiny as adopted child: to be given up to the praise of
his Father's glory, the glory of his holiness. Thus he

pleads with his Father that his name may be "hallowed," glorified before all creatures, that his love and goodness may triumph.

This desire is shared by all the adopted children, as are all the petitions of the "Our Father," because all are inspired by the Spirit of adoption. The children of God experience them within themselves increasingly, according to the extent that they are under the influence of the Holy Spirit. And thus we become increasingly aware of our fellowship with the other children of God; we say "our" Father, for we see in God not only our own Father, but the Father of all the adopted children, our brethren. We long for our Father to be known for what he is: Creator of heaven and earth, infinite in holiness, purity, love, justice, forgiveness, and all his perfections. We want all these qualities of our Father to be known, acknowledged, glorified, magnified by all, for he is the Source of unending blessings and of all holiness. That is why in the first petition the child asks above all things that the Father's name should be hallowed.

Then the child's desire to share his knowledge and love of the Father leads him to pray: "Thy kingdom come." His Father is King, but the child wants his Kingship to be acknowledged throughout the whole world. The Father is the only Source of life, and his child has an intense desire that as many as possible should share that life and inherit the riches of grace and love which the Father keeps for his own children. The sharing in his plenitude of life and in his holiness is "the mystery of his will" for his children and gives them a place in his kingdom where all things are reestablished in Christ (Eph 1: 9–10). So the child longs for all mankind to be "heirs indeed of God, and joint-heirs with Christ" (Rom 8: 17).

"Thy will be done." Once the child has gained some insight into the wisdom, love, and care that lie behind his Father's will, he experiences a deep desire that his Father's will should be done in all circumstances "on earth as it is in heaven." He wants that will to be done in himself, in every aspect of his life now and forever, regardless of what it may cost; and not only does he want this in himself, but in the whole world. This is sharing the Son's constant willingness to do his Father's will, making it the nourishment of his daily life. Of course, this desire springs from love, for love means identity of will. In the case of the child it means submitting his will to that of the Father, not because he has to, but because he wants to. Such a petition as "Thy will be done" is characteristic of the true child.

"Give us this day our daily bread." This petition comes from a sense of dependence upon our Father. A child needs his daily sustenance in order to grow. In this world we need strength, fortitude, perseverance, all sorts of things both material and spiritual. And so we ask our Father for what is necessary for every moment of natural life and, still more, supernatural life. This again is a willing dependence, not a grudging acceptance of a fact that we know is true, and we do not go into long descriptions of our needs. We have been told by our Master:

> Be not solicitous therefore, saying: What shall we eat, or what shall we drink, or wherewith shall we be clothed? For after all these things do the heathen seek. For your Father knoweth that you have need of all these things (Mt 6: 31–32).

And so we have confidence in our Father. This childlike trust is another characteristic of a true disciple of the only-begotten Son, who is growing into his likeness. It rests on faith and hope and love and does not depend on natural motives at all. The child of God has that attitude which leads him to insist that even if he could live without his Father's help, he would still prefer to be dependent on him for everything, as in truth he is. So he is both truthful in acknowledging his own helplessness and eager to accept that condition. According to the teaching of our Master, we must keep our eyes on this day, not looking too much into the future with its possible problems, dangers, and needs. We know that our Father will continue to care for us after this day, and we ask with confidence, as a child does its human father, knowing that he can and will supply all our needs. Thus we shall learn to resist the temptation to be agitated about the future, we shall live for this day, and in no better way could we express our implicit trust in our Father.

"Forgive us our trespasses." The Christian with his fallen nature, living under pressure from the world, will fall into sin many times. Therefore he always stands in need of forgiveness. It is again essentially as a child that he must ask, and at the same time as one who needs to forgive his brethren before he can ask forgiveness for himself: "as we forgive them that trespass against us." The petition assumes in fact that the child has already forgiven his brethren everything. For once he has seen what forgiveness means, for the Father and for himself, the child recognizes that he cannot possibly be forgiven unless and until he has forgiven others. Our Lord has taught us a very important lesson about the Father in his parable of the king's servant who would not forgive a fellow-servant his debt, when he himself had been forgiven much (Mt 18: 33–35). The king in the parable says: "Shouldst not thou then have had compassion also on thy fellow-servant even as I had compassion on thee?" And he hands the wicked servant over to be severely punished. Our Lord's comment could not be more explicit: "So also shall my heavenly Father do to you, if you forgive not everyone his brother from your hearts."

This is where many children of God fail: their pleading for forgiveness is of no avail because they have not completely forgiven others who are, after all, children of the same Father. We must understand that we cannot go to our common Father unless we are ready to forgive our brethren, from the bottom of our hearts, and in every detail. There is no proportion between the act of forgiveness on our part and on that of the Father, because he is God. How great is our need of mercy from the Father we have offended! A true child of God never forgets that the Father's forgiveness of his sins depends on his own willingness to forgive others the harm they may have done him. For this petition does not deny that our brethren may offend or hurt us. Many people are discouraged because they do not understand this. We shall be hurt by others, but no matter how true this may be, our forgiveness must be complete. The efficacy of our Father's forgiveness where we are concerned depends on the sincerity of our forgiveness of others.

"And lead us not into temptation." We are open to temptation both from within and from without. As all temptations urge us to act in ways that do not befit a child of God, all sin can be seen as a denial of our true nature as his children, and likewise of our responsibilities. That is why we add: "but deliver us from evil." It really means "from the evil one," in the same sense as that of St. John's first epistle, where sinners are seen as children of the evil one, and sin as his work. The devil is a formidable opponent who is most anxious that we should repudiate our adoption and become children of darkness instead of children of light. Even though the action of his powerful intellect and will is controlled by God's providence, the devil tries his utmost to entice us away from our Father. But it is a fact that the more a child becomes animated by the Spirit of adoption, the more does he become aware of the reality of the devil's power and thus alert to oppose it. The devil is indeed the prince of darkness, having great forces of evil at his disposal, which he adapts in a marvelous way to each person he tempts in order to draw him away from the Father.

The child of God recognizes, therefore, how much he needs the Father's help to resist temptation, for the Father alone has power to control the devil and to defeat his purpose. In this way "deliver us from evil" ceases to be a routine formula and expresses a living and actual desire, an intense desire, that nothing should separate us from the Father and so bring to naught our adoption and all its fruits. For the child of God, nothing is evil except whatever intrudes between himself and his Father, or whatever tends to separate them. Thus in the last petition the child begs to be delivered from everything: the world, the devil, his own fallen nature, that might endanger the relationship that his adoption at baptism has established with the Father. "Whosoever is born of God, committeth not sin: for his seed abideth in him, and he cannot sin, because he is born of God. In this the children of God are manifest, and the children of the devil" (1 Jn 3: 9–10).

The more a child loves his heavenly Father, the more he longs for all these desires expressed in his prayer to be fulfilled. His filial love gives him that unshakable confidence in his Father's faithfulness that the Epistle to the Hebrews describes as "the strongest comfort . . . the hope set before us: which we have as an anchor of the soul, sure and firm" (Heb 6: 18, 19). Linked with the child's desire for his Father's name to be hallowed, for his will to be done, for his kingdom to come, is the desire for the protection of his state of adoption. Nothing must interfere with this close, loving relationship with the Father: not lack of nourishment, nor lack of forgiveness on the child's part, nor temptations. The child knows his need for nourishing daily bread, for forgiveness and strength.

And so we have seen that in the first half of the "Our Father" the child looks at his Father and longs for all that a loving child must desire for his Father's glory; we have seen, too, how the second half of the prayer concentrates on the protection and deepening of that child's adoption. Thus we are reminded of the great necessity there is for us to eliminate anything which might lead us to repudiate our adoption, which is our only means of life and happiness.

"Amen" sums up all our desires. It endorses and reinforces them, by adding this emphatic "so be it." "Amen" is not simply a means of bringing our prayer to a conclusion; too often we treat it merely as a full stop. How often it is used in the Book of Revelation, always in a very effective way. For instance, it is used as a means of assent, agreement with what has been said: "To him that sitteth on the throne, and to the Lamb, benediction, and honor, and glory, and power, for ever and ever. And the four living creatures said: Amen. And the four and twenty ancients fell down on their faces, and adored him that liveth for ever and ever (Rev 5: 13–14).

Indeed, it seems as if it can be a song of praise in itself: when the ancients and four living creatures "fell down and adored God that sitteth upon the throne, saying: Amen. Alleluia" (Rev 19: 4). So at the end of our supreme prayer to the Father, "Amen" gathers together all the petitions that have gone before in a very special way, and emphasizes our desire that they all may be truly fulfilled: *Fiat.*

20

The Bread of Life

Believe me when I tell you this; the man who has faith in me
enjoys eternal life. It is I who am the bread of life. Your
fathers, who ate manna in the desert, died none the less; the
bread which comes down from heaven is such that he who
eats of it never dies. I myself am the living bread that has
come down from heaven. If anyone eats of this bread, he shall
live for ever. And now, what is this bread which I am to give?
It is my flesh, given for the life of the world.

JOHN 6: 47–52 K

Our loving Father reserves to himself the right to feed his
children now, just as he did in the wanderings of the
Exodus. The miraculous circumstances of the manna pre-
figure those of the Eucharist. God suspended the ordinary
law at that time: that man should earn his bread by the
sweat of his brow; and he allowed no settling down; the
Israelites might not even look after themselves in the
matter of food—he alone fed them. As long as they remained in the desert, they ate the manna which he sent
them every day. It fell like dew, white and sweet, and there
was always enough for each family.

> And Moses said to them: This is the bread, which the
> Lord hath given you to eat. This is the word, that the
> Lord hath commanded: Let every one gather of it as
> much as is enough to eat (Ex 16: 15–16).

Likewise, as long as we, the new Israel, are traveling
through the desert of this world we are given the Eucharist. We are not to rely on natural food, for the supernatu-

ral life is sustained and strengthened only by supernatural food.

Our Master tells us that he is our food, come down from heaven, sent by the Father to give us life. Now, life in the Gospel does not generally mean physical life. Too often we do not go deeply enough into its meaning; we look at things too humanly. Our immediate reaction, for example, if someone told us that a friend died last night would not be that he had committed a mortal sin, but that he had died physically. Yet we must understand our Lord supernaturally when he talks about life and death. Life, for him, usually means supernatural life. As second Person of the Blessed Trinity, he draws his life from the life of the Father, for all the Persons of the Blessed Trinity share one life. In Christ, God made man, this divine life is communicated to his human soul as habitual grace, the plenitude of the divine life. It is this life which, after baptism, we draw from the Father through Christ: supernatural life or grace. This life is fed by our Lord with his own Body and Blood in the Eucharist.

To live is to act; so what does this life enable us to do? It enables us to live according to our nature as adopted children of God: to will, to love, to think, to act supernaturally. But in the Hebrew idiom, loving and knowing go together, and so we get the definition of eternal life in our Lord's words: "Eternal life is knowing thee, who art the only true God, and Jesus Christ, whom thou hast sent" (Jn 17: 3 κ). Eternal life is to know and love the Trinity. Our Lord gives himself to us in the Eucharist in order to feed this life and knowledge within us, to increase it each time. Each time we receive him, we must let his life take possession of us: we in him and he in us. His thoughts must become our thoughts, his desires our desires, his love our love. The movements of our soul must become more and more identified with his. That is true union of wills and of love.

This means, of course, a gradual transformation, and it does not happen all at once, even when we do not put obstacles in the way. But why is it that people can go to Communion every day for many years without growing in holiness? Surely it ought to make a tremendous difference to them. The reason is that they are not willing to let our Lord take complete possession of them, to change their ways of thinking, their desires and interests, into his own. Our mind has to be conformed to his, and this requires a very deep-going detachment from self. Too many people, for instance, are afraid of losing their own personality, but, as we have seen, this is foolish. Our Lord does not crush what is unique in us; instead he sanctifies it. Let us make ourselves like soft wax to our Master's touch, when he comes to us in Holy Communion, so that he can impress his features upon us. We shall become intimate with him only if we are able to share his way of looking at things, his perfect, eternal desires, and his attitude to the Father as Son.

Let us take an illustration of this. There are two boys: one is interested only in the cinema, the other only in fishing. They may meet every day for a long time, but they never become friends because they do not share the same interests. There is a barrier between them because they have nothing in common. But if the fisherman takes an interest in the cinema, trying to share the other boy's interest, they are likely to become friends. And if both try, they will soon become very close friends, because they will understand each other.

Now, our meeting with our Lord every day in Holy Communion should be a personal and very intimate one. His great, unchangeable, perfect interest and desire is the glory of the Father, and so we must learn to share it: this leads to intimacy, to identity of love. We must beg him to teach us, to sanctify us, so that we too shall have this deep desire to glorify the Father. Then indeed our Lord can take possession of us. That is what he comes for, to live in us, not merely to pay a polite visit. We are to live his life: he is to think, will, desire, and love in and through us. Of course, this needs great detachment from self. There are few people in whom Holy Communion attains its end perfectly, because most of us dislike giving up everything that might be an obstacle to perfect union with him. But how worthwhile such a sacrifice is, how small compared with the immense reward.

The Father, then, intensifies his own life within us by giving us his Son as food. This means that we live the life of our heavenly Father to the extent that we have the life of Christ flowing vigorously in us, uniting us to him and to the Father. Each Holy Communion is essentially Trinitarian: a sharing in the life of the Holy Trinity. So the effect of it is that we become more filial, more possessed by the Spirit of adoption. It gives us a longing for our Father as the Son had, not only as uncreated, only-begotten Son, but as man too. He explains this to his disciples: "You have heard me say that I am going away and coming back to you. If you really loved me, you would be glad to hear that I am on my way to my Father" (Jn 14: 28 K). He wants us to share this feeling for home as being the place where our Father is. If he is truly living in us, he communicates it to us, and the knowledge it brings is sweeter than the taste of manna:

> The Father himself is your friend, since you have become my friends and have learned to believe that I came from God. It was from the Father I came out, when I entered the world, and now I am leaving the world, and going on my way to the Father (Jn 16: 27–29 K).

Holy Communion makes us "taste, and see that the Lord is sweet" (Ps 33: 9), just as the manna of old was sweet both to the taste and as a proof of the Father's loving care for his children. The author of the Book of Wisdom expresses this double sweetness perfectly:

> Thou didst feed thy people with the food of angels, and gavest them bread from heaven prepared without labour; having in it all that is delicious, and the sweetness of every taste. For thy sustenance shewed thy sweetness to thy children (Wis 16: 20–21).

The manna was therefore meant to be food for the soul as well as for the body: from it the Israelites learned more about their Father and his love. Only the Holy Spirit could give this new light and deeper insight which would show the people the hidden depths of meaning in the obvious outward signs. The Father does the same today, most of all with the Eucharist, but even in other things. The Holy Spirit enables us to find in our physical food the sweetness of God's love and care, for it may be produced in a natural way, unlike the manna, but it comes to us from our Father's hands all the same. It is the awareness of this, and our gratitude to him, that makes it nourish soul as well as body.

Our Father also gives us spiritual food in the Scriptures. These words too have to be transformed by the Holy Spirit if they are to feed, enlighten, and sustain our souls. He helps us to assimilate them, and this does not depend so much on our own eagerness in studying Scripture, but on his enabling our minds to be sustained by it. We can live on it for a whole lifetime, always being shown new light and new depths. The dead letter of human language is transformed by the Holy Spirit into living food which we make our own by contemplation. For in contemplation the word of God becomes the food of our souls, deepening in them the theological virtues, because God himself is both the end and the source. Union with God is the goal of it all, and the illuminations, the inspirations, of the Holy Spirit are in order that the soul may come closer to the Trinity.

What has been said of the words of Scripture applies still more to the Word of God himself. For the words are as it were merely crumbs of the Word, who was spoken in silence from all eternity. All the words of God, all his creation, were spoken by him first of all in his Word. In Holy Communion the Holy Spirit helps us to absorb the Word Incarnate as food of our soul. He is indispensable in this process of assimilation and growth, because without him to transform us, our mind cannot become the mind of Christ. The transformation is slow, imperceptible, but gradually, with each Communion, we find ourselves thinking and acting in a more Christlike way. It is most important to become as sensitive and docile as possible to him, otherwise our Communions will not bear this fruit.

Thus we shall come to learn and experience the sweetness of God. In Holy Communion the sweet Word of God is our joy, sustaining us in our journey through the desert, healing our ills, strengthening and encouraging us. Though we may have no sensible consolation, the very thought of his presence is sweet. The Jews were prepared for the manna by being three days without food. St. Catherine of Siena, hundreds of years later, used to say: "I am hungry" for Holy Communion. We too must experience this hunger for God if he is to reward us with his sweetness.

The sweetness of Christ springs from his soul. Our soul is to become conformed to every movement of his, and will be pleasing to the Father only insofar as it is so. This is the reason for all the benefits ever bestowed upon us. We are to share the intense desires of his soul, and how grateful we should be that he lets us know what they are. At the beginning of the Last Supper, St. Luke tells us, our Lord said: "I have longed and longed to share this paschal meal with you before my passion" (22: 15 K). But it is St.

John who reveals the depths of his Master's desires, in the account of his priestly prayer. Just as his supreme revelation of God in action is the crucifixion, our Lord's supreme revelation in speech is this prayer after his institution of the Eucharist.

We see there our Lord's desire for union among his disciples. The Eucharist was to become for them in later years the chief sign of that union of love with him and with one another which he asked. And this union is based on that existing between himself and his heavenly Father:

> I dedicate myself for their sakes, that they too may be dedicated through the truth. It is not only for them that I pray; I pray for those who are to find faith in me through their word; that they may all be one; that they too may be one in us, as thou Father, art in me, and I in thee; so that the world may come to believe that it is thou who hast sent me (Jn 17: 19–22 K).

To the extent that we make our own the union of the Father and the Son, we shall be united among ourselves. This union is based on a sharing of the same life, not on any compromise or even agreement of ideas. A union of "give and take" is only natural, a matter of courtesy, social obligations, and so on. It is not what our Lord desires. Only if we all become Christlike can there be true unity.

Now, this is the ideal; we have to approximate to it as closely as we can. Our unity must grow from within, not be imposed from outside. This is the oneness that is fed and nurtured by Holy Communion: the Christ-life is being built up in us and shared with one another. And this union is based on that inexplicable union within the Trinity: the union of two persons, Father and Son, which cannot be described in sense images that have no part in it, the union of two Persons breathing forth the Holy Spirit, the Fruit of their mutual love.

Just as much as the Son is in us, the Father is in us, too. This is another reason why we should long to be united with Christ: in him we are united to the Father and are allowed to share in the love which passes between them both. We are able to call the Father by the same name which his Son used: *Abba*. We can ask the same favors from the Father, for we want only what his Son wants. Our Lord says that when the Holy Spirit has taken possession of his disciples: "Believe me, you have only to make any request of the Father in my name, and he will grant it to you. . . . At the time I speak of, you will make your requests in my name; and there is no need for me to tell you that I will ask the Father to grant them to you, because the Father himself is your friend" (Jn 16: 23, 26 K).

With each Communion, the Holy Spirit can make us more and more aware of our relationship with our Father as his adopted children. He will give us the sense of being loved by him with the same love as he has for his only-begotten Son. And the fruits of this are the same in us too: the Son's utter loving submission to his Father's will, and his intense desire that the Father should be glorified by all creation and especially by mankind.

21

Gift of Love

*I have revealed, and will reveal, thy name to them; so that
the love thou hast bestowed upon me may dwell in them,
and I, too, may dwell in them.*

JOHN 17: 26 K

At the end of his priestly prayer after the Last Supper, our
Lord expresses the supreme desire of his heart, the one
thought which dominated his life on earth. He has, he tells
us, made known the Father to us so that the Father's love
may dwell in us. Our Lord has made the Father known,
not only by his teaching, his actions, suffering, death, and
resurrection, but above all by being the Son: revealing
himself as Son of the Father, so that we should see the
Father's perfections in him. For instance, we see his mercy,
and this is the Father's mercy too, the same in both.

This growing insight is continued by the Holy Spirit, in
order that the Father's love may dwell in us. Thus, because
we are adopted children of the Father, our outlook becomes essentially trinitarian, akin to the outlook of our
Lord, Son of the Father.

"... that the love thou hast bestowed on me may dwell
in them ..." What is it? It is uncreated love, not created
love; the Father has none. The Son, as man, has created
love, the charity in his Sacred Heart, but as Eternal Word
his love is eternal and uncreated. The Father and the Son
therefore have this mutual eternal love, whose infinite,
uncreated, eternal fruit is the Holy Spirit. So this love of
which our Lord speaks can mean only the Holy Spirit: He
is to dwell in us, be active in us, remain and reproduce the
Father's love in us, and the Son's love with its infinite

desires and longings. We should love the Son through, with, and in the Holy Spirit: then we shall love him with the Father's love.

The Holy Spirit dwelling in us produces some of the movements of love which the Father has for the Son. He draws us into the experience of them because it is the Father's love for the Son which is actually producing these inclinations in us. If his love has a certain power over us, we shall begin to experience this. There arise in us desires for the Son which can come only from the Father. He has them because He loves the Son infinitely. The great and mysterious fact is that the Father's love is in the soul which is dominated by the Holy Spirit. The child of God experiences these desires, coming from love, because they are so vital. They are summed up in the desire to see the Son glorified, and that becomes the true root of all genuine apostolic zeal. This intimacy with the Father is essential. The more childlike we become, the more sensitive we become to the heart of the Father. We see more clearly what he desires, or what he abhors, just as we have learned to do with people in our human relationships.

There is therefore a deep desire in the soul that the Son should be glorified—irrespective of what may happen to the person concerned. There is a deep desire, too, that the Son should be loved and trusted; all this is done by the Father. One of the ways in which the Father glorifies the Son is to produce these effects in souls so there will be in us a selfless desire that the Son of God and our Redeemer should be known, adored, and praised. The Father is communicating his own longings for the Son to our soul, and we identify ourselves with them, translating them into adoration, prayer, sacrifice, fidelity, love for the Son, through the Holy Spirit.

The Son has revealed the Father to his adopted children, and the Holy Spirit continues to make Him known in us. He wants to bring us to the Father. We must not therefore allow ourselves to forget the Father by over-concentrating on the Son. If we truly concentrate on the Son, we shall recognize that he is leading us to the Father, and the Father back to the Son. We must become Son-like, having the attitude of the Son to the Father, in our human way, and thus we shall become intimate with the Father, as St. Catherine of Siena did. Then we can say spontaneously: "Abba, Father." It is only to the extent that the Spirit of adoption masters us, that we see his Father as our Father. The Father responds to us then, and takes us into his intimacy. When a human child responds to its father's love, an intimacy grows up which is clearly seen and expressed without effort or strain: it is simply a turning to its father. So is this intimacy between the adopted child and the Father.

The Son is the "Sweet Word of the Father." When we share his love for the Son, in glorifying him we shall give deep satisfaction to the heart of the Father. Thus our soul turns more and more toward Christ; it must do so, because the love of the Father will never allow us to forget him, just as the love of the Son will always lead us to the Father. It is a mutual love, because the Spirit of love dominates the soul, communicating himself, mastering it. This is the truly consecrated soul: drawn into the depths of the mystery of the Trinity, at the frontier of faith and vision.

Many people are unaware of these truths; just as they are unaware of the indwelling of the Spirit, they are unaware of this movement of the Spirit. Yet children of God can experience it if they allow themselves to be molded by the Holy Spirit and so enter into the intimacy of the Father. This is not the privilege of a few, but it is meant for all in whom the Spirit dwells. This is what our Lord means. The action of the Holy Spirit is to transform the soul in communicating himself. We must, therefore, allow ourselves to be mastered: this demands that we should always be at his disposal. It demands great detachment, humility, and purity. There must be no resistance, for we must allow ourselves to be formed, guided, enlightened by the Holy Spirit. Thus the will of the soul takes part in the love of the Father and the Son, is carried by the movement of the Father's love, and goes out to the Son with something of the intensity of the Father's love for the Son. This is a completely unemotional experience; a longing to glorify the Son, to adore and praise our Savior, Redeemer, and Beloved.

These are the wonderful things done by the Father in the adopted child whom he has drawn into intimacy with himself. He begins by allowing the child to understand something of his love for the Son. When the child responds, the Father gives insight and makes him aware of the Father's love moving in him toward the Son, and he allows his soul to be carried by this steady current of love toward the Son.

When our Lord asks his Father that his love, the Holy Spirit, may dwell in us, he asks that he too may dwell in us. Now, in his human nature our Lord cannot dwell in us longer than the species remain after Holy Communion; but as the Eternal Son, Word of God, he can always dwell in us. All three Persons of the Trinity dwell in us, in every soul in a state of grace, living the life of adoption. The Three Divine Persons do indeed dwell in that soul, abiding in that person whom they love.

Our Master does not dwell in us inactively: he comes to bring about a radical transformation of mind and heart—as far as we allow him. He transforms our mind into his mind, our way of thinking into his way of thinking, outlook, wisdom, prudence, knowledge—but only if we detach ourselves from our un-Christlike outlook. We have to open our mind to the Sweet Word of God, to do in our mind in a little way what he did to his human mind at the Incarnation—although his mind was never like our minds, blind, spoilt, darkened; his was a perfect human mind, and he had the Beatific Vision. Our Lord makes our will like his, too, gives it a new orientation, not centered on self but on God; he gives it a capacity to love him and the Father and the Holy Spirit. He makes our hearts like his, with something of his capacity for loving the Father, infusing his created charity into us from his Sacred Heart. Our Lord, therefore, in order to bring about this complete transformation, must dwell in us. We, having nothing of our own—"Blessed are the poor"—are given infused charity to love God as the Persons of the Trinity love themselves.

As the transformation of the soul progresses, a desire to give God a gift commensurate with his infinitude is aroused and deepens. The soul, growing in love, looks round for gifts to give to the Trinity. All love does this; it must give, express itself in giving. We look around to see if we can find anything to offer, but our hands are empty, what have we to give the Trinity? Our natural talents, intellect, natural affections, are not gifts we can offer, for they are human, unworthy as such. They are even compatible, in themselves, with hatred for God. Yet, according as charity masters us, we want more and more to give God something worthy of God. But there is only sinfulness, infidelity, negligence, half-heartedness, mediocrity, meanness. We could give infused charity, but even charity becomes dissatisfied with itself, because it is created and therefore still not even commensurate with the infinitude of God.

The light of God can give us the answer to our longing. The worthy gift, commensurate with the infinite majesty, goodness, and holiness of God, is nothing of our own, and yet it is possessed by the soul urged on by charity.

It is the Holy Spirit, because he is given by the Father and the Son to us as adopted children of God.

We must take the word given literally: just as the Son

was given to us, so is the Love of the Father and Son given, and that Love is the Holy Spirit. He is truly mine because the Father has given him and the Son has given him.

The Father understands that I want to give a worthy gift to the Son.

The Son understands that I want to give a worthy gift to the Father.

The Father gives me Love to give the Son.

The Son gives me Love to give the Father.

Only because I am given Love can I give him to the Father and the Son.

Our longing to give comes from charity. The more we see how infinitely good God is, and how little we have to give him, the better we see that the Holy Spirit is the gift we long to give.

We go to the Father and give the uncreated Love of the Son.

We go to the Son and give the uncreated Love of the Father.

They accept, they cannot refuse, because the Gift is uncreated Love. I can give him because they have given him to me to give them. I can give God to God: the only worthy gift. The giving can go on, all day long, an unceasing giving, and an immense joy. The soul cries out with amazement at this: the infinite condescension of God, showing how we can give infinite compensation for all that our Lord has suffered for us. This is the gift which is commensurate with each divine perfection: goodness, mercy, majesty, holiness. This is the height of the mystical life because we are drawn into the heart of the Trinity, the mutual giving of love between Father and Son, and it is a foretaste of eternal life in heaven. Identifying herself completely with the Gift, the soul finds an inexpressible joy in being able to give God to God.

All of us are called to this, but few fulfill the necessary

conditions for making the Holy Spirit our Gift. We all believe that the Holy Spirit dwells in us, but few really understand and see what it means, for that is a special grace. Yet this grace is offered to all; we must desire it, and wish to give this Gift to the Father and the Son. When the Father and the Son give us the sense of truly possessing the Holy Spirit as our own, there is only one desire left: to give the Holy Spirit to them.

God gives, first of all, faith, hope, and charity. According as these virtues transform me, do I see that all I possess is given by God. Then comes the light to see that more is given: the Holy Spirit himself. This awareness of the acceptable Gift fills the soul with spiritual joy. It is the grace which our Lord laid down his life to give us, and he is anxious to give it to anyone who is willing to sacrifice self, to be detached. We are not pure enough to receive it, therefore we must become mortified, detached, pure. St. John of the Cross tells us to look at this, and think how mean we are, closing our souls to it. But this is the only way to the supreme joy of sharing the love between Father and Son.

No amount of theology can give this. It is given only to the childlike in mind and heart, utterly open to God, a condition which is rarely fulfilled because we prefer to be mediocre, popular, or academically successful, when what we need is the mind and heart of Christ. That is why the saints gave up all things, because there is nothing else comparable on earth to this beginning of the joy of heaven. On earth it is precarious, but in heaven there is no chance of losing the vision. And this vision will be the living at home with the Father, Son, and Holy Spirit, in spite of their infinity, as a little child, utterly at home, more than anywhere else, sharing God's own intimate life and wisdom and love in the Trinity.

22

The Language of Heaven

And the tempter coming said to him: If thou be the
Son of God, command that these stones be made bread.
Who answered and said: It is written, Not in bread alone
doth man live, but in every word that proceedeth from
the mouth of God.

MATTHEW 4: 3–4

When a child of God enters heaven, he feels immediately at home with his Father. He has learned to love him and to speak the language of heaven while he has been in exile on earth: that is what our prayer does for us. Let us, then, look at this language, not seeking for anything new or startling about it, but to remind ourselves of some of its principles. So often prayer is made into a problem, but this is quite unnecessary. There is no problem about prayer if we have the right attitude to God; that is the starting point.

Our attitude should be that of a child toward his Father, and that is what our prayer should spring from, not from the sense of obligation. Those who pray only because they know they ought to, have no spontaneity in it; they are easily wearied and soon reduce it to the minimum. But a child has no artificiality in his attitude to his Father; he speaks from his heart and mind. He expresses himself in many ways besides words: smiling, crying, asking, standing close by his Father silently—all are quite natural. A child asks many questions, because so much is going on inside his head, but in everything he turns first to his Father.

In active prayer, the child speaks or expresses himself somehow. This distinction between active and passive prayer can be somewhat artificial, but it is often helpful to clarify matters. In active prayer the Holy Spirit gives the desire to pray and stimulates it in a hidden way, so that however much we think the prayer is our own he is at the bottom of it, but it is chiefly the child's own effort. The Holy Spirit plays an indispensable part, but the child's part predominates.

Passive prayer comes wholly from the Holy Spirit: we "undergo" prayer. The more he is at work in our soul, the more sensitive we are to his inspirations, the easier will he be able to pray in us. He brings about movements of adoration, wonder, silence, praise, and so on, especially through his gifts. For instance, through the gift of understanding he may give us insight into some action of God in Scripture, which produces in us a movement of admiration; he inspires us, and we make the movement our own as soon as we are aware of it. Or again, he may enlighten us about God as he is in himself, his attributes, the Blessed Trinity, and we are moved to adoration, gratitude, contrition, or whatever it may be. At times the promptings and inspirations of the Holy Spirit are so overwhelming that they are inexpressible, and we adore in silence. This gives great honor and glory to God. Thus we undergo this kind of prayer, but we are also identifying ourselves with it.

This prayer presupposes great sensitiveness and liberty of spirit. If we are too clumsy, too impure, too blind, we are not able to receive this passive prayer, for it requires agility and openness of mind and heart. A stringed instrument is a good comparison. It only has to be touched for it to bring forth notes, with all the rich tones of a good instrument, not any tinny, untuneful sound. The whole soul then responds like this to the touch of the Holy Spirit. When it is true, this is an easy prayer. There is no fatiguing effort of concentration to keep the thoughts from wandering away, and no need to concentrate on points of meditation. Meditation may be necessary to begin with, but we must not be attached to it, becoming chained by it when we could be free. The *Imitation of Christ* says that there are so few contemplatives because there are so few who are willing to renounce themselves.

But this form of prayer is subject to fluctuations. Sometimes the Holy Spirit moves a child of God to the depths of his soul, so that for days he lives under this influence. On the other hand, the Holy Spirit may leave that child completely dry, and he may have to fall back on active prayer. We never know what he will do. We need to be detached even from his promptings; that is, we may desire them, but we should not be disturbed when he withdraws them. And in their absence we must not fall back into daydreaming or vagueness. To begin with, the "flashes" of passive prayer come occasionally, while active prayer is more usual. Later on, passive prayer increases, until it is almost continuous; it becomes quite normal, and active prayer becomes the exception.

The Old Testament is most illuminating on this subject of prayer. When the children of Israel saw manifestations of their Father's power or mercy, they burst into songs of praise. Although they might use the same words that they had used before, it was always a new song, a *canticum novum*. We too can do this, because we have fresh inspirations from the Holy Spirit, giving us a foretaste of heaven, where there will be an everlasting *canticum novum*. Other people, pagans, saw the wonderful deeds of God, the same things as the children of Israel, but only these saw the manifestation of God himself in them. We too can experience the urge to praise our Father, under the influence of the Holy Spirit, so great an urge that we need to ask all creation to join in, like the three young men in the fiery furnace. The Israelites found inspiration in the prayers of their fathers; they used their words again, just as our Lady did in the *Magnificat*, her *canticum novum*, her "new song."

The Holy Spirit speaks his admiration of God through us, if only we let him inspire, enlighten, and guide us. His inspirations should come to us and master us, finding nothing to hinder them, for we accept them willingly. We may well use the words of holy Scripture, even in passive prayer: if they have been burned into our soul, they will constantly come back into our mind. This shows that we have been using Scripture as it is meant to be used, as a means of knowing God, and as nourishment for our soul.

Our life of prayer, at whatever stage it is, will always be undernourished, sterile, weak, spasmodic, and artificial unless it is fed by the word of God. This means especially the New Testament, in which the Word of God himself is speaking to us, acting, suffering, dying, and rising from the dead for us. It applies also to the Old Testament, for the whole of Scripture is valuable food for our prayer. In the Exodus, the Father gave food to his children in the desert; they needed bread to survive on their march to the promised land, and so they received manna. This prefigures both the Eucharist, essential food of our souls, and the word of God, which nourishes our spiritual life.

One of the reasons, therefore, why a person's prayer is anemic, lacking in strength and depth, may well be that it is not nourished properly: it is living on a starvation diet. Our prayer cannot continue to grow from its seedling state and mature unless we return constantly to the word of God. We know that in order that it may become our food, the Holy Spirit has to change it into nourishment for us. The power of assimilation must be given by him, for without this it remains a stone instead of bread. When the word of God in Scripture is transformed into nourishment by the Holy Spirit, it feeds us and makes us strong. Some examples will show how he does this in practice.

He throws a deep and searching light on some particular text. For St. Teresa of Avila, one of these was Psalm 88: *Misericordias Domini in aeternum cantabo*: "I will sing the mercies of the Lord for ever." This remained the chief nourishment of her prayer for ever afterward; we might say even for eternity, for surely she has been singing it in heaven ever since. She saw aspects of it in the Old Testament and in the New, and especially in the crucifixion of our Lord. She responded with all her soul, with a longing to sing of the mercies of her heavenly Father, to speak about them to others, to praise God for them, and she has been given all eternity to do this.

St. Thérèse of Lisieux was profoundly influenced by the words of our Lord: "Unless . . . you become as little children, you shall not enter into the kingdom of heaven" (Mt 18: 3). Millions have heard those words, but have not been moved by them; they have not nourished their life of prayer on them. Yet upon St. Thérèse these words made a great impact and became the focal point of her prayer. The Holy Spirit gave her that light, and she responded and grew to maturity in the spiritual life through her childlikeness.

Sr. Elizabeth of the Trinity found the words in the Epistle to the Ephesians: *in laudem gloriae*, "unto the praise of glory," God's glory; and, combined with the words of our Lord on the indwelling of the Trinity, they formed the center-point of her life of prayer. Her spiritual life became very vital, enlightened, and deep, enriched by her understanding of those texts, which had come alive for her.

There are many other texts in both the Old and the New Testament which could take on a rich meaning for us, according as the Holy Spirit moves us. An example might be taken from Isaiah, chapter six: *Sanctus, Sanctus, Sanctus, Dominus Deus Sabaoth*, "Holy, holy, holy is the Lord of hosts" (c). It is quite easy to imagine that the Holy Spirit can seize the mind, heart, soul, and imagination of one of God's children and throw light on that text, making it something living, haunting him for the rest of

his life. For this child of God the words can be an inexhaustible source of inspiration, generosity, mortification,
consecration, provided that he responds to that light with
all he has. It will never cease to strengthen him, for the
words are so searching, so deep-going when they are truly
understood. The text embraces his whole being; his spiritual life is no longer divided, as it were, into compart-
ments—prayer, reading, the sacraments, and so on—but
is now unified, seen wholly in the light of that text. The
Mass contains it, too, so right at the center of everything
these words are found, a living source of holiness, little-
ness, courage, and fidelity. What a grace: to be haunted by
the holiness of God. What a responsibility also: to be a
living reflection of the holiness of God, in soul and body,
mind and heart, speech and action, and then to live thus
for all eternity.

All the saints have found such texts for themselves, with
the light that the Holy Spirit gives unfailingly. St. John of
the Cross had the Canticle of Canticles, which led him to
the heights of union with God, for the Holy Spirit made it
a spring of water welling up into eternal life. Such texts
can accompany children of God throughout their lives. St.
Augustine loved the words "The Word was made flesh," so
much that it seems he could not get away from them, to
the point that when reading his work we sometimes wish
he could. But the text possessed his soul; he saw something there which captivated him: again this was the work
of the Holy Spirit. We say that text very often, but does it
move us so much? It will if it is transformed by the Holy
Spirit into food for our souls, to make us grow up as
children of God.

We saw how texts from the Old Testament were absorbed and assimilated by our Lady, until they became
her natural means of expressing the movements of her
soul. The *Nunc dimittis* of Simeon can be compared to the
Magnificat in this, for there we find Simeon using the

words of Jacob to his son Joseph in the Old Testament, and also words from Tobias and Isaiah for his personal prayer. Jacob had said to Joseph: "Now shall I die with joy, because I have seen thy face, and leave thee alive" (Gen 46: 30). Simeon, filled with joy when he holds the Messiah in his arms, blesses God and says: "Ruler of all, now dost thou let thy servant go in peace, according to thy word . . ." (Lk 2: 29 K). As the servant of Yahweh, Simeon begs his Master to give him freedom from this life, now that he has seen the long-awaited Savior. He looks on the "Ruler of all" as absolute Master, in deep humility, and he uses the same words as our Lady: "according to thy word." Simeon had been promised that he would not die without seeing the Messiah; now he can be at peace—what he longed for has been granted: "for my own eyes have seen that saving power of thine which thou hast prepared in the sight of all nations"; as Isaiah had said, the whole world would see the salvation of Israel. Simeon has meditated on God's promise, with the help of the Holy Spirit, and so the words come out spontaneously, his own prayer.

"This is the light which shall give revelation to the Gentiles, this is the glory of thy people Israel." In Isaiah, salvation is promised also to the gentiles, the "not chosen" people. Simeon sees that the same Light is to be the salvation of both them and the old Chosen People of Israel. But this Light is the greatest glory of God's own people; the Son of God arises from their race to illumine the whole world.

Nearly half of Simeon's words are drawn from the Book of Isaiah between the chapters 40 to 52. Such words as these: "Behold, I have given thee to be the light of the Gentiles, that thou mayst be my salvation even to the farthest part of the earth" (49: 6) have struck Simeon, and through the Holy Spirit's guidance he has made them his own. In the supreme moment of his life, as he holds the

Redeemer and blesses the Father, these words come to his lips. They are the perfect expression of his very deepest feelings.

This is an excellent example of how Scripture can nourish prayer. It is found often in the prayers of the New Testament: our Lady, Simeon, Zachary, the people who quote the prophecies about the Messiah, all show how they have nourished their souls on Sacred Scripture. We should be doing the same in our own lives. The Church says the *Nunc dimittis* every night at Compline because we should have lived each day in such a way that we can ask God to let us depart in peace, with the same loving trust that Simeon had.

In Scripture there are prayers that everyone can and should use: words that can be adapted to all our needs, our longings, and our feelings. In fact we shall find that the further our prayer departs from Scripture, the more anemic, the more self-centered and superficial it will become. We have to ask the Holy Spirit to enlighten us: this is what he is sent for. We need to find in Scripture some text, or passages, that will be the support, the inspiration, and the driving force of our life. It will help us to face our daily life with its times of darkness, trial, and temptation. We can incorporate it into our personal life, become a living realization of that text. Then those words, which express the Word of God himself, are transformed by the Holy Spirit into nourishment. This is what happened in the lives of so many saints: they found in Scripture the inspiration to give themselves generously, wholeheartedly, always, whether it was hard or easy. The words they chose were engraved on their hearts, and they formed their lives around them, making them a pattern not only for their time on earth, but for eternity too. Their prayer became the natural breathing forth of love and understanding, nourished by their special text, enlightened by the Holy Spirit. Let it be so for us too.

23

"Blessed Be God"

*Zachary was filled with the Holy Ghost, and spoke in
prophecy: Blessed be the Lord, the God of Israel; he has
visited his people, and wrought their redemption.*

LUKE 1: 67–68 K

Zachary is another example of a person whose prayer has
been nourished by the Scriptures. The thoughts expressed
in his *Benedictus* come from the very core of the Old
Testament and show how perfectly the New Testament
fulfills the Old. Enlightened by the Holy Spirit, Zachary,
with a lifetime of meditation on Scripture behind him,
gives us the whole history of the salvation of mankind, the
working out of the Father's plan for his children. He
shows us that from ancient times up to the present day,
there has been a succession of divine interventions in the
world. The Father visits his children by intervening in
their lives, penetrating into their inmost depths. For instance, he is said to have visited Sarah, turning her sterility
into fruitfulness, enabling her to have a child. We find in
the Book of Exodus that he visited his Chosen People,
sometimes to chastise them, sometimes to bestow favors;
but whatever he did, it was done for their salvation, their
deliverance. Everything the Father did and promised was
for the good of his children, no matter what it was, the
favor of victory or the punishment of exile: he chastised
them in order to save at least a faithful remnant.

Especially after the Babylonian exile, a new note is
heard in the announcing of God's visitations, in the voices
of his prophets: God would visit his people in an unheard-
of way, in such a way that all the preceding ones would be

seen as preparations. The Holy Spirit purified and enlightened Zachary's mind so that he sees this supreme visitation in the Incarnation: God becoming man in the womb
of Mary. She sings her canticle with a deep understanding
of what the Incarnation means, in terms of God's perfections and ways, as learned from the Old Testament. So
Zachary, having been in Mary's presence for three months,
sees the Incarnation as the supreme visitation which God
had promised and prepared for such a long time. Zachary,
then, gives us a bridge from Old to New through his
prayerful understanding of Scripture; he sees our Lady,
Ark of the Covenant, with the Old and New Testaments
linked in her womb. Let us see how he expresses his
vision.

"Blessed be the Lord, the God of Israel; he has visited
his people, and wrought their redemption." This is the
characteristic reaction of a good Israelite: he is sensitive
to the goodness of God and remembers the deeds that the
Father has always done on behalf of his children. He is
overwhelmed by the thought of God's becoming man,
and his reaction is to praise and bless him. This is the
supreme rescue of his people: the Incarnation is by far the
greatest of all God's wondrous deeds. Thus the Holy
Spirit gives Zachary a deep understanding of the Father's
ways.

"He has raised up a horn of salvation to us, in the house
of David his servant, according to the promise which he
made by the lips of holy men that have been his prophets
from the beginning." Zachary sees in this visitation above
all another proof of God's faithfulness, his keeping his
promises. The Father was ever true to his word, and is so
supremely in sending his Son who is his Word. He has
given his people the power of salvation, says Zachary,
using the symbol of the horn as the traditional one for
strength and power. One prophet after another, especially
Isaiah, had promised that God would visit his people in a

decisive way, and this was echoed by the Psalmist, whose language Zachary is using in his own canticle.

We can pause here and feed on this thought. What, for instance, is better nourishment for the prayer of petition than this conviction that our Father keeps his promises? There is strength in such solid faith in God's word. What he has promised, he will do, no matter how impossible it may seem at the moment; nothing is impossible to our Father. If we ask him for favors, we know he has the power to answer. He answers the prayers of his children for sanctification and salvation. We have never been shown that this is not so. What is more astonishing than the visitation of the only-begotten Son of God in the Incarnation? Or day by day to us in the Eucharist? Each Holy Communion should be an intervention of his in view of our sanctification, with lasting effects upon us. He visits his Church; he is faithful to his promise to remain with us for ever. Then we too can burst into a song of blessing and praise to him for his faithfulness, like our Lady and Zachary.

"Salvation from our enemies, and from the hand of all who hate us. So he would carry out his merciful design toward our fathers, by remembering his holy covenant." This is what the Father had promised in the Old Testament. Zachary is identifying himself completely with his own people. God has promised to rescue them; he shows his mercy in keeping his promise because his faithfulness is rooted in his mercy and holiness. He remains faithful in spite of our faithlessness; only infinite mercy can do this. The history of the Chosen People, as of every soul, is full of unfaithfulness, halfheartedness, rebelliousness, waywardness. Yet the Father loves his children in such an unselfish way: he is exacting because he is God, but at the same time, that is why he is faithful and unselfish.

God is mindful of his covenant, his holy alliance with his Chosen People. There is a much more holy alliance

197

between God and ourselves, the Chosen People of the New Testament. This is sealed by the Precious Blood of his own Son, our Master: a new and everlasting covenant and testament. What is the core, the content, of both alliances, the old foreshadowing the new? "He had sworn an oath to our father Abraham, that he would enable us to live without fear in his service, delivered from the hand of our enemies, passing all our days in holiness, and approved in his sight." Zachary sees his central duty, the heart of religion, as the worship of God by his people. Therefore God has promised to deliver them, so that they may worship him in holiness. This is the purpose of his visitation in the Incarnation. We are delivered from the hand of the devil and sin, set free from hostility and slavery, as were the Israelites so many times, that we may worship the one true God in holiness. The purpose of the Incarnation is to make us holy: reflecting the holiness of our Father, his Son, and the Holy Spirit.

"And thou, my child, wilt be known for a prophet of the most High, going before the Lord, to clear his way for him." God has his own ways among men, and sometimes those ways have to be prepared by others—such is his wise and holy will. Looking at the infant John, his father sees the greatness bestowed on him by the choice of God. He sees the uniqueness of his little son in that he is to be the prophet of the most High, the most exalted title after that of Mother of the most High. It is no wonder, then, that our Lord spoke in such glowing words of the greatness of St. John the Baptist. All the prophets were sent to prepare his way, but none of them so immediately as John.

How is John to prepare his way? "Thou wilt make known to his people the salvation that is to release them from their sins." We too are called to do this. In the apostolate of everyday life, we have to prepare the way of God among his children, always remembering that they belong to him, not to us. We have to show them that

salvation lies in the forgiveness of sin—that is the knowledge we all need. This was what John did, and why he said
so often, "Repent, be baptized," as a symbol of their
repentance. Thus observance of the law gives place to
faith under the new covenant.

"Such is the merciful kindness of our God, which has
bidden him come to us, like a dawning from on high."
Salvation is the work of the tender mercy of our Father;
Zachary is talking to his little child, but he is speaking to
all of us too: the work of God's tender mercy is shown in
his forgiveness of our sins, our deliverance from original
sin and the blindness of our own personal sins. Again the
word "visit" is used. This time the visitation of God seems
like the sun rising in the sky. Our Lord was not yet born,
and Zachary saw the womb of our Lady as the horizon
from which the Sun would rise in the East, coming to the
full splendor of noon.

"To give light to those who live in darkness, in the
shadow of death, and to guide our feet into the way of
peace." The coming of the Light of the world is to bring
salvation, a dispelling of all the darkness of sin, and the
cloud of death which oppresses mankind. Our Lord is the
Sun who enlightens our path so that we may walk confi-
dently in the light, as St. John says in his First Epistle.
Then we shall find ourselves in the way that leads to peace
in the Messianic sense, the sum total of everything, spiritual and material too, which the Messiah brought us.

It is no wonder that Zachary, chastised for his lack of
faith, dumb for nine months, having meditated on his
failure in faith, should have been ready to see these truths
so clearly. One has to be humbled in order to see. Humility makes the soul much more responsive and sensitive in
the depths of her being to the Holy Spirit. Prayer is bound
up with humility: the more we recognize our utter dependence on God, the more we shall turn to him in everything. Humility is truth: we see ourselves as we really are,

little dependent children; thus it eliminates all pretensions to be either better or worse than we are. Humility helps us to see ourselves as far as possible as our heavenly Father sees us, and so it brings childlikeness, simplicity, and sincerity. It prevents us from living in a fictitious world, for it keeps our feet on earth, our head and heart in heaven. We recognize that everything we have, any talents or graces we have been given, all are pure gifts. Therefore we should always love humility: "Jesus meek and humble of heart, make my heart like unto thine." Christ is so sweet, as Word Incarnate, because of his gentleness and humility, and we must measure our love for him by our love of humility. We can even learn to love being humiliated. What humiliations he had to suffer out of obedience to his Father and love for us! And it is extraordinary, in a way, that we should have the impertinence to think in terms of humiliations: if we were really humble we should see ourselves as so small and sinful that what might appear humiliating is received by us as merely something that befalls us. We should be too little, too low, to be capable of humiliation.

The Incarnation is a wonderful reminder of our utter dependence upon God. Our Lord made himself as dependent as he possibly could, by becoming a helpless child. He did not choose, he took everything, and gave himself into the care of a woman and a foster-father. So God, infinite in majesty, comes into this household as the weakest one. It is important that we should see this dependence as being deliberately chosen by him, because the Father willed it. And it is one of the most important of the lessons he came to teach us.

So Zachary was given insight into the things of God through the lesson of humility, and through his loving study of the holy Scriptures, enlightened by the Holy Spirit. We too can use the words of Scripture to express our blessings of God for having blessed us so much.

Zachary's words, our Lady's, or Simeon's fit in so well with the movements of the Holy Spirit in our own soul that they will express our inmost thoughts and feelings. They will be sincerely ours, not someone else's, a new song. They must come from the depths of our being, hidden till now, and opened up only by humility. Blessed be God, always and everywhere, above all for the supreme visitation of the Incarnation. He has visited us, and he has never left us; he remains with us in the Blessed Sacrament. He never ceases to be the Key of David, opening up our prison of conceit and self-reliance to the light of humility and truth, leading us out of the shadow of sin and death into everlasting life.

Blessed be God for being God, and for being so infinitely merciful, faithful, and loving in his Fatherly goodness to us, his adopted children.

24

The Spirit of the Liturgy

The kingdom we have inherited is one which cannot be
shaken; in gratitude for this, let us worship God as he would
have us worship him, in awe and reverence; no doubt of it,
our God is a consuming fire.

HEBREWS 12: 28 K

Since the word of God is the food of our personal prayer,
it is not surprising that the liturgy draws its words almost
exclusively from holy Scripture. For the liturgy, when it
fulfills its true purpose, expresses our desire to worship
God as his creatures, and still more as his children, in and
through Christ.

One of the most striking consequences of the relationship between the Father and his adopted children in the
Old Testament is his gift to them of a definite liturgy. It
was their duty to worship him, to pay him as God the
homage they owed him as his people. The liturgy he gave
them fulfilled a need: he must demand worship, and they
felt the urge to worship, love, serve, and obey him as God.
Thus they were prevented from falling into idolatry with
its often hideous sacrifices by the ceremonial rites which
he directed, as well as by the alliance he made with them.
He gave them a priesthood, sacrificial rites, the Psalms, a
whole liturgy concerned with himself and his holiness, as
such books as Leviticus show. This liturgy may seem crude
to us, but in his infinite wisdom the Father knew what best
suited each stage in the history of his people. It was
different in the time of Solomon from that of the wandering in the desert or the exile, with the Ark of the Covenant, a movable temple.

This liturgy of theirs was very clear-cut. Only when worship was paid him in this particular way did God accept it, and this, except for occasional exceptions, kept them from going astray. Through that liturgy the Father sanctified his children, and this was its main purpose from his point of view. From their point of view it was the means they were given to fulfill their duty of worship to their God. So all these rites, the flutes, the cymbals and psalms, the ceremonies, were used by God to sanctify them. The people through this liturgy "sanctified God," in the Biblical sense: that of worshiping God for all that he is. They paid homage to his transcendence as the God of holiness, of infinite strength, of tender mercy and providence.

All this foreshadows the liturgy of the New Testament in a way that only God in his infinite wisdom could devise. In the Old Testament the high priest entered the Holy of Holies once a year with the blood of victims; no one else ever did. The high priest alone was allowed to come close to the majesty of God, under the shadow of the wings of the two cherubim. This prefigures the liturgy of the New Testament: our Lord, dying on the cross, entered heaven carrying his own Precious Blood as offering. The Passion and death of Christ, prepared for by the old sacrifices, are the focal point of the liturgy of the new alliance. After that comes the liturgy of the Church, which lives under the new alliance, and this in its turn foreshadows the liturgy of heaven, which was glimpsed by St. John in the Book of Revelation. There they sing the Canticle of Moses, in a marvelous continuity of liturgy stretching from the Old Testament, through the New, to the Holy of Holies of heaven.

The essential elements in the Old Testament liturgy were invisible. There were many outward signs, prayers, movements of the body, the use of ashes and so on, but they were meant to signify interior dispositions and unseen realities. God used the liturgy to sanctify them, but this is invisible: you cannot see the sanctification of a soul. Likewise the essence of the homage rendered, the spiritual dispositions of the worshipers, are invisible. It is not just a matter of movements or words; there has to be a spirit in them, or else it is only a mockery. The two elements, outer and inner, have to correspond if the worship is to be sincere. For the liturgy was not made for angels, but for human beings: body and soul together, and the body is the instrument through which the soul works. Those signs of repentance in the Old Testament: the ashes on the head, the mourning, could be done without any life and soul being put into them; they could become meaningless gestures. That is the great danger which besets all liturgy, old or new.

We have to bear these things in mind, for we too have a complete liturgy, with definite words and gestures: we have a Sacrifice, the sacraments, psalms, vocal prayers, and so on. The danger that these outward actions may become meaningless is always there. We have to go behind them, sometimes into their history, in order to make sure that they are expressing the spirit within us. This is where the Holy Spirit comes in. He alone can give us insight into, and understanding of, the liturgy and what it all means in the sight of God and the Church, because he alone knows the deep things of God. We need not only to study the history of it all, but, more important, we must go to him for light on the meaning of the liturgy. What do we understand by a Christocentric liturgy? What does it mean here and now in terms of the human heart, mind and body? What is its impact on me, on my life at present? It is the Spirit of the liturgy, the Holy Spirit himself, who must teach us these things, for he is behind it all: behind the liturgy of the Old Testament and that of our Lord's life, death, and resurrection which begins that of the New. The Holy Spirit urged our Lord to offer himself as Priest and Victim to the Father for the sanctification of mankind. He will dispose us to make our liturgy, which is one with Christ's, living worship. And through it he will sanctify us. We need the Holy Spirit if our worship is to glorify the Blessed Trinity, and we need him to give us the right dispositions for it.

It is no use being interested in the liturgy from the point of view of its symbolism or history only: this serves no purpose unless we are docile to the Holy Spirit, sensitive to him, for he is the Spirit of the liturgy. However keen we may be on the outward things, only the Holy Spirit can make our liturgy serve its purpose truly. Only he can turn lifeless observances into the expression of our living desires. In the power of the Holy Spirit we are able to worship the Trinity through, with, and in Christ: this is true liturgical worship. Mere enthusiasm is not enough. The Holy Spirit is to the liturgy what our soul is to our body: without him it has no soul. The more "liturgical" we become, the greater is our need of docility to him. It is those who are possessed by the Spirit of adoption, who know how to say "Abba, Father," who are able to unite themselves to Christ, offering himself to the Father at Mass, that are truly liturgical.

The Holy Spirit, then, enlightening our minds by the light of faith and his gifts, gives us a glimpse of the stupendous majesty and holiness of God. At the same time, he gives us insight into our duty as creatures to worship him with reverence, submission, and love. We must always remember that there is a line of distinction between God our Creator and ourselves his creatures which can never be blurred, but which gives direction and orientation to our minds and whole life. The Holy Spirit gives us insight into his transcendence, which gives such tremendous dimensions to our adoption, for it reveals still more the length and breadth, height and depth of his love.

The better we come to know God as Father, the more we love and adore his infinite being, his majesty, holiness, and transcendence. Our spirit of childhood, the spirit of adoption, will not let us forget these attributes, and familiarity will never dull our response to them. He who has adopted us is so perfect, so deserving of homage, praise, and worship. The greatest joy of the child of God springs from a realization of this greatness of the Father. Thus the Holy Spirit blends within that soul a deep reverence for God with great trust in and love of the same God who is our Father. "Hallowed be thy name"—may your name be "sanctified." The child recognizes that everything he has is God's gift, and he experiences an increasing desire to give him glory and praise, to acknowledge his holiness, and to worship him. These are his by right: "Blessing and glory and wisdom and thanksgiving and honor and power and strength belong to our God through endless ages, Amen" (Rev 7: 12 K). The more we absorb the Spirit of adoption, the more we want our Father to be worshiped in reverence, with awe and filial submission.

This is why we find the spirit of the liturgy at its most perfect in the soul of Christ. No one has ever worshiped God as perfectly as his only-begotten Son, and so the more we become like that Son, the more perfectly we shall be able to worship God. We too shall desire to vindicate the holiness of the Father, to be submissive to his will, even to carry the cross and die on it. These marvelous things the Spirit can do in us if he is allowed to master us, and he gives us a longing and a need to express them.

In order that we may correspond to these desires, the Holy Spirit also gives us the virtue of religion, the highest moral virtue which is especially concerned with the worship of God both inwardly and outwardly, and with his glorification. He implants this virtue in our wills so as to strengthen them and help them to correspond to the urge of love. This virtue of religion gives to our wills the inclination to worship our Creator-Father as creature-children, and therefore it goes hand in hand with filial love. We cannot have an immense love of our Father and a weak virtue of religion, for they grow together.

This virtue is perfected by piety, one of the Holy Spirit's seven great gifts. Piety is particularly aimed at transforming the whole debt of homage that we owe to God as creatures into a loving debt that we owe to our Father as his adopted children. Thus the virtue of religion is accompanied by filial piety, loving gratitude, and homage to the Father for all his perfections, and this is expressed in a worship inspired by the Spirit of adoption, who is the Spirit of Christ and of his Church. The liturgy of creatures is therefore transformed into the liturgy of children of our heavenly Father.

That is the essence of the liturgy, and that is why only a child of God has the true spirit of the liturgy. A person who is wanting in the spirit of adoption, of childlikeness, can be liturgical on the surface but lacking in meaning to the Father. It is not incense, genuflections, and ceremonies that the Father looks for, but the worship, honor, and glory given him by his children. This is manifested by the outward forms of the Mass, the sacraments, the saying of Office, the prayers, undertaken by the children of God.

The basic act of the virtue of religion, perfected by the gift of piety, is the act of devotion, which is not just an emotional attraction toward spiritual things but the deepest and most sincere homage of the creature-children to their Creator-Father. In this devotion the child gives himself wholly to God in an act of utter submission so that henceforward his will is ever prompt, alert, ready to honor, praise, thank, and glorify God as Father and Creator in all his majesty and holiness. This surrender is what the Father is looking for in our liturgical actions, and that is what all those actions laid down by his Church, following his Son, are intended to convey.

God often says in the Old Testament that he does not want man's sacrifices of lambs and bulls, but rather his will. The Psalmist expresses this idea in these words put into God's mouth: "If I should be hungry, I would not tell thee: for the world is mine, and the fulness thereof. Shall I eat the flesh of bullocks? or shall I drink the blood of goats? Offer to God the sacrifice of praise: and pay thy vows to the most High" (Ps 49: 12–14). It is the loving submission that only a child can give to his Father that God wants. He asks for ourselves; only thus are we "devoted" to him, when we have turned our whole will toward him, completely and as permanently as we can make it so in this life. This is both the sacrifice and the essence of the liturgy. And it is to this end that the Holy Spirit gives us his gift of piety and the virtue of religion. The theological virtues of faith, hope, and charity are, of course, called into play, for this worship that comes from the very roots of our being, from the depths which only the Holy Spirit can open up, is completely centered on God himself. It is through the gift of piety and the virtue of religion, directed and inspired by the theological virtues, that the Holy Spirit reaches those depths.

This is another reason, therefore, why the Holy Spirit must be allowed to master the children of God. When he is at work in us, our whole life becomes a liturgy. Every act in it becomes a liturgical act; and the specifically liturgical worship laid down by the Church, the flower of all the rest of our life. Things which seem to be merely outward actions can thus become signs of our inward submission to our Father as his child. So everything is integrated into the framework of our continuous and all-embracing act of surrender to the Father.

That is what we mean by liturgy, by religion, and by devotion. Unless there is this total surrender, including all the details of life, it is merely a succession of isolated acts; there may be liturgical acts, but they are not part of the whole. The complete giving of the whole human person to the Father, the total surrender of the will, ensures a unity of homage and adoration, expressed by the liturgy. It is a marvelous thing that God, through the Holy Spirit, gives us both love for the Father, as adopted children, and the perfect means of expressing it. There is no need for us to wonder what to do: we know that provided we offer the liturgy of his Son and of his Church, in his Spirit, our worship is acceptable. Once more we are conscious of the Father's infinite mercy in sending us his only-begotten Incarnate Son: he has shown us in his Body and Blood what it means to worship the Father and love him as his child. We, as adopted children in the Church, are doing the same things as the Son: we say the Psalms, spend hours in prayer, as he did, and we have his own Sacrifice, to offer infinite adoration, praise, and thanksgiving. All our liturgical acts, our Masses, our signs of the cross, are acceptable, provided we do them in the Spirit of the Son, with utter, unreserved giving of ourselves to him; then they will all be integrated, all our actions will be true expressions of our attitude toward our heavenly Father, that of utter loving submission to him as his child.

Then there is in our liturgy a note of joy and gratitude to God for being our Father, in all his transcendent holiness and perfections, who has in his abundant mercy and goodness given us, his Church, the perfect way of showing how much we want him to be acknowledged, loved and worshiped as supremely holy. The glory of God thus becomes a constant preoccupation: we are always seeking means to glorify our Father in all the details of our lives: "Abba, Father, glorify thyself."

This is what it means to have a liturgical spirit. It is the Spirit of adoption within us, who urges us as children of God to consecrate ourselves, through, with, and in his Son, utterly to his glory, praise, and adoration. And this is a genuine foretaste of the heavenly liturgy in which we shall continue for all eternity to give praise, honor, and glory in Christ to our heavenly Father for his infinite majesty, holiness, and mercy, and all his numberless perfections.

25

The Perfect Sacrifice

*Therefore doth the Father love me: because I lay down my
life, that I may take it again. No man taketh it away from
me: but I lay it down of myself, and I have power to lay it
down: and I have power to take it up again. This
commandment have I received from my Father.*

JOHN 10: 17–18

If perfection of the adopted children of God is measured
by their likeness to his only-begotten Son, they should
meditate constantly on that act of all-embracing submission which constitutes the heart and soul of Christ's
worship of his Father. This will help them to understand
and imitate it, and thus to worship their heavenly Father
as his adopted children should. Earlier, in examining
what our attitude as a child ought to be toward the
Father's will, we kept the Son's obedience before us as
our model. Now it is time to enter more fully into his
supreme act of utter loving submission to the Father, to
see it as the core of the liturgy and of our whole life as a
child of God.

Throughout his whole life, the Father's will was embraced by the human will of his Son, completely, with
nothing held back at any moment:

Wherefore when he cometh into the world, he saith:
Sacrifice and oblation thou wouldest not, but a body
thou hast fitted to me. Holocausts for sin did not please
thee. Then said I: Behold I come; in the head of the
book it is written of me, that I should do thy will, O
God (Heb 10: 5–7).

The fullness of his submission is something most important for us to understand. It included every detail of his life: our Lord willed with the full capacity of his human will whatever the Father willed, at no matter what cost to himself in terms of poverty, fatigue, suffering, tears, blood, death. Even when things might have seemed unimportant or unconnected with the salvation of mankind, he did not say "mankind can be saved without this," but he surrendered himself in every detail, fully, for there could be no halfheartedness in him. This is the example we must follow if we are to become like him. Nothing mattered but his Father's will, and his perfect appreciation of the holiness and wisdom of that will called forth unceasingly our Lord's utter loving submission. Yet at no time was this so clearly and perfectly manifested as at his crucifixion, and especially in the total shedding of his blood, completed and symbolized by the piercing of his heart by the lance. All his blood was shed, in conformity with the fullness of his submission to the Father's will.

The fullness of our Lord's surrender involved also unwavering constancy. His submission was an attitude which dominated his whole life, and which led him to his death, making of it the perfect sacrifice that was to replace all the sacrifices of the Old Testament. At the same time it led to his Resurrection. It is necessary that we should see that the Father's will was not merely that our Lord should die, but also that he should rise, and this even more than his Passion and death. There is a danger, when we talk of our Lord's submission, that we may think of his pain and humiliation, forgetting that the Father's will was, above all, the everlasting exaltation of the Son at his right hand. That is why before he suffered he prayed to his Father: "And now glorify thou me, O Father, with thyself, with the glory which I had, before the world was, with thee" (Jn 17: 5). Knowing that the bestowal of that everlasting glory was his Father's will, he desired it, and rejoices in it for all eternity.

What a mistake it would be, therefore, to exclude the thought of this glorious exaltation from the all-embracing submission of the Son, and to think of it merely in terms of suffering and death. The Father willed the incarnation, Passion, and death of his Son because he desired his glorification as Savior of the world. He now possesses that glory which is the fruit of his submission in his life, Passion, and death. "Ought not Christ to have suffered these things, and so to enter into his glory?" (Lk 24: 26). And this glory immeasurably surpasses his sufferings. So we must not think of the Father's will as being set on suffering, or as being only demanding and exacting, as if it never desires or gives joy. We must see the resurrection and everlasting exaltation of our Lord as being just as much the Father's will. Our Lord is glorified as the one Person who took away sin, who reconciled all mankind to the Father, thus gaining for him numberless adopted children, which all the sacrifices of the Old Testament could never do. His joy is everlasting, and that too is the Father's will.

It is the same for ourselves. We must not think of our heavenly Father as a Person who wills only sufferings and hardships for us, or demands only submission to his commandments. Our heavenly Father is a Father who desires, wills for his children everlasting glory, this above all. He desires therefore our sanctification, with the mortification that is implied in this because of the Fall. He wills our death in view of our glory; in a way, he desires it, because then he can give us everlasting joy. We cannot measure the joy we shall receive by the suffering we have now; there is no proportion between the two: eye has not seen nor ear heard the welcome the Father gives to the children who love him. Like the Son, the adopted children suffer in order to enter into their glory; the suffering is allowed because it purifies them. The death of a child of God can be precious in God's sight only if that child is purified, all dross burnt away by fire, to leave the gold.

The Son's submission is, above all else, loving. It was not the forced submission of a slave to his master, but the submission of a Son who is only too eager to give it and to accept the consequences out of love for his Father. "Behold I come . . ." Behold: what a word to be spoken by such a Son to such a Father. He did not have to be urged, and his attitude is perfectly spontaneous: Behold, here I am. My submission alone will take away the sins of mankind and restore them to you, Abba, as your adopted children. So the Son came forward eagerly, knowing what the Father desired, knowing also that his loving submission would lead to his death, making of it the perfect sacrifice to take away all sin. "Behold I come to do thy will, O God." That was the motto at the head of the book of his life, and as the book was unrolled and all the details of his life followed one another, his Father's will evoked the utter loving submission of his human will.

This cannot be emphasized too much: our Lord submitted as Son, and his human will was drawn into the divine relationship of the Son with his Father. What is so important for us to understand is directly connected with this fact, for the same Father has adopted us and demands of us utter submission, but he wants us to give it as children, not as slaves. He wants that utter loving submission of the children to the Father who has adopted them into his own family, which alone transforms acceptance of his will into worship. Then the whole of life becomes an unceasing liturgy: one continuous act of worship, homage, and praise, as St. John saw it in the Book of Revelation. In union with the Son, every act is transformed into an act of deepest love: the utterness of our submission is the utterness of our love, just as it was with him.

In his supreme act of loving surrender, our Lord offered

himself as Victim of sin, and yet at the same time he was High Priest of the new covenant. How is this? At the Incarnation, his human nature received the fullness of the priesthood, through being united to the divine Word. All through his life, from the first instant of his incarnation, Christ was both Priest and Victim, because it was at that instant that he made his all-embracing act of utter loving submission to his Father's will. However, it was in his Passion and death that his Victimship and Priesthood were manifested most clearly, because this was the climax and consummation of his self-oblation.

On the cross our Lord as Priest and Victim offered himself to his heavenly Father, shedding his blood, which was thus separated from his Body, at the Father's bidding. It is this too that reveals his Sonship most clearly to the eyes of faith: "Indeed this man was the Son of God" (Mk 15: 39). "The world must be convinced that I love the Father, and act only as the Father has commanded me to act" (Jn 14: 31 K). It was as Son that he shed his Blood, died, rose again, and thus redeemed mankind and glorified his Father.

The Father's will was that his Son should be the Savior of mankind through dying on the cross. If his Father had willed him to redeem mankind in any other way, by being beheaded, for example, our Lord would have accepted it with an equally loving and complete submission. This inward offering of himself is the core of his sacrifice.

Now, in every true sacrifice there are four essential elements, and all of these are in the sacrifice of the cross. There is a priest, a victim, an interior offering, and the outward expression of it. The outward action must express the inward attitude, or else it has no life or meaning. Our Lord, dying on the cross, showed outwardly his inward loving submission to the Father by all his words and actions: Father, into your hands I commend my spirit. The task is finished, I have obeyed your will. He offered himself as Victim, but he was Priest too, both then and now:

> Having therefore a great high priest that hath passed into the heavens, Jesus the Son of God: let us hold fast our confession. For we have not a high priest, who can not have compassion on our infirmities: but one tempted in all things like as we are, without sin (Heb 4: 14, 15).

This inward offering of himself gives meaning to all the outward elements of his sacrifice: his hanging for three hours, the shedding of his blood, the piercing of his heart, all reveal him as Priest and Victim.

Clearly, then, the sacrifice of the cross is unique from every point of view. Priest and Victim are one and the same Divine Person: the Incarnate Son of God. Our Lord was not offered to God by Pilate, or the Jews, or the soldiers, but by himself. It is inconceivable that there could be a sacrifice more perfect, more acceptable to God. And now we can see, in the utter loving submission of Jesus, a marvelous continuity from Bethlehem to the cross. Both manifest the same submission in different circumstances. But although it was not capable of increasing in depth or maturity or generosity, being perfect at all times, on the cross it was given its supreme expression. There, our Lord's utter loving submission and his Sonship were most strikingly, overwhelmingly revealed.

If we are to understand the unity of the sacrifice of the cross and the Mass, we must focus our attention on our Lord's interior offering of himself in utter loving submission to his Father. There is no question of a new sacrifice: our Lord does not suffer and die again, for he is glorified. The sacrifice of the Mass does not repeat, but commemorates the sacrifice of the cross. Now the history of Protestantism shows that we must be careful in interpreting the word "commemorate," and make it clear that the Mass is not a merely symbolic or figurative commemoration of the cross or the Last Supper. The commemoration of the cross in the Mass is itself a real sacrifice, a reminder of the sacrifice of the cross by being itself numerically one and the same sacrifice.

How is this possible? There is no question of physical death, or the shedding of our Lord's Blood now, so in what way does it commemorate and remind us of the sacrifice of the cross? We must recognize the same essential element in both; that is, the utter loving submission of our Lord to his Father's will is absolutely identical in both. There is no difference whatever in the interior oblation of the Son's will to his Father, for the glorified Christ has the same utter loving submission to his Father's will now as at the first moment of his Incarnation and as on the cross. Likewise, there is in both exactly the same Priest and Victim. The human priest is only the instrument of Christ the High Priest. Christ offers himself to his heavenly Father in every Mass just as he did on Calvary, although now it is through a human priest.

On the cross the outward expression of his inward oblation took the form of the shedding of his Blood and his physical death. This is no longer possible, because Christ is beyond death. In the Mass he cannot die as he did on Calvary, but he dies in another way. He dies sacramentally in virtue of the first consecration, "This is my Body," being separated from the second consecration, "This is my Blood." Therefore, although the physical Body and Blood of the Victim are not separated, they are sacramentally separated. Because our Lord's Body and Blood are now physically inseparable, as he is glorified, his whole humanity is really present in both. Sacramentally, however, they are separated when the priest pronounces with Christ the words of consecration. These words signify in the mystery of the sacrament the same utter loving submission to the Father's will with which our Lord came into the world. Christ himself, then, in each Mass, offers himself to the Father, expressing the utter loving submission of his will to his Father sacramentally by the double consecration.

The Mass, being identical in substance with the sacrifice of the cross, has infinite value. Each Mass gives infinite adoration, thanksgiving, and reparation to the Father, independent of the dispositions of the Church or the priest, because Christ is offering it. It is obvious, then, that there is no more perfect way of adoring God than to offer Mass, in which his Incarnate Son is Victim with the High Priest himself. There is no more perfect way of thanking God for all that he is, and for all his mercy toward us. Nothing on earth can equal it. Each Mass, too, because of the infinite dignity of Priest and Victim, is more pleasing to God than all sins taken together could be displeasing to him: it is perfect reparation. Blessed be God for making us his children and for giving us the sacrifice of the Mass, because now we can offer him a sacrifice that is worthy of him and acceptable to him. The fruits of the Mass, therefore, are infinite, but in us they are limited by our dispositions and by the fact that we are creatures. Our capacities vary, and when each Mass offers us forgiveness of sins, remits punishment due to sin, obtains for us spiritual and even temporal goods if they are useful for our salvation, our response is the measure of its fruitfulness in us.

One day the time will have come when the last Mass has been said and when there will no longer be a sacrifice properly so called. But then the Lamb of God, our Savior, in a perfect act of adoration and thanksgiving will continue to offer himself and his whole glorified mystical Body to his heavenly Father. That is the adoration and thanksgiving with which the Church associates us already in each holy Mass, when we say: *Sanctus, sanctus, sanctus,*

Dominus Deus Sabaoth, "Holy, holy, holy is the Lord God of hosts."

What should be the fruits of these thoughts on the sacrifice of the cross and the Mass and their essential identity? One of the more important is a deep devotion to the consecration. We should see it for what it is; it must be the moment when we penetrate most deeply into the soul of him who is both Victim and Priest, seeing there the ever-living utter and loving submission of himself to his Father. Then, and only then, shall we have a living remembrance of his self-oblation on the cross: "Do this in commemoration of me." It will be the focal point of our daily life, as it is of the whole liturgy and life of the Church.

We should have a devotion to the consecration primarily because it is Christ's sacrifice, not because he then becomes present on the altar. The sacrifice of the Mass was not instituted merely to make it possible for us to receive Communion, to have Benediction, to have our Lord really present with us. The consecration is the quintessence of the sacrifice of the Mass because it is the moment when Jesus Christ, High Priest of the new covenant, offers himself to his heavenly Father in a most perfect act of adoration; the other results follow on from that. But at that moment it is as if we were present at the foot of the cross, for we are present at the sacramental death of our Master. When he offers himself thus, the whole Church unites herself to him in his oblation. And we need this living remembrance of his sacrifice if as adopted children we are going to unite ourselves to him by making, in our turn, the utter and loving surrender of our will to the will of his Father, who is also our Father. His dispositions must be in us then, for we can unite ourselves to him at the consecration only in this way.

The Mass therefore must be the outward expression of our utter loving submission to the Father: only this will suffice to make it our sacrifice, as well as that of the Son. The whole atmosphere of the Mass must be filial: the Son offering himself to his Father, and we, as adopted children, uniting ourselves at the moment of consecration to his self-oblation. In union with the Son, therefore, we offer to the Father his Son's Body and Blood in sacrifice, and at the same time offer ourselves through, with, and in him. This act of union must be so deep and living that it irradiates our whole life and makes itself felt decisively in all our activities throughout the day. Then the sacrifice of the Mass will always keep our minds turned toward our Father's will, whatever it may demand. "Thy will be done as it is in heaven." And where is it more perfectly done than in the glorified soul of the only-begotten Incarnate Son in heaven? *Anima Christi sanctifica me.* Soul of Christ, sanctify me.

When the Son finds the minds and wills of the adopted children who receive him in Communion so perfectly attuned to his own, in harmony with his deepest desires, what can he do but pour out his Spirit into them? The Spirit will make them cry out, or whisper: "Abba, my Father; Abba, Father, not as I will but as thou wilt." The Spirit will give them strength to suffer and die as victims of the same Father's will, the strength which the Son had, and his desire. The Son finds joy in coming to a soul with the same desire, the same determination as his own, to suffer and submit, utterly and lovingly. Only the true adopted child, who is mastered by the Holy Spirit, has the same longings as the Son, whose deepest desire is expressed in his priestly prayer: "Father, . . . glorify thy Son, that thy Son may glorify thee. . . . For them do I sanctify myself, that they also may be sanctified in truth" (Jn 17: 1, 19).

26

The Springs of Charity

You have only to live on in me, and I will live on in you.
The branch that does not live on in the vine can yield no
fruit of itself; no more can you, if you do not live on in me.
I am the vine, you are its branches; if a man lives on in me,
and I in him, then he will yield abundant fruit; separated
from me, you have no power to do anything. . . . My Father's
name has been glorified, if you yield abundant fruit, and
prove yourselves my disciples.

JOHN 15: 4–5, 8 K

It is to the heart of the Trinity that we must go to find the sources of charity. In the Trinity the Father and the Son love one another with an infinite, eternal, uncreated love; and as the infinite, uncreated fruit of their mutual love, they breathe forth the Holy Spirit. Now, in human beings supernatural love can come only from the Spirit of Love, and it has to be grafted by him upon the will, because of itself human nature, even when sinless, has only human love. At the Incarnation the human heart and will assumed by the Son received from the Holy Spirit the plenitude of supernatural love, which we call charity. Our Lord, therefore, as God, possessed the Holy Spirit himself, infinite uncreated Love, and as man, the fullness of charity. It is from his human heart that all his followers, the children of God, draw their charity. It can truly be said that they love one another with his love. The Holy Spirit communicates it, a constant flow of supernatural love from the heart of Christ into the hearts of the adopted children.

Charity, then, is an infused virtue: it cannot be drawn from our own resources, and must not be confused with the natural affection of a human being. A person can love very deeply without charity, but this is purely natural love. Charity depends not upon personality, temperament, talents, or an affectionate nature, but upon the Holy Spirit. Infused into our will, charity makes our heart, in a little way, like our Lord's. It is quite outside the natural order and can be possessed by anybody: by those who spend their lives teaching theology or by those who peel potatoes, there is no discrimination—all depends on whether supernatural love dominates the whole person.

When we love with charity we are passing on to others Christ's gift of love to us; it is both ours and his. It is rather like a little child giving his mother a birthday present provided by his father, but the mother accepts it as the child's own gift. By giving love in this way, we do not lose it; we multiply it, for each of such acts increases it. Each time it takes a deeper hold on our own will and profoundly influences our attitude toward others, because we are learning to love them as Christ loves them.

In order to illustrate true charity, we might imagine two mothers. A mother living in a state of mortal sin may yet love her children with a deep maternal love. But this remains purely natural love; it is not charity. A mother who is in a state of grace will have, in addition to her maternal love, the supernatural love which makes her deeply concerned with the salvation of her children. Their spiritual welfare will seem to her even more important than their material welfare. Charity makes us look at people from God's point of view; it opens our eyes to their spiritual qualities and blinds us to the trivial things which do not really matter. For instance, we shall value others more for their spiritual qualities, such as humility or justice, than for their intellectual or practical gifts. St. Paul, in his famous chapter on charity in the First Epistle to the Corinthians, says:

I may have utter faith, so that I can move mountains; yet if I lack charity, I count for nothing. I may give away all that I have, to feed the poor; I may give myself up to be burnt at the stake; if I lack charity, it goes for nothing (13: 2–3 K).

St. John of the Cross, following the same line of thought, says that in the evening of life we shall be judged on love. It is the only thing that matters. What we have done will be important only if we have put love into it; the actions in themselves are worth nothing. Therefore we must take care that our charity is alive and growing; we must pray for it to be increased and keep it in the foreground of our thoughts. We shall understand all this well enough when we are dying, for then all else fades away.

An important aspect of charity for us to remember is that just as our infused charity is identical with that of our Lord, our charity for God and our neighbor is one and the same. There is only one charity upon which we can draw. From this we can see that the charity which is infused into us must of necessity have the same tendencies and give rise to the same desires and aspirations as our Lord's. One of the principles which can help a great deal in our understanding of the spiritual life is that which shows that things identical in nature have the same pattern of structure, the same tendencies, and the same basic activities. Apple trees are the same in nature wherever you plant them: they will always produce apples and not pears or gooseberries. Even if there are many varieties of apples, and in each variety no two specimens are alike, they are all apples with the same basic structure and properties. The more charity fills our hearts, the more Christlike are our desires and all our actions.

In our Lord these supernatural desires and tendencies completely dominated his will because, besides being given the plentitude of charity, there was nothing whatever to hinder it in possessing complete mastery and full maturity. But in us, things are different. For in us there are many obstacles which make it difficult for charity to penetrate and master our will, and to communicate to it fully its own tendencies. This is because our will, without necessarily turning away from God, can easily remain under the sway of self-love with its self-centered tendencies and preoccupations and thus prevent charity from taking root deeply in it and from becoming its driving-force.

We know, however, that our Lord, the only-begotten Son of the Father, was perfectly God-centered. The charity infused into his soul gave him a most intense desire to glorify his heavenly Father at no matter what cost to himself, even when it meant laying down his life. His charity is the Incarnate Son's love for his Father as it is infused into his Sacred Heart. This brings his human will into perfect unison with the uncreated eternal love which he as Son gives to the Father in the Holy Spirit from all eternity.

This adaptation of his human heart to his infinite love is the explanation of our Lord's supreme desire as Incarnate Son to glorify his Father. So much was this so that, from the very first instant of his incarnation, he placed his whole human nature with all its powers, its sensitivity, his soul with all its natural and infused endowments, and his Body and Blood, wholly and unreservedly in the service of this aim. To such lengths was he impelled to go by his love of the Father and his glory.

Our Lord's love is essentially the love of the Son, and it is this filial character which gave his whole life its all-embracing orientation and consuming intensity. Even his desire to redeem mankind was subordinate to his desire to glorify the Father: it was the task he was given to do, in the accomplishment of which he gave supreme glory to his Father. Not that our Lord loved his Father and was, so to say, by obedience forced to love mankind. No, his love for mankind was contained in his love for the Father. But it was his love for the Father which determined the unfolding of his life from its beginning to its end. Because he loved his Father, our Lord longed to redeem mankind, thus giving them the power to become the adopted children of his Father, and becoming himself the "eldest-born among many brethren" (Rom 8: 29 K). This was his Father's loving design, and the Son made it utterly his own. Thus we have come to the deepest spring of charity: the heart of the Trinity.

Since the charity of the adopted children is identical with the charity of the Incarnate Son, their charity is first and foremost a filial love: the love of a child toward the Father who in his infinite love has adopted him. This filial love makes the child go out more and more frequently, wholeheartedly, toward the Father. The more he opens his will to the influence of charity, the more preoccupied he becomes with the glory of the Father and subordinates all else to it. This is learned gradually through experience. So the adopted child comes to have the same desires as the only-begotten Son, through possessing in charity the Son's love of the Father. As our hearts become more and more like our Lord's, we may well find ourselves borrowing his words to express what is now our great longing, too: "Abba, glorify thy name" (Jn 12: 28). This in itself is a marvelous fruit of the child's love for his heavenly Father. Yet there are many others.

The adopted child's love for the Father also produces in him a deep desire for personal holiness. He begins to see that the glory he will give to the Father on earth, and for all eternity in heaven, will be measured by his likeness to the Son, for that is holiness. He will give the Father joy by being a faithful disciple of his Son. "In this is my Father glorified, that you bring forth very much fruit, and become my disciples" (Jn 15: 8). Only in this way is the desire for holiness safeguarded against being a self-

centered desire for self-improvement, or for the fulfillment of one's personality: rather, it is a wholly God-
centered desire. Thus it gains in purity and strength.
Then there may come a time when the adopted child will
in some mysterious way understand that the Son is glorifying the Father by producing his likeness in him, and the
Father glorifying his Son by making his child's adoption
perfect in virtue of the death and resurrection of the Son.
"Father, glorify thy name. A voice therefore came from
heaven: I have both glorified it, and will glorify it again"
(Jn 12: 28). The Father glorifies his name again in all his
adopted children because their adoption was secured
with the price of his Son's Precious Blood.

Therefore a true desire for personal holiness wells up
from the filial love of charity. It is centered upon the
Father and inspires every effort of the child in virtue,
every mortification, every sacrifice. Its qualities are recog-
nizable from St. Paul's description:

> Charity is patient, is kind; charity feels no envy; charity
> is never perverse or proud, never insolent; does not
> claim its rights, cannot be provoked, does not brood
> over an injury; takes no pleasure in wrong-doing, but
> rejoices at the victory of truth; sustains, believes, hopes,
> endures, to the last (1 Cor 13: 4–7 K).

The child of God is determined to become holy because
his Father is holy: his own holiness will be a reflection of
his Father's holiness, and this will glorify the Father in,
with, and through the Son. So he will become like the
Son, who did not seek his own glory but the glory of the
Father, who sent him. In this way the child is given a
glimpse into the mind and heart of the Son: the Holy
Spirit communicates to him the Son's thoughts and
longings. In experiencing these, the adopted child begins
to understand the Son, to enter deeply into his mind and

heart and unite his own with his Master's. Nowhere is this experience so unmistakable as in the consuming desire which the child finds in himself to glorify the Son's Father, who through adoption has become his Father, also.

There can be no doubt, then: the quest for holiness is a necessary fruit of a child's love for the Father. This quest may not be abandoned for any reason, however praiseworthy it may seem. No matter what demands are made upon his time and energy by the needs of the apostolate, the child of God must persevere in his quest for holiness. Our Lord's words are quite clear: union with him is all-important:

> I am the true vine, and it is my Father who tends it. The branch that yields no fruit in me, he cuts away; the branch that does yield fruit, he trims clean, so that it may yield more fruit. You, through the message I have preached to you, are clean already; you have only to live on in me, and I will live on in you. The branch that does not live on in the vine can yield no fruit of itself; no more can you, if you do not live on in me (Jn 15: 1–4 K).

The closest possible union with our Lord is the only perfect means of glorifying God. And the more intimate this union is, the more our filial love will urge us on. We know so well that our Father desires the holiness of each one of his children.

27

Brotherly Love

This is my commandment, that you should love one another,
as I have loved you. This is the greatest love a man can shew,
that he should lay down his life for his friends;
and you, if you do all that I command you,
are my friends.

JOHN 15: 12–14 K

Although the quest for holiness has priority in the life of
each child of God, his infused charity, filial love, is of
course also a brotherly love. So much so that, when we
talk about charity, we often mean specifically the love of
our neighbor, and which, as has been seen, is not the same
as mere natural affection. But charity is a brotherly love
only because it is first and foremost a filial love. An
adopted child of God loves his brethren because they are
children of the same Father and brethren of Christ. He
loves them because the Father loves them, since it was for
them too that the Father sent his Son to make them sons
by adoption:

> Then God sent out his Son on a mission to us. He took
> birth from a woman, took birth as a subject of the law,
> so as to ransom those who were subject to the law, and
> make us sons by adoption (Gal 4: 4–5 K).

It is as St. John puts it in his First Epistle: "Everyone
who believes that Jesus is the Christ is a child of God,
and to love the parent is to love his child. If we love God,
and keep his commandments, we can be sure of loving
God's children" (1 Jn 5: 1 K). This sums it up perfectly;

we love the brethren for the "family likeness" that we see in them. The love an adopted child gives his brethren, then, is not a natural personal affection but the love of charity: the same love with which the Incarnate Son loves them. This is because, and only because, the Son has first given it to us, that we might give it to others. Then we can obey his commandment to love our brethren as he loves them.

What does the child's love for others generate in him? The same desire as that of the Son: their sanctification and salvation. He will want his brethren to have the power they need to become true children of God. For they are all either actual or potential children: actual, when adopted and living as children of God; potential, when they have either not yet received the Spirit of adoption or have repudiated it by turning their backs upon the Father. Whichever they are, a true child of God wants them all, without exception, to remain or become children of the same Father. In this way the Father will be glorified, and they will all enjoy the inestimable gifts which the Father bestows on his adopted children, especially the gift of his Son and of his Spirit. The child will not only express this longing in prayer, but he will use all the means at his disposal to help the actual children to remain faithful to their Father and to become better children, and to bring the potential children to the home of their Father. Then all may be one in the common possession of the same Father, the same Savior, the same Spirit, and the same abiding home.

Filial love is thus inevitably also an apostolic love. It is indeed the mainspring of genuine apostolic zeal. It is the zeal of Christ, given by him to his brethren and disciples: zeal for the glory of his Father, and therefore the salvation of mankind unto the praise of his Father's glory. It is essentially supernatural: a fruit of infused charity, which urges the children of God to gain other children for their

Father. It does not seek its own glory, but only that of the Father: "Not to us, O Lord, not to us; but to thy name give glory" (Ps 113b: 1).

We find in St. John's Gospel an incident which will illuminate this point and supply some more details in connection with it. In chapter four, we find our Lord talking to a Samaritan woman by Jacob's well, making himself known to her as the Messiah. This woman believes and accepts him, and because she opens her heart to him, our Lord transforms her into an apostle. He arouses in her the desire characteristic of an apostle, to call others to "come and have sight" of him. He "has told me all the story of my life," she tells her acquaintances; this is what impresses her most. He has penetrated her soul, and she wants to bring others to him. Now this is a fundamental lesson for us: the great thing is to draw people to our Lord himself; we can do this only by showing them what a wonderful Person he is, and that this Person, divine and human, is the center of our faith.

When the disciples come back from the city, where they have been buying food, they try to make our Lord eat, but his reply is meant to teach them something very special: "My meat is to do the will of him who sent me, and to accomplish the task he gave me" (Jn 4: 34 K). He has a spiritual hunger and thirst which they must learn to share. Thus our Lord allows us to enter into his heart, to see the love for his Father that makes him long to glorify him, in perfecting our adoption. The salvation of the world through his loving obedience to the Father's will, that is his task and the basis of ours also. We help to continue his work by bringing others to him, just as the Samaritan woman did. And our Lord longs to receive them, to give them life. When he sees the people coming along the road in the distance, he speaks of the spiritual harvest waiting to be reaped:

Lift up your eyes, I tell you, and look at the fields, they are white with the promise of harvest already. The wages paid to him who reaps this harvest, the crop he gathers in, is eternal life, in which sower and reaper are to rejoice together. And here the proverb fits, which is true enough, One man sows, and another reaps. The harvest I have sent you out to reap is one on which you bestowed no labour; others have laboured, and it is their labours you have inherited (Jn 4: 35–38 K).

Our Lord tells the apostles that this is the harvest they must reap, and, just as others have sown it, they in turn must sow for others to reap. The wages of this labor is eternal life, both for the sowers and the reapers, and after giving their life on earth for it they will rejoice together for eternity in their reward. In some way we are all meant to be either sowers or reapers. Very often our work is to sow the seed, not to see the harvest, the growth and fruition, and we have to trust that someone else will reap it. This is particularly true of those who work with children, or whose apostolate is mainly carried out by example or in very hidden ways. Our life as a sower must be spent in hope. We sow as well as possible, knowing that our work may possibly be spoilt in the growing time, but we leave everything to be cared for by our loving Father, who watches over all. Our place in the Church is not spectacular, but our Lord may sometimes give us insight into what it means to him and to his Father. It is indispensably part of the redemptive pattern because there can be no harvest which was not first sown.

One man sows, and another reaps. The Samaritan woman had been prepared for our Lord by people long before, who had taught her about the Messiah. This reminds us that it shows a lack of spiritual insight if any of us count "our" converts; in fact, someone else has sown the seed that makes them ask for instruction. Often the seed is sown unknowingly by somebody's quiet example, or a word of faith or sympathy, even some chance remark. Therefore a truly supernatural outlook will make us reap humbly, and sow with trust in our Father's providence. It is God who gives the sun and the rain and makes the seed grow; we are only his laborers.

A deep charity is thus presupposed: the whole-hearted consecration of oneself to the glory of the Father in close union with the Son through his Spirit. All vainglory is absolutely rejected. Apostolic zeal is not a display of talents in any field, academic or practical. It is not a quest for personal popularity or an ever-widening circle of friends. It is not a relentless effort to get one's own ideas or opinions widely accepted. On the contrary, it is a love which urges us to place our whole being, body and soul, with all its powers and gifts wholly and unreservedly in the service of the Father's glory. The true apostle needs a mature spirit of childlikeness, of simplicity and single-mindedness, so that his absolute dedication to the Father's glory makes him acutely aware of how much more needs to be done. This leaves neither desire nor time to calculate—even if it were possible—in precise detail what he has done.

This understanding of genuine apostolic zeal is of the greatest importance. A child of God must never forget that his apostolic zeal will bear fruit only to the extent that he is used by the only-begotten Son himself. All initiative must come from Christ through his Spirit, and all the completion must come from him, too. The Son in his mercy cannot use an adopted child to any extent if success would merely make him conceited. If he took to himself the glory which is due to the Son, success would gradually prepare his downfall. Our Lord cannot desire this in any way, or be instrumental in bringing it about. The Son can freely use the adopted children in his work of sanctification and salvation only to the extent that they too seek only the Father's glory, and in no way their own. Then the Son can bless their work. In an adopted child whose zeal is pure and ardent, there is no limit to what the Son can and will do through him, and to the glory he will give to his Father by bearing much fruit.

We can see from all that has been said how imperative it is that if we are to be true apostles, we should be imbued with charity that is deep and supernatural. If we thirst for charity, we must go to our Lord, especially in his Passion. We need to remember St. John's description of the crucifixion, which shows us so movingly our Lord's total gift of his love and himself:

> Jesus drank the vinegar, and said, It is achieved. Then he bowed his head, and yielded up his spirit. . . . And so the soldiers came and broke the legs both of the one and of the other that were crucified with him; but when they came to Jesus, and found him already dead, they did not break his legs, but one of the soldiers opened his side with a spear; and immediately blood and water flowed out (Jn 19: 30, 32–34 K).

Our heart too must someday be pierced, so that we may pour out our charity upon others, as our Lord did. We must offer them water to drink, as Rebecca did in the Old Testament, but now it can be the water of life, if we lead them to Christ who is Life. For this we need a heart on fire with charity, like his. Only when we have something of his love for them can we give our brethren anything worthwhile. They will sense this, finding that in our love there are some of the qualities of his.

Charity alone, then, secures first that the driving force of our apostolic activity is the glory of the Father in virtue of a close union between the Son and ourselves: "Abide in me and I in you." Second, it ensures that we in no way sacrifice our own spiritual life, its vitality and growth toward maturity, to our activities, because the glory we must give to the Father is above all the glory of our own holiness. And third, charity ensures that our work is truly apostolic in the sight of the Father because we are laboring for the sanctification and salvation of others wholly and unreservedly for his glory.

The love of our brethren must always spring from our filial love of the Father. We must love them and each must dedicate himself to the others because they are or can become the children of the same Father. This includes both their spiritual and material welfare, everything, because we also love them individually and personally, as our Lord does, for charity does not make us love people in the abstract, but as they really are. A child of God cannot claim to love the Father if he is indifferent toward his Father's children either collectively or as individuals. Over and over again in his First Epistle, St. John repeats this message, which he learned from his Master:

> God is love; he who dwells in love dwells in God, and God in him. . . . If a man boasts of loving God, while he hates his own brother, he is a liar. He has seen his brother, and has no love for him; what love can he have for the God he has never seen? No, this is the divine command that has been given us; the man who loves God must be one who loves his brother as well (1 Jn 4: 16, 20–21 K).

A Christian, child of God, is by definition one who loves the Father, and this is revealed by his deeds. The fruits of the divine life in him are that his actions are just and that he loves his brethren. "Love one another," this is the quintessence of St. John's lesson, and it shows how completely his mind has been formed by our Lord.

All this goes to show how important it is that the child of God should have grown up in the things of God, and matured considerably, before embarking upon apostolic activities. If he starts out with a spirit of self-reliance and with a self-centered orientation of life, he may conceivably spend a great part of his life in a multiplicity of activities, having little to do with the glory of his Father and much to do with his own. Thus the outcome of it all may well be that he has glorified the Father neither in himself, because he has neglected his personal sanctification, nor in others, because his activities may prove sterile in the sight of the Father. Therefore all the adopted children of God, but especially those most engaged in apostolic activities, must always remember the Psalmist's words: "Unless the Lord build the house, they labour in vain that build it. Unless the Lord keep the city, he watcheth in vain that keepeth it" (Ps 126: 1). These words are given a definite sanction by our Lord himself when he said to his disciples: "He that abideth in me, and I in him, the same beareth much fruit: for without me you can do nothing" (Jn 15: 5).

28

The Religious Vows

*Love not the world, nor the things which are in the world.
If any man love the world, the charity of the Father is not in
him. For all that is in the world, is the concupiscence of the
flesh, and the concupiscence of the eyes, and the pride of life,
which is not of the Father, but is of the world. And the world
passeth away, and the concupiscence thereof: but he that doth
the will of God, abideth forever.*

I JOHN 2: 15–17

The vows can be approached from two angles: first, in
relation to baptism and the other sacraments, and second,
in relation to the world and other Christians living in the
world.

We must not allow the religious vows to usurp, at least
in our minds, the place of baptism or any of the sacraments. The vows do not make us children of God, but
baptism does. The vows are intended to help us to live as
true children of God, but it is necessary to become children of God first, to be re-created in baptism. This spiritual childhood is shared with the whole Church. There is
no distinction, from this point of view, between priests or
religious or laity, and so we have to keep the religious vows
in perspective, as being subservient to baptism and its
vows.

We have to live, all of us, fully as children of God in
every aspect of our lives, and living thus we have to grow.
Now, just as we do not receive our life from the religious
vows, we can grow and reach the full stature of Christ
without them. The evangelical counsels are not indispensable for the child of God to live as such. It is the sacra-

ments which are of the greatest importance, and especially the Eucharist makes us grow in the virtues and
become more and more like the Son of the Father. The
vows are helps toward Christlikeness, but not indispensable ones.

Therefore, we must never, never look upon the vows as
more important than the sacraments. Those, especially
baptism and the Eucharist, far outweigh the vows in importance, and unless we understand this we create a gulf
between religious and the laity. There is indeed a very
important link between the religious life and the sacraments in that it is meant to make access to the sacraments
very easy, so that religious may make the fullest use of
them and so grow up quickly and mature as children of
God. But we are all, whether religious or not, members
of the same Mystical Body of Christ. The Father and his
Son do not want to divide the adopted children into "elite"
and "common folk." They want them all to be one in their
sharing of the divine life, one family, one Body. And so,
religious can never stand aloof and deplore things in the
world. They have a positive task: that of giving light and
love to the world, for no child of God whatsoever can be
indifferent to the cause of Christ and his Mystical Body.

All children of God live in the world of darkness, just as
their Master did, but like him they cannot be of that
world, which is composed of those who hate him, who
refuse to accept him as the Father's Son and our Redeemer. For the laity this can be a grave problem; for the
more alive they are to their obligations as children of God,
the more aware they become of the pressure of the world
and the dangers to which they are exposed. For some of
them, the desire to live constantly as a child of God,
coupled with an acute awareness of the obstacles, may
contain the seed of a religious vocation. However, most
children of God have to live in a world of sin and hatred,
poverty and greed, and boundless ambition, and not be of

it. The children of God have to change that world, be the salt of the earth, beacons of light, and not merely keep their heads above water. Each child of God is an apostle, sent by Christ his Master, who prayed to his Father: "Keep them from evil."

Now this is the agonizing position of the child of God: to be faced, day after day, with the choice of loving the Father and renouncing the world, or of renouncing the Father and loving the world. It has always been so. The world exerts a very great pressure which can be blatant or subtle but which does everything possible to entice the child away from his Father, to follow its Prince. The world also means the gratification of self in rebellion to the Father's will. It is the purveyor of various means of gratifying self thus, which St. John sums up in the three concupiscences: of the flesh, of the eyes, and the pride of life. The work of the world in this respect is made easier because there are desires in us, like a fifth column in our fallen nature, always on the point of betraying us into enemy hands. The world has plenty of means to satisfy the desires of our flesh; there is no need to look for them, they are pressed upon us. They are almost inescapable, for we are never allowed to forget them. The world is busy day and night, likewise, to cater for the desires of the eyes, for things aroused by what we see. Millions of dollars are spent on advertisements which stimulate the desire to possess the things we see, and we should have to go about blindfolded in order to escape them. The world is only too anxious to encourage the pride of life: the desire for self-aggrandizement, human glory. All this pressure is brought to bear on the children of God, urging them to go their own way in a false independence, in defiance of the Father's will.

The child of God cannot altogether escape the world, and he receives all the strength he needs to resist its pressure and to remain faithful to his Father. Yet he is weak: he does not always respond to grace, and the danger of being seduced remains grave. Therefore he needs encouragement, not consisting of pious words but of the living examples of children of God who actually live as such. He needs the example of those children who have gone as far as to bind themselves to the three evangelical counsels, which are in direct opposition to the three concupiscences that sum up the desires of the world. Chastity is opposed to the concupiscence of the flesh, poverty to the concupiscence of the eyes, and obedience to the pride of life. The laity are entitled to this encouragement, and it is one of the reasons for the existence of the religious in the Church. These children of God show the others, by their renunciations, that it is possible to live in the world and not be of it.

A tremendous responsibility rests with religious, not only to sanctify themselves, but to see their own lives as the examples needed by others trying to live and grow as children of our heavenly Father. This is what our Master wants of his religious. By calling them to the religious life, he wants them to become so other-worldly that their life is a living, inspiring example to those children that the world tries to tear away from the Father. For unworldliness, taken positively, means other-worldliness: mind and heart always going out to the Father; a deep likeness to, and union with, his Son. If religious give this example, the children of God will find, as in fact they do, in the example of their lives strength and inspiration to help them to remain faithful, resisting the attraction of the world that is at enmity with the Father and his Son, Jesus Christ, our Redeemer and Brother.

Now, religious do not make their life an inspiration by becoming like people in the world. There is sometimes a tendency for people to try to be both religious and worldly for the sake of the apostolate, but this is dangerous. The spirit of the children of God is free, but it is unworldly, other-worldly in heart and mind. When this spirit is fully expressed in it, the religious life is a magnificent reinforcement of the baptismal vows both in practice and as regards example.

In addition to their baptismal vows, therefore, religious take the three vows of poverty, chastity, and obedience, and thereby accept the evangelical counsels as the norm of their life. In virtue of these life-long, binding promises made to God, many of his children take their baptismal vows a stage further, renouncing not only things that are evil, which all children of God do, but also things that are good. These renunciations of things that are good and sacred constitute the most precious offerings an adopted child can make to his heavenly Father, and religious profession is meant to be an offering, a genuine sacrifice, an outward and public act signifying the complete interior self-oblation. In making this offering, a religious is not a person who ransacks his house and his personality to look for things he wants to get rid of. He does not go to his heavenly Father and say: "Abba, I do not want these things, you can have them." No, he is a person who says: "Abba, these things are precious: marriage, parenthood, possessions, freedom of action, all are precious to me. They are to me what gold, frankincense, and myrrh were to the Magi. I want to offer them to you unreservedly, unconditionally, in close union with your beloved Son's utter and loving surrender of himself to you. I unite myself to him in sacrifice for love of you, so that my life too may be transformed into one life-long act of deep adoration, praise, thanksgiving, and reparation, unto the praise of your glory."

A religious profession made in this spirit is the greatest offering a child can give to his heavenly Father. He is enabled to do so by the same infused virtue of religion, actuated by charity, whereby the Incarnate Son offered himself at the first instant of his Incarnation, and on the cross, continuing to do so in the Mass. This is why the taking of the three vows at a final or solemn profession is a deeply liturgical act. It is a sacrificial act, in homage to the infinite majesty and holiness of our heavenly Father, corresponding to the holocaust of the old covenant, and it constitutes a perfect act of charity, thus obtaining forgiveness of sin and the punishment due to sin.

At a final or solemn profession, therefore, a religious makes the gift of his whole life and self to God. The time beforehand is a preparation for the offering, to enable him to make it intelligently, knowing what he is doing. He needs that time to gain the experience of religious life, and of himself in that life, which helps him to take the vows prudently and justly. The profession is an all-embracing act of surrender and dependence urged by a deep love of the Father, offered to him in homage. At the same time, we must remember that while it is true that a religious takes vows once and for all, it can also be said that he goes on taking them all his life. It would be a mistake to think that final profession happens once, and that then all the work is done. It is only the beginning.

At profession the basic renunciations are made. But fidelity to one's profession is a continuous process, demanding fresh renunciations, not independent of those basic ones, but as so many concrete applications of them, which never cease to be called for until the moment of death. The very fact that religious have a great responsibility laid upon them make it fitting that the act of profession itself should be surrounded by a certain solemnity. But the ceremony, whether it be splendid or austere, must not blind them to their later responsibilities: they have to resist the temptation to take back in little ways what has been given in a big way, to nibble away at their obligations, to shift the responsibility for their observance of the vows onto superiors, thus gradually undermining their sense of personal responsibility. These are things which prevent the vows from achieving their purpose, which is Christ-likeness: the growing up of the child of God into an ever-increasing likeness to the only-begotten Son. It is therefore the actual living-out of the vows that is the decisive and searching test of loving fidelity, and the measure of their effectiveness. Each religious is responsible for keeping his own vows: they are his vows, and his alone.

This carrying out of the vows with personal responsibility and life-long fidelity depends upon that grace which is promised by God to his religious. They know when they take their vows that he will always give them the grace they need for each day of their religious life. Though the graces they receive at the moment of final profession are, in the measure of their dispositions, more abundant than they can possibly recognize, those graces are not confined to the moment itself, but are assured for the whole of their life "until death." God has guaranteed that the graces his children need to remain faithful to their promises will always be given them. It is important for all God's children, but especially religious, to have a deep trust in our Father's faithfulness. When he promises graces, we shall receive them. We need have no anxiety: however difficult it may be to be poor and pure and obedient, God is always there to give his children abundant help. The Spirit of adoption assures us of his faithfulness in such words as these:

> God is faithful, who will not suffer you to be tempted above that which you are able: but will make also with temptation issue [a way to escape], that you may be able to bear it (1 Cor 10: 13).

> God is faithful: by whom you are called unto the fellowship of His Son Jesus Christ our Lord (1 Cor 1: 9).

To understand the true place of the religious vows in the spiritual lives of those called to make them, we must go back again to baptism. If we keep before ourselves the overriding importance of the sacrament of baptism, we shall see the vows and the whole of the religious life in perspective. We have seen that at baptism we are made children of God and are given all the virtues we need to live and grow up as such into a perfect likeness to the Incarnate Son. The producing of this likeness is the purpose of all God has given, and all Christ has suffered for us. This too is the purpose of all the graces we are given, but above all, of charity. The perfection of our likeness to Christ is measured by the perfection of our charity, not in isolation from the other virtues, but as their mother and queen.

All adopted children without exception are called to the perfection of charity. In this, religious are on exactly the same footing as lay Christians, for the ultimate purpose of their life is the same: to become full-grown children of God, reproducing all the virtues of the Incarnate Son, especially his charity, and thus to reflect his likeness. Moreover, as far as the essential and indispensable means to this likeness are concerned, the graces they are given, the sacraments and infused virtues, there is no distinction between all children of God. Where religious do differ from other Christians is in being given additional means, first the vows, and then, connected with them, the many observances which protect them. By their vows, religious bind themselves for life to live in accordance with the evangelical counsels, in order to break down the obstacles that make perfect likeness to Christ so difficult to attain in the world. The vows remove the obstacles of the pleasures of the flesh, of the disposal of earthly goods, and of the disorder of the will. At the same time, the religious renounces many good things which may easily become obstacles, or which may lead him away from the Father.

Religious want to give themselves wholly to God. The vows give them freedom to do this. They are additional means, to the essential ones we already have, for becoming Christlike. The purpose of the vows is therefore positive: likeness to Christ and union with him, which will bring their adoption to perfection. This relation of the vows to the child's likeness to Christ, the only-begotten Son, become so clear when the eyes are fixed on him, and it can be seen clearly how the evangelical counsels find their highest perfection in him.

Christ was utterly poor. There was no greed or covetousness in him, no trace of attachment to earthly goods. Therefore to become like him, the adopted children must be poor in spirit, and nothing helps so much to achieve this as the vow of poverty. They take it because they want to be poor like him, because they want his poverty to enter their lives and become their own.

Christ was utterly pure, utterly consecrated to his heavenly Father, wholly self-given, fully God-centered. A religious takes the vow of chastity, renouncing even the lawful pleasures of the flesh, because he wants to be like Christ in his total, exclusive self-giving to his heavenly Father. Any hindrance to this God-seeking attitude is removed. The vow of chastity is taken, not because the religious dislikes the idea of marriage, but solely because he wants to give himself to his Father with the utter self-giving of Christ.

Christ was utterly obedient. His whole life was lived in perfect conformity to the utter and loving submission of his will to the Father's will until death. The religious takes the vow of obedience because he wants to be like Christ in his obedience. Through it he imitates the Son as closely as a human person can: he submits his whole life in all its aspects to the Father's will through obedience to his lawful superiors, in accordance with the constitutions of his religious institute. In this way all his actions converge on the fulfillment of the Father's will. This is why the vow of obedience is the greatest of the three and the most efficacious in producing a greater likeness to Jesus crucified in the adopted child. Therefore the desire to be like Christ must remain the driving-force behind all observance of the vows. No religious must allow himself to drift into human reasons for his obedience—fear or personal affection, for instance. This is to abuse the vow of obedience. He must obey because he wants to be like Christ, obedient unto death, and not make his vow, that precious thing, subject to his whims and moods. If each religious has a sense of responsibility in his obedience, he will keep his eyes fixed on Christ, because he loves him, and because he loves the Father who adopted him.

Our Lord was poor, pure, and obedient unto death. It is one of his inestimable mercies that he has invited so many of the adopted children of his Father to share in his poverty, chastity, and obedience more fully. If they respond generously and faithfully, they will be given a deep insight into the basic law of the Christian life. It is this: if we want to live, we must die. We cannot live unless we have died first. This is the mysterious law whose truth is most fully experienced by religious when they recognize that they begin to live and mature to the extent that they begin to die to self, so as to live to God.

The deeper they plunge into the renunciation made at profession, in union with Christ, the more they die to self and live to God. They come to religious life in order to live, even if it means that they must die for the sake of life. They want to live so much that they are ready to die, for the deeper they plunge into the death of renunciation, in union with the crucified Christ, the more joyful and glorious their resurrection will be: first the hidden resurrection of mind and heart from the death of selfishness into a life of union with God, and then its completion, the glorious resurrection from death in the body to everlasting life. They die to live, and live to praise, adore, and thank the Blessed Trinity for all eternity. Every religious who keeps his vows willingly, generously, and faithfully, will die, but then find life growing and maturing into a wonderful union with God:

> Risen then with Christ, you must lift your thoughts above, where Christ now sits at the right hand of God. You must be heavenly-minded, not earthly-minded; you have undergone death, and your life is hidden away now with Christ in God (Col 3: 1–2 K).

St. John tells us that we shall be "like him." But we have to die like him first, so that we may be alive like him. What we shall be like we do not know, but we do know that we shall be *like him*. This thought can be a great inspiration to our Christian life, whether we are religious or not, for all sacrifices, all renunciations, are in order that we may become like him. They are to make us live and mature as children of God, in deepening union with his Son, our beloved Master, Jesus Christ.

29

Chastity

*He who is unmarried is concerned with God's claim, asking
how he is to please God; whereas the married man is
concerned with the world's claim, asking how he is to please
his wife; and thus he is at issue with himself. So a woman
who is free of wedlock, or a virgin, is concerned with the
Lord's claim, intent on holiness, bodily and spiritual;
whereas the married woman is concerned with the world's
claim, asking how she is to please her husband.*

I CORINTHIANS 7: 32–34 K

As it would lead us too far afield to deal with all three
religious vows in detail, it seems best to confine ourselves
to one of them. We shall take the vow of chastity, trying to
see it in its proper perspective, with its concrete demands
as well as its glorious fruits. Why choose chastity rather
than obedience or poverty? It is because the vow of chastity is least understood and is often attacked because it
raises problems, in certain human situations agonizing
problems, such as are not raised by the other two vows.
These problems cannot be dealt with adequately on the
level of emotional reactions or on the level of physiological
or psychological analysis, without also an understanding
of the religious life as a whole, and still less without an
understanding of God's all-powerful help. They can be
resolved only in the context of the religious vocation taken
in its entirety; to isolate them from this context is to
distort them, to give them false proportions and make
them incapable of a radical and lasting solution.

The religious vow of chastity was never meant to be
wrenched out of its context: it is an integral part of a

pattern which must be seen as a whole if its constituent elements are to be understood. Above all, it must never be considered without constant reference to Christ himself, because it is he who gave us the basic pattern of the religious life, insisted on its renunciations, its distinctive character, and its reward. Our Master knew perfectly well that not everyone would understand his counsel of chastity, for when he gave it he said: "He that can take, let him take it" (Mt 19: 12). But Christ not only gave us the basic pattern of the religious life, he was himself the supreme embodiment of it, being utterly poor, obedient, and pure.

Christ was utterly pure, wholly concerned with his Father's claim, and always intent on pleasing the Father in all things. He was totally given, fully God-centered. A religious in his turn takes the vow of chastity, renouncing even the lawful pleasure of the body so as to imitate our Lord. He wants to be concerned with God's claim, to concentrate on being pleasing to God, and so he dedicates himself wholly to God's glory and the salvation of souls.

Now, we must be careful not to express the vow of chastity exclusively in negative terms: not to get married, not to have children, not to have personal friends, not to have friendships at all. This would be a mistake, for the aim of the vow is positive: to love God with the whole heart and soul and strength, and to love others in and for God. The vital point to grasp is that chastity is not self-centered: its purpose is to make the religious God-centered. This shows that the virtue of charity and the vow of chastity are closely linked. The religious promises chastity because he loves, and this love urges him to take every possible step to remove all obstacles that might hinder the ripening of that love into intimacy with God. He sets out therefore on a lifelong quest for the love of God. He opens himself more and more to God's love and his gifts, seeking too the power to love others for his sake. A religious must see his vow in this positive way, otherwise he will never have the courage to keep it faithfully until death.

We must not, however, go to the opposite extreme. Although we have to concentrate on the positive aspects, we must not forget the negative side of the vow. Our Lord meant it to be a renunciation—there is no question about that. He saw the evangelical counsels as so many ways of renouncing self, so as to open oneself more fully to God and his love, to foster charity toward God and our neighbor. When the vow of chastity is analyzed, we find that the religious renounces the gratification of three basic human urges. These urges are not sinful in themselves, but we must remember that religious renounce not only sinful things but also good things by their vows.

First, he renounces a physical urge. It is nonetheless human, for it has roots deeply embedded in human nature, and for this reason it cannot simply be discarded like an overcoat, or lightly brushed aside. In taking the vow of chastity, a religious renounces the gratification of this urge completely and utterly until death. It must not be underestimated, for strength is needed in order to remain faithful, and this can be difficult, especially if adolescence has awakened and stirred it.

Second, by the vow of chastity the deep human urge to love and be loved is renounced. For women it may be more a matter of wanting to be loved, and to be with the person loved. Still, the urge to give oneself body and soul to the person loved is universal, deeply human, and there is nothing at all sinful in it as such. After all, the sexual instinct is not a purely animal instinct: it is human and therefore bound up with the affections. It enters deeply into the human personality and involves the whole person. It is a marvelous instinct, humanized by the deep mutual affection, embracing body and soul, which should accompany it.

In renouncing this way of receiving love and giving himself to the person loved, a religious causes within himself a natural loneliness. It is impossible to make such a renunciation without it. There is in any case an irreducible core of loneliness in the human person in virtue of the radical uniqueness of his personality: no two human beings are identical. Then this inevitable loneliness is much accentuated by the vow of chastity. Here especially we must keep in mind its positive purpose: to love God and to be loved by him. Chastity does much more than separate, for it opens the person more and more to God's love, enlarging the capacity for his love and his gifts. If any religious loses sight of this purpose, he is asking for trouble. It is possible to take the vow of chastity and then to stop loving God, or striving to love him more, or else to refuse to comply with his demands. Of course, love makes demands on anyone's self-giving, but it can be refused. Then the sense of loneliness might indeed overwhelm the heart of a religious and lead him to look for solace outside God, away from his vocation. And it may start innocently, but it might gradually undermine the spirit of the vow. This vow is taken in order that the religious may learn to love God with the love with which God loves himself, and to love his neighbor with God's love for him, not merely with that natural affection which lies within anyone's grasp. Natural human affection is not charity, and charity is not natural affection.

We need to remind ourselves here of the fact that the love we give God, which he expects us to give to him and to our neighbor, is supernatural love, God's own love; and that we cannot give supernatural love unless he has first given it to us. We can give him love only to the extent that we have opened ourselves to his love. Then divine love enters our heart, takes possession, and gives it new dimensions. This is true for all God's children. Now, the vow of chastity does not destroy the power of loving.

Instead, it purifies it and harnesses it to charity, giving it an all-embracing orientation toward God. Nor does chastity mean the destruction of the desire for love, because the heart's infinite capacity for love is God-given. Chastity, when preserved and deepened by charity, secures for it an immense influx of love, which comes to it directly from the Sacred Heart of our Lord.

Last, we come to the third urge which is renounced by the vow of chastity, the urge to become fathers or mothers. Again, this desire is not just a superficial accessory to human nature and so cannot be simply eliminated all at once. It is a deeply human desire implanted in us by God himself and therefore is not sinful as such. By the vow of chastity, however, it is renounced utterly and completely until death.

This vow, then, involves a tremendous sacrifice. Religious renounce precious things, those urges implanted by God in human nature. The vow does not uproot them—that is why it must be observed wholeheartedly and faithfully until the end. It must be clearly seen and accepted as a sacrifice, and one which the unceasing loneliness of advancing years may well make more rather than less costly. Such a renunciation goes deep. There are people who say that in the framework of the modern world the vow of chastity demands too much. They think that instead of making something greater of human nature, it has a stunting or unsettling effect on the personality. Of course, if a person takes a vow of chastity in a spirit of presumption and self-reliance, he is courting disaster. No one is meant to take it trusting only in his natural strength of character and will-power. This will not enable him to remain utterly faithful to his vow throughout his life on earth. God's power is what is needed, not mere human will-power. No one ever said it was possible to be faithful relying only on the resources of human nature. Pride and chastity are ill companions. Our Lord said that all things were possible to him, but to him alone. We need to remember St. Paul's words: "He whose power is at work in us is powerful enough, and more than powerful enough, to carry out his purpose beyond all our hopes and dreams" (Eph 3: 20 K). Defeatism is wholly incompatible with faith in God's infinite mercy and power.

If the vow of chastity demands such searching renunciations, there is no doubt that its fruits and rewards will be commensurate. The generosity of the Father can never be outdone by the generosity of his children, but always infinitely surpasses theirs. Yet religious must not expect to see reward and fruits the moment they take their vow of chastity. A fruit tree does not bear fruit the moment we have planted it. Time is needed, so that it may mature; it needs watering and pruning, care and protection; then it grows up and produces fruit. Likewise the fruits and rewards of the vow of chastity take time to mature. When a religious has remained faithful to it and has done all he can to protect and deepen the spirit of his chastity, he will learn how wonderful God is in all his ways. He will see how sweet and wise God is in the way he fills the emptiness of the purified heart. He will wonder at God's understanding of all the longings and aspirations of the human heart, and such wonder is sweet: "No eye has seen, no ear has heard, no human heart conceived, the welcome God has prepared for those who love him" (1 Cor 2: 9 K). This means absolute faithfulness and a giving of the heart to God that is unconditional and unreserved. A most exacting demand, indeed.

What does the religious discover through his faithfulness? He finds that he is becoming more and more God-centered. The opposite of this is to become self-centered, which is to misuse and frustrate the vow of chastity, and which, if it happens, becomes fertile soil for temptations and aberrations. The religious who is God-centered, however, finds that his sense of loneliness is taken away, for he begins to live in company with God. He experiences in himself that stillness of soul which is one of the precious fruits of the vow and spirit of chastity. It is an utter serenity, undisturbed by fluctuations of emotions or passions. This is the stillness of a soul which is held by God, absolutely calm and at peace in the harmony of its sanctified powers. All its powers are engaged, each in its own way, in the love of God and of others. There is a sense of liberation too, from the restlessness of pride and concupiscence into the singlemindedness and wholeheartedness of total self-giving. This is the stillness of a soul wholly intent on the life of the Blessed Trinity within it; intent on listening to the Father speaking his sweet Word in the silence of its inmost depths; intent on giving to the *Abba* the love of his Son, and to the Son the love of his *Abba*, thus entering into their mutual exchange of love in the stillness of inexpressible wonder and joy. The religious finds in himself this stillness of soul because the Holy Spirit, the uncreated Flame of Love, has taken possession of his will and transformed it. His soul becomes resplendent with the perfections of the Blessed Trinity, reflecting them for the praise of their glory.

Charity, perfected by chastity, transforms the loneliness of a chaste religious into deep intimacy with the three divine Persons within him. Gradually his spiritual life becomes profoundly trinitarian: he will begin to live more or less intermittently with the three divine Persons, becoming more and more sensitive to their indwelling and to the immense love it implies. He will have become a fully-grown, mature child of his heavenly Father, for nothing is so conducive to genuine maturity in childlikeness as chastity of body and soul. As a child he will have found his true and everlasting home within himself, there where his beloved Three dwell. There the Father is progressively transforming the substance of his soul into an abundant spring of divine life and fatherly tenderness. There the sweet

Word is transforming his intelligence into an overflowing spring of wisdom and insight. There the Holy Spirit, the living Flame of Love, is transforming his will into a living flame which will burn through, with, and in the Spirit, with the mutual love of Father and Son, and with their love for their children.

The religious is thus sharing God's own life and has a genuine foretaste of heaven. And so his heart begins to ache for its consummation. He utters cries of longing for the hour of his death, of his going to the Father, so that he may plunge himself for all eternity into the endless depths of the mystery of the Blessed Trinity, Father, Son, and Holy Spirit.

30

Homecoming

Then I saw a new heaven, and a new earth. The old heaven,
the old earth had vanished, and there was no more sea. And
I, John, saw in my vision that holy city which is the new
Jerusalem, being sent down by God from heaven, all clothed
in readiness, like a bride who has adorned herself to meet her
husband. I heard, too, a voice which cried aloud from the
throne, Here is God's tabernacle pitched among men; he will
dwell with them, and they will be his own people, and he will
be among them, their own God. He will wipe away every tear
from their eyes, and there will be no more death, or mourning,
or cries of distress, no more sorrow; those old things have
passed away. And he who sat on the throne said,
Behold, I make all things new.

REVELATION 21: 1–5 K

A true child of God looks forward to death as the indispensable condition of meeting his Father face to face, of
being at home with him, unmolested by temptations, for
ever. As his charity grows, the child's fear, resulting from
his past sins, is cast out, and his contrition is surpassed by
his longing for the Father. Death is a lovely thing for those
who love the Father: "I rejoiced at the things that were
said to me: We shall go into the house of the Lord" (Ps
121: 1).

Nowadays it is often considered morbid to long for
death, but it is not necessarily so. In the normal develop-
ment of the spiritual life, a child of God will come to long
to be with his Father for all eternity; he will long to see
and possess him. When the moment of his death is an-
nounced he is thrilled with joy, because he is about to

meet the Father he loves so much, the Father he desires to see and love and glorify. It is the moment for him to pass into eternity, where he can no longer offend his Father, and where he can praise him for ever.

It is, of course, the Spirit of adoption who gives us this consuming love for the Father which leads to the desire for heaven. If we love the Father very deeply, we shall long to be with him in heaven, for it is natural to us to desire to be with the person we love. Now, unless we desire heaven for this reason, the thought of it will not have much effect on our life, for love is the whole secret. Theologians and preachers sometimes discuss the problem of how to make the thought of heaven attractive to people, because, in order to produce and foster in them a spirit of other-worldliness, their minds and hearts must focus on heaven and eternal life. We have to acknowledge the fact that people do not seem to find it particularly stimulating; often they are too immersed in this world, too ignorant of the great truths of faith, for the thought of heaven to touch them. Therefore it is very important for all adopted children of God to recognize that heaven means being with our Father, and that while we are on earth we are journeying toward our true home.

According as the love of the child of God for his heavenly Father gains a deeper hold on him, he finds himself longing more and more to be with the Father in heaven. That is, the childlikeness infused by the Spirit of adoption deepens his desire for heaven, because the child's love increases as the Spirit masters him. At the same time and in the same degree, the child of God will look upon his life on earth as an exile, a vale of tears, because his Father is not yet to be seen. There is always a precariousness about life here, because of the danger of losing the Father, of being enticed away from him by the pressure of the world. The child who loves his Father wants to get away from the dangers, not because he is afraid of them, but simply because of the precariousness of his possession of God among them. All this is the work of the Holy Spirit. Many people in the world have little sense of its being a vale of tears, or an exile, for they are satisfied by their prosperity and material comforts, and feel at home here. They are just as mistaken if they think of heaven as an escape from this world, in a negative way, because they want to avoid troubles or suffering. It is the desire to be at home with the Father that is the essence of exile, and only the unworldly children possess that.

The more we love the Father, the more impatient we shall become with the limitations of faith. We begin to desire the reality, to know the Father fully, possessing him and being possessed by him, and to love him with a pure love. The attraction comes not from without but within; there is no means of desiring heaven truly except that of allowing the Holy Spirit to enlighten and guide us. It is he who gives us that intense joy which goes with the news that death is imminent. What child would not rejoice on hearing that his Father is close at hand. It is not the mere pinpricks of daily life which make it an exile and give us the desire to go home to *Abba*, but the longing for the consummation of a life filled with love for him.

We do not know exactly what the child of God will experience when he enters heaven. But we can be sure that he will know the Father through the light of glory, that the Father will give himself wholly and entirely to his child for ever, and the child will be overwhelmed by this deep and personal possession. Vision will perfect faith, for it never denies faith; the truths are all fulfilled. The child will be thrilled to see all the Father's perfections, of which he had only a foretaste on earth. How much more will he taste them in heaven. And he will feel utterly at home in spite of all the Father's infinite perfections, for this *is* his Father, and the child *is* his child in spite of all his limitations as creature. He will be perfectly at home in glory with his transcendent and holy Father in the heart of the Holy Trinity.

The child feels at home because now he has grown up into the likeness of the only-begotten Son and receives his glory from him. The glory of the child of God has its origin in the very depths of the divine nature. The life which he received at his baptism has gradually transformed and perfected his human nature, conforming him to Christ, and flowers in the light of glory. Thus his eternal destiny is fulfilled:

> All those who from the first were known to him, he has destined from the first to be moulded into the image of his Son, who is thus to become the eldest-born among many brethren. So predestined, he called them; so called, he justified them; so justified, he glorified them (Rom 8: 29–30 K).

The whole purpose of our destined glorification is suggested, again by St. Paul, in his Epistle to the Corinthians: "It is given to us, all alike, to catch the glory of the Lord as in a mirror, with faces unveiled; and so we become transfigured into the same likeness, borrowing glory from that glory, as the Spirit of the Lord enables us" (2 Cor 3: 18 K). In commenting on these words, the Greek Fathers compare us to precious stones plunged into the full light of the sun; they reflect the sunlight and detail it, each in accordance with its capacity and purity. So with us, even on earth, but still more in heaven, for our sun is the divine glory and our souls are so many precious stones plunged in the radiation of that glory by which and in which we are transfigured. In heaven we shall see reflected in each others' faces a ray of that divine glory.

All things will be new. It is this newness that is so striking in St. John's vision of heaven. The old universe will have disappeared, "folded up like a scroll" (Rev

6: 14 K), and yet heaven will not be strange to us. It will be our universe, because it is that of the Son, the Word who became man in order to lead us home to our Father. It will be a city, a community, a new Jerusalem, where we shall all live with new minds, new hearts, new wills. At the resurrection we shall even have new bodies transfigured by the light of glory. Then our adoption will be brought to its perfect completion.

The child in heaven will be filled with the desire to sing the *canticum novum*, the new song of praise and glory to the Father, and on earth he has only a foretaste of what this is like. The new light of the Beatific Vision will evoke in him an upsurge of praise. The *Magnificat* is only a faint echo of that new canticle which every child of God will sing to the Father in heaven. Each new experience of the light of glory will inspire a new canticle. And yet the children of God are learning to sing their new song while they are on earth. We read in the Book of Revelation that the saints will sing the canticle of Moses; the same words which will carry a far greater load of praise and gratitude and glory in heaven than they ever did on earth. So it will be with all of us.

The child's new song expresses his joy in seeing at last the transcendent perfections of the Father in all his holiness. The child recognizes the condescension of Infinite Majesty in adopting him on earth, in guiding, training, sanctifying, and preparing him for heaven. Now he has invited that child to enter heaven, to be with his Father for all eternity. God has had regard for his littleness and given him the power to glorify the Trinity for ever.

As far as is possible to a creature, the child will now perfectly understand the otherness of God and his infinite transcendence. He will see his Father for what he is, and see what he has done for his child, because the infinite distance between God and his creature is the measure of all the Father has done for his child. And so the child will have a corresponding desire to give praise and glory to his Father, especially in all his holiness. Like the four living figures in Revelation, he will want to cry unceasingly: "Holy, holy, holy is the Lord God, the Almighty, who ever was, and is, and is still to come" (Rev 4: 8 κ). All long to sing the holiness of their heavenly Father, now so clearly seen, possessed, and shared. That is why St. John's Book of Revelation rings with praise: "And every creature in heaven and on earth, and under the earth, and on the sea, and all that is in it, I heard crying out together, Blessing and honour and glory and power, through endless ages, to him who sits on the throne, and to the Lamb" (Rev 5: 13 κ).

The true child of God desires this life of praise so much that he begins to carry it out on earth. He cannot wait for heaven, but he begins even now with his limited under- standing and insight to glorify his Father's transcendent holiness. He is on fire to see his Father's glory acknowl- edged throughout the universe:

> Let all thy works, O Lord, praise thee: and let thy saints bless thee. They shall speak of the glory of thy kingdom: and shall tell of thy power: To make thy might known to the sons of men: and the glory of the magnificence of thy kingdom (Ps 144: 10–12).

Above all, the child longs to glorify his Father by becom- ing like the only-begotten Son, who is himself "the flash- ing-forth of his glory, and the very expression of his being" (Heb 1: 3 w).

And who, of all the adopted children, is most like the Son? It is, of course, his mother, most perfect of the adopted children, greatest and most loving. Let us think of what her homecoming must have been like, and that will help us to understand our own. Our Lady's Assump- tion has not been described for us, but if we think of it as the first moment of her homecoming to the Father, and of the fulfillment of her life of union with the Trinity, we shall recognize what a sublime mystery it is.

When our Lady entered heaven she met the Father, with whom she had worked so intimately in the Incarnation of his Son. And in that first moment of vision she saw what the Holy Trinity had done in, for, and through her, and her love in all its intensity went out toward the Trinity. Then too, the immense love of the Trinity embraced her and established an everlasting union. This is a moment of silence, of inexpressible joy, and yet it must contain our Lady's desire to bless the Trinity for all their blessings bestowed upon her. She must have experienced a great urge to bless the three Divine Persons with whom she had collaborated in the redemption of mankind. We call our Lady "blessed," but of course we are in doing so blessing God: the two go together, and indeed it is impossible to call anyone blessed without blessing God too—the recognition is the very meaning of it.

We know that our Lady received God's greatest blessings. The Holy Spirit prepared her to be the mother of the Son in a perfect way, because her motherhood is very close to the Fatherhood of God, a distant reflection of it. This is why she had to be immaculate: to be as close as a human being could be to the Father in his holiness, so that she could be Mother of God. That is her greatest title, and yet she remains his adopted child. She reflects for us the perfections of the Father, and our Lord's birth from her reflects his eternal Sonship of the Father. How much, then, must our Lady have blessed the Trinity when she came home to them in heaven. And how much reason we have also to bless them, to share our Lady's desire to bless them, both for her and with her. We have to think of that first blessed moment when our Lady held in her arms the Child who was both Creator and Savior, and yet also her Son. No one else can say to him "my Son," except the Father; he allows her to share that privilege. And yet still more should we love to think of her homecoming to the Father, the Son, and the Holy Spirit, whom she had loved so much on earth. At that even more blessed moment, faith became vision, hope became possession, and love was intensified and rewarded with deep union with God for all eternity.

Our Lady wants us to add our blessings, our praise and thanksgiving to hers, even now on earth. Nothing could please her more than that we should join with her in blessing the Trinity. This is one of the elements in the new song, the *canticum novum*, that we learn to sing in preparation for heaven. Let us bless the Trinity for all they accomplished in her, for we are meant not merely to pray to our Lady, asking her to help us, but also to share her love and blessing of God now, as we shall in heaven. This is no self-centered devotion, for it makes us go out of ourselves and enter into the mind and heart of our Lady, while we learn to share her attitude toward the Trinity. True devotion to our Lady will always lead us ultimately to the Trinity: if it does not, we have not understood our Lady and her relation to the Trinity and all she owed to the infinite mercy of God. At her Assumption, she was glorified for ever through her vision and possession of the Blessed Trinity, and her love and glory are surpassed only by those of her Divine Son. She shows us something of what is in store for us, for with her we can say "our Father" and long to be at home with him, and with her and all the adopted children of God.

Now we can see why heaven is a home only for its own children; that is, for those who love God as their Father and in whom he sees the likeness of his only-begotten Son. No outsiders can come in, for there the adoption, which must first take place on earth and mature on earth, comes to fruition. Only if we feel at home with the Father on earth can we feel at home with him in heaven. For this we must take his Son's words seriously: our Lord said that unless we become as little children, we cannot enter the kingdom of heaven. We cannot see God, nor praise nor glorify him, except as little children, because the distance between God and ourselves is infinite. The Holy Spirit alone can carry us across that gulf, but for this we must be truly childlike in mind and heart so that he can master us completely. If we are utterly loving and submissive, he will give us a true desire for death, for this exile on earth to end, and for our homecoming. He will teach us that part of our joy in heaven will spring from our new-found, perfect, and everlasting ability to glorify our heavenly Father.

It is not surprising, then, if the Father has been so close to our mind and heart and soul, if the desire to glorify him has filled our life on earth, that with the thought of possessing him for ever we cry out: "Abba, Father," "Come, Lord Jesus." And then, when the moment of our homecoming arrives, we shall enter into the family of heaven to glorify the Father, Son, and Holy Spirit—to whom be glory for ever and ever. Amen.

INDEX OF SCRIPTURE REFERENCES

Index of Scripture References

INDEX OF SUBJECTS

children of God
  baptism and, 100
  Blood of Christ and, 90
  charity and, 243
  as disciples, 84–91
  failure of, 168–69
  faith and, 154
  fear and, 158–59, 161
  formation of, 59–66
  fortitude and, 159–60, 161
  freedom of, 32–33
  holiness of, 225–27
  Holy Spirit and, 100–101,
    166
  humility and, 103–4
  obedience and, 126
  "Our Father" and, 165–71
  piety and, 155–56, 161
  religious vows and, 236–39
  Son and, 107
  Spirit of adoption and,
    160–63
  temptation and, 169–70
  unworldliness and, 238–39
  See also adoption by God
children of Israel. *See* Chosen
  People
Chosen People
  covenant and, 68–73, 197–98
  disobedience of, 22–23
  faithfulness and, 68–73
  filial love of, 69
  formation of, 22–23, 59–65
  God's Fatherhood and, 19–
    25
  God as Spouse of, 72–74
  lack of faith of, 62–65
  merciful love of God and,
    35, 37

of New Testament, 23
obedience of, 69
power of God and, 26–29,
  80–81
providence and, 52–53
wisdom and, 49
wondrous deeds of God
  and, 17–18, 27–29
See also Old Testament
Christ. *See* Son of God
Christlikeness
  infusion of, 106
  religious vows and, 237,
    242, 243, 244–46
  of saints, 106
Church
  apostles and, 146
  faith and, 62
  holiness of, 147
  Holy Spirit and, 48
  merciful love of God and,
    37, 38
  mysteries of faith and, 119
  power of God and, 32
  providence and, 56
  wisdom of God and, 45
Clementissime Pater, 99
Cloud, Luminous, as symbol
  of faith, 65
commandments, 22, 59
concupiscence of eyes, 238–
  39
concupiscence of flesh, 238–
  39
conscience, 118
Consummatum est, 132
contemplation
  our Lady and, 82–83
  wisdom of God and, 47, 98